America &
Alfred Stieglitz

A COLLECTIVE PORTRAIT

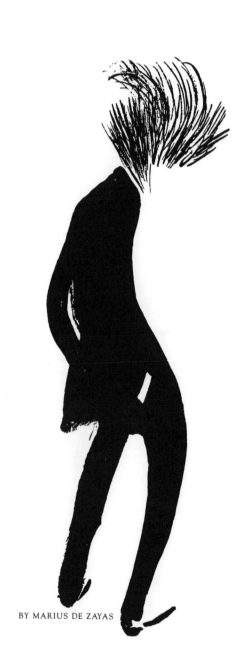

BY MARIUS DE ZAYAS

America &
Alfred Stieglitz

A COLLECTIVE PORTRAIT

Edited by

Waldo Frank
Lewis Mumford
Dorothy Norman
Paul Rosenfeld
Harold Rugg

New, Revised Edition

AN APERTURE BOOK

APERTURE, INC., PUBLISHES A PERIODICAL, PORTFOLIOS

AND BOOKS TO COMMUNICATE WITH SERIOUS PHOTOGRAPHERS

AND CREATIVE PEOPLE EVERYWHERE.

A COMPLETE CATALOGUE WILL BE MAILED UPON REQUEST.

SUBSCRIPTIONS TO THE PERIODICAL ARE $28 FOR

FOUR ISSUES ($30 IN CANADA AND FOREIGN COUNTRIES).

ADDRESS: ELM STREET, MILLERTON, N.Y. 12546.

THE TEXT OF AMERICA AND ALFRED STIEGLITZ HAS BEEN

REPRODUCED IN ITS ENTIRETY FROM THE ORIGINAL EDITION.

THE ILLUSTRATION SECTION HAS BEEN RE-CONCEIVED

TO PROVIDE A RICHER UNDERSTANDING OF

ALFRED STIEGLITZ, HIS WORK AND THE WORK OF

OTHER ARTISTS HE SUPPORTED.

And a man shall be as an hiding place from the wind, and a covert from the tempest; as rivers of water in a dry place, as the shadow of a great rock in a weary land.

And the eyes of them that see shall not be dim, and the ears of them that hear shall hearken. ISAIAH 32: 2, 3

Verily, verily, I say unto you, Except a corn of wheat fall into the ground and die, it abideth alone: but if it die, it bringeth forth much fruit. JOHN 12: 24

Contents

Dorothy Norman: *Preface*   9

The Editors: *Introduction*   12

PART ONE

William Carlos Williams
The American Background   17

Lewis Mumford
The Metropolitan Milieu   27

Paul Rosenfeld
The Boy in the Dark Room   38

R. Child Bayley
Photography Before Stieglitz   51

Herbert J. Seligmann
291: A Vision Through Photography   58

Dorothy Norman
An American Place   67

PART TWO

Ralph Flint
Post-Impressionism   81

Harold Rugg
The Artist and the Great Transition   91

Evelyn Howard
*The Significance of Stieglitz for the Philosophy
of Science*   100

Waldo Frank
The New World in Stieglitz   106

Portfolio   113

VARIATIONS ON THE THEME

Elizabeth McCausland
Stieglitz and the American Tradition   115

The Man and the Place

John Marin: *The Man and the Place*   118
Marsden Hartley: *291-and the Brass Bowl*   119
Arthur G. Dove: *A Different One*   121
Charles Demuth: *Lighthouses and Fog*   122
Jennings Tofel: *A Portrait*   123
Edna Bryner: *An American Experience*   125
Dorothy Brett: *The Room*   127
Victoria Ocampo: *A Witness*   129
Harold Clurman: *Alfred Stieglitz and
the Group Idea*   130
Gertrude Stein: *Stieglitz*   136

Photography

Paul Strand: *Alfred Stieglitz and a Machine*   137
Evelyn Scott: *A Note on the Esthetic
Significance of Photography*   139

City Plowman

Jean Toomer: *The Hill*   143
Sherwood Anderson: *City Plowman*   146

Chronology   150

List of Exhibitions   150

Selected Bibliography   152

Notes on Contributors   154

Acknowledgments/Picture Credits   155

Index   156

LIST OF ARTISTS WHOSE WORK IS ILLUSTRATED

D. O. HILL

JULIA MARGARET CAMERON

J. CRAIG ANNAN

ALVIN LANGDON COBURN

BARON DE MEYER

ROBERT DEMACHY

CAPTAIN PUYO

RENÉE LE BÈGUE

THEO. AND OSCAR HOFMEISTER

PROFESSOR HANS WATZEK

HUGO HENNEBERG

HEINRICH KÜHN

EDUARD J. STEICHEN

CLARENCE H. WHITE

FRANK EUGENE

GERTRUDE KÄSEBIER

PAMELA COLMAN SMITH

AUGUSTE RODIN

HENRI MATISSE

CONSTANTIN BRANCUSI

PABLO PICASSO

ALFRED MAURER

MAX WEBER

ARTHUR G. DOVE

PAUL STRAND

MARIUS DE ZAYAS

PAUL CÉZANNE

HENRI DE TOULOUSE-LAUTREC

ELIE NADELMAN

MARSDEN HARTLEY

ABRAHAM WALKOWITZ

CHARLES DEMUTH

S. McDONALD WRIGHT

GASTON LACHAISE

JOHN MARIN

GEORGIA O'KEEFFE

ALFRED STIEGLITZ

Preface

Stieglitz was to be seventy on January 1, 1934. When Paul Rosenfeld and Waldo Frank came to tell me of their plan in relation to his birthday, I could wonder only why no one had thought of it before. Their suggestion that we do a book about Stieglitz in honor of the occasion appealed to me at once, as it did to Lewis Mumford and the educator Harold Rugg when they were asked to be co-editors. The twenty others invited to write for the proposed volume were equally enthusiastic. Clearly some fitting homage was in order during the lifetime of so eminent an artist—especially one who had devoted himself with unflagging dedication to gaining support for other living artists.

In our initial statement of purpose, we announced our desire to prepare a structured organism rather than a haphazard collection of tributes. The book we envisioned must provide a powerful sense of the still-living man and his ever-present impact on others. It must describe his contribution to the creative life of America and analyze the facts, significance and technique of his work and influence, their historical and spiritual importance. A large part of the volume should consist of lyric interpretations by writers and artists of varying temperaments who, through their contact with Stieglitz, their critical ability and talent for expression were deemed best equipped to round out the publication. We hoped to include relevant documentation, reproductions of photographs by Stieglitz, and key works by others he had exhibited, first at his now legendary 291, next at The Intimate Gallery and An American Place.

Happily we discovered that those who already had written about Stieglitz—his way of life, his photographs, his battle for modern art— were eager to say more. Others who were planning to put into form what they felt about him also were desirous of writing for what became *America and Alfred Stieglitz.*

When Carl Van Doren chose our completed manuscript as a Literary Guild selection, he issued an eloquent statement: "There was bound to be, sooner or later, a book on the Age of Stieglitz. He is a distinguished artist in his own right, recognized more than forty years ago as a genius in photography. He has had throughout his life an extraordinary gift for perceiving talent in various arts wherever it showed itself and an equal gift for encouraging those artists who deserved it. In a sense he has been both a critic and a patron. But he has been so much more than this that those terms as ordinarily applied fail to characterize his accomplishment."

Van Doren described the volume as "an account of an important movement in American art during the past generation, associated with Alfred Stieglitz as its central and fertilizing figure, but extended in all directions to include numerous phases of artistic impulse and achievement." The new book, he added, represented a study of what had been occurring in the United States and Europe, and pointed out the connections between them, as well as contemporary developments "in science and philosophy in their efforts to give form and expression to the new civilization which is obviously replacing the old."

Because Van Doren saw the "collective portrait" only in early autumn and wanted it distributed in time for Christmas, 1934, it had to be manufactured with inordinate speed. The design was necessarily hurried and the small reproductions were by no means ideal. We feared that Stieglitz, a meticulous craftsman, might be highly critical. On the contrary, he found the unpretentious pictorial section quite adequate under the circumstances and was overwhelmed by both the book's content and the spirit of Van Doren's treatment of it.

Francis Henry Taylor—later to become Director of the Metropolitan Museum of Art—observed in his review of the volume that Stieglitz, a truly great man, probably had "been right in the matter of contemporary aesthetics more often than any other critic and 'patron.'" Stieglitz, he noted, "was the champion of the new and the difficult to understand, a law unto himself with courage that is vouchsafed to few of us in the arts."

3

Stieglitz has been widely heralded as the father of modern photography. Yet photography signified something far more to him than taking pictures with a camera. It became an obsession, a philosophy, a way of life—a religion. It served as an essential instrument in his search for truth.

Stieglitz was a photographer in whatever he did, no experience being complete for him until he had *seen* it, put it into form, in picture or in word. He said of the camera that it brought the invisible to the surface. He brought wonder to the surface—and self-delusion: "To see the moment," he proclaimed, "is to liberate the moment."

Stieglitz was a man in love with truth. It shocked him that the world rebelled against the telling and hearing of the entire truth. He challenged people to say what they really saw and felt, rather than what they thought they should see and feel; to distinguish between what they really did and what they said or thought they did. From early childhood he failed to comprehend how people who said they believed in one thing could do the reverse. He detested the double standard, the discrepancy between an uptown and downtown morality.

He expected nothing of others save that they tell him the truth, without fear: "Only by telling each other the truth can we help one another. Only by being true to oneself can one be true to the other: can one be true to time. Only in being true to all moments can we be true to any." He said, "The sole democracy I recognize is that 'All true things are equal to one another.'" He believed that where there is no conscience, there can be no art. "The goal of the artist is to be truthful and then to share that truthfulness with others."

Stieglitz was a man in love in manifold ways. "When I make a picture," he said, "I make love. Unless what is created communicates the pristine quality of the first kiss—unless it is born of a sense of awe and wonder—it does not deserve to be called a work of art." Yet it was never art in any narrow sense of the word about which he cared: "Whether it be scrubbing a floor or painting a picture, only doing the best job of which one is capable finally can fulfill. And then one must aim to surpass even that: to hit not only the target but the center of the center of the target, and then the point beyond that. . . . If we cannot lose ourselves to something beyond, we are bound to be disappointed."

He spoke of beauty as the universal seen—as the sole reality for one of his temperament. "Beauty," he believed, "begets beauty. Love begets love. Art begets art. Truth begets truth." But he knew also that the work of art we seek to create, like truth itself—like the total possession of the loved one—is ever beyond absolute attainment: "The true thing can never be brought completely to light. The more beautiful it is, the less completely can it be brought to light." And so art, for Stieglitz, like love, was "born of heartache."

Tell him that you loved a particular picture by a living painter and you would elicit a heated response: "But what are you ready to do for the artist who made it? Will your admiration procure a loaf of bread, a single crumb? The act came first and only then the word."

It was because Stieglitz looked upon modern art—including photography—as a great liberating force that he dedicated himself to celebrating and protecting those who created it. He wanted to procure respect for the living artist, and a living wage. He challenged people to grow beyond bargaining for art or thinking about it in terms of private ownership and investment. "When," he asked, "will the public learn voluntarily to protect for itself its most sacred heritage? What is of interest to me is to awaken people to having a sacred feeling about certain things that cannot be bought, cannot be touched." The sense of touch was sacred to Stieglitz. His greatest pictures portray with awe an equivalent of what he felt too sacred to touch, yet he knew well that, unless what one creates possesses a sense of touch, it will not be art.

Art, in Stieglitz's view, like love, transcended theory. He abhorred dogma and labels, attempting always to discover what he called basic laws of life: "I am attracted by life, not doctrine. All isms contain a grain of truth. Each is but part of a passing phase." He responded warmly to Goethe's "Life is green. Theories are gray."

Stieglitz early concluded that all else we can accomplish is futile, unless we recognize life's basic laws. Even though he insisted that "that 'all else' may be the living—the experience necessary for the eventual crystallization termed 'Seeing.'"

He affirmed the fact that our ability to "see ourselves without pity for self or resentment toward others" signals the "beginning of peace within—the only Peace. Not as theory—but as life itself—swinging *with* the universe—not for."

Stieglitz was convinced that he had discovered several basic laws of importance, one of them having to do with equivalence. At first he referred to his cloud photographs as "equivalents." Next he used the word to describe all of his photographs. Finally he termed all art an equivalent of the artist's most profound experience of life.

Stieglitz was indeed obsessed by a search for truth. Yet his equally powerful aversion to isms protected him from becoming doctrinaire himself, either about that quest or any other. In the 1921 catalogue for an exhibition of his photographs, he called attention to how the document did not contain any of "the following, fast becoming 'obsolete' terms . . . *Art, Science, Beauty, Religion . . . Abstraction, Form, Plasticity, Objectivity, Subjectivity, Old Masters, Modern Art, Psychoanalysis, Aesthetics, Pictorial Photography, Democracy, Cézanne, '291', Prohibition.* The term *Truth* did creep in but may be kicked out by anyone."

Over the years an increasing number of art exhibitions, college courses, doctoral theses and other writings have been focusing attention upon Stieglitz. Since some of those responsible for such undertakings have lacked the opportunity of knowing the man at first hand or have failed sufficiently to study his work and existing documentation about him, facts and interpretations have become somewhat distorted at times. It is to be hoped that this publication, created by those who knew their subject and his work, will aid in setting the record straight.

Fortunately, it has been made possible to provide a new Appendix. Since the original one had to be compiled at the last moment with undue haste, errors inevitably were introduced. Neither the amended Chronology, Bibliography, nor the List of Exhibitions have been extended beyond the date of the original edition. No changes have been made in the remainder of the book. The few inaccuracies to be found in the main text have been considered too minimal to warrant correction at the risk of disturbing the book's original flow.

Dorothy Norman

December, 1974
New York

Introduction

THIS BOOK IS NOT A COLLECTION OF TRIBUTES, it is not a symposium of opinions, it is not a compilation of facts about a man. The life of Alfred Stieglitz has been lived in active relation with the world; his work has been in the deepest sense a communal work. This book is an attempt to express the nature of the career of Alfred Stieglitz by being, itself, in spirit and form, a communal work, a work organic with its subject.

It begins with a study of the cultural background, the specific Pioneer-Puritan culture, from which all creative work in the United States derives, directly and indirectly; and with a portrait of the nineteenth-century city of New York which was the fruit of that culture, the scene of the modern revolt and emergence from it, and the specific matrix of the life of Stieglitz. A biographical interpretation of the man follows, a first intimate sighting of his person; then an account of the medium—photography—in which he achieved his most impersonal expression, and portraits of the gathering places of men and of art, and of the human relations, in which he has fulfilled his creative purpose. This is Part One: it may be said to present the body of the subject in concrete social terms. Part Two draws the ideological dimensions and continues the historic lines through our immediate and urgent present into the future before us. It studies, specifically, the movements of art in the period spanned by Stieglitz, linking his work and that of his group with the work of Europe; it portrays the intellectual and educational directives at home, epitomized under such terms as Pragmatism and Instrumentalism, and the place and symbolic share therein of Stieglitz; finally it endeavors to situate Stieglitz, as the leader of a communal creative movement, within the march of modern thought and within the central preoccupation of our era: the creating of a new civilization, a new culture, a new world. This concludes Part Two: the Theme. But in the judgment of all who know him, an essential aspect of the creative work of Stieglitz is his relationship with individuals and his effect upon them. This indeed is the color and music of the man, and no collective portrait would be complete without its recording. Hence, the last division of the text: *Variations on the Theme*. It is really a collection of brief portraits of persons mirrored within their own experience of Stieglitz. Since for fifty years Stieglitz has lived in constant intimate contact with the lives and works of men and women, these variations of the theme in the modality of sensitive Americans, South Americans, Europeans, are integrally of the theme itself.

Of course, the idea of such a book as this had to start in the heads of specific individuals. But as soon as it was abroad it nourished itself, it took on body like an organic being. The idea made certain contributors inevitable; once exposed to it, they responded. Others proved themselves inevitable by spontaneously coming forward with collaborations that belonged in the communal undertaking. The specific subjects of the collaborators were innerly determined by their own nature and by the nature of their relationship with Stieglitz.

Such a process could not be precise. The cultural life in America that Stieglitz's work has shared, nurtured, and projected, and which this book was designed to express, is not delimited like a biological body; nor could it be logically controlled beforehand like the summation of an epoch that had already flowered. This life, after all, and Stieglitz himself (as the book reveals), is largely a *potential*. There have been contributors whose work, for one reason or another, could unfortunately not be used in this book, as its final form evolved; there are others whose contributions, although they may at first appear to break the march of the whole, were felt in reality to be organic with the book; and there are doubtless other potential collaborators who, because of time or distance or lack of knowledge on our part or theirs, have not made their contribution.

These imperfections of trial and error are of the world which Stieglitz has helped to keep alive within our American time. Yet our book, however inadequate, at least begins to articulate that world; and, by its variety of vision and its community of structure, to embody it. It is, in itself, a proof that the spirit lives in America today. And this concerns us more (as it does Alfred Stieglitz) than the book's personal subject.

This world which Stieglitz has embodied and projected through nearly fifty years of intricate creative action is, we feel, important in the precise sense that Man is important; in the precise sense that the struggle toward truth is important; in the sense that America, as a favored soil where truth may be sought and where Man may live, is potentially important. And this book we feel is significant, perhaps, in that it reveals this world through the collective portrayal of a contemporary whose life has been an incarnation, singularly perfect, of the struggle toward truth, an incarnation indeed, in humble modern form, of Man . . . and in American terms and on American soil.

THE EDITORS.

September, 1934,
New York.

PART ONE

William Carlos Williams

The American Background

THEY SAW BIRDS *with rusty breasts and called them robins. Thus, from the start, an America of which they could have had no inkling drove the first settlers upon their past. They retreated for warmth and reassurance to something previously familiar. But at a cost. For what they saw were not robins. They were thrushes only vaguely resembling the rosy, daintier English bird. Larger, stronger, and in the evening of a wilder, lovelier song, actually here was something the newcomers had never in their lives before encountered. Blur. Confusion. A bird that beats with his wings and slows himself with his tail in landing.*

The example is slight but enough properly to incline the understanding. Strange and difficult, the new continent induced a torsion in the spirits of the first settlers, tearing them between the old and the new. And at once a split occurred in that impetus which should have carried them forward as one into the dangerous realities of the future.

They found that they had not only left England but that they had arrived somewhere else: at a place whose pressing reality demanded not only a tremendous bodily devotion but as well, and more importunately, great powers of adaptability, a complete reconstruction of their most intimate cultural make-up, to accord with the new conditions. The most hesitated and turned back in their hearts at the first glance.

Meanwhile, nostalgically, erroneously, a robin.

It is conceivable that a new language might have sprung up with the new spectacle and the new conditions, but even genius, if it existed, did not make one. It was an inability of the mind to function in the face of overwhelming odds, a retreat to safety, an immediate defensive organization of whatever sort against the wilderness. As an emergency, the building up of such a front was necessary and understandable. But, if the falsity of the position is to be appreciated, what they did must be understood to have been a temporary expedient, permissible only while a new understanding was building.

Thus two cultural elements were left battling for supremacy, one looking toward Europe, necessitous but retrograde in its tendency —though not wholly so by any means—and the other forward-looking but under a shadow from the first. They constituted two great bands of effort, which it would take a Titan to bring together and weld into one again. Throughout the present chapter, the terms native and borrowed, related and unrelated, primary and secondary, will be used interchangeably to designate these two opposed split-offs from the full cultural force, and occasionally, in the same vein, true and false.

The English settlers, on the northeast coast, were those most concerned in this division of the attack, but it was they who would establish the predominant mode and its consequences. Further south, and it is important to note that it was to the south and in California, where the climate was milder, that this bolder phase of the colonization had its brief flowering, an attempt on a different scale was instituted. Under the Spanish the sixteenth-century universities, bishoprics, and works of a like order, constituted a project diametrically opposed to what the English understood. What they seemed to have in mind was no colony at all, but within the folds of their religious hegemony an extension of Spain herself to the westward. But the difficulties were too great, too unimaginably novel to the grasp of their minds for them to succeed.

From geographic, biologic, political, and economic causes, the Spanish conception ended in failure, and the slower, colder, more practical plan of lesser scope out of northern Europe prevailed. North America became, in great measure, a colony of England, so to be regarded by the intellect and fashion of the day. While on the part of most of the colonists there would be a reciprocal attitude toward "home." The immediate cultural aspect, in dress, music, manners, soon developed a disdain for the local, as became a colony looking back toward fashion brought to it by its governors and copied in America wherever possible.

Nowhere is the antagonism of the times toward local initiative better shown than in *An Official Report on Virginia (1671)*, by Governor Sir William Berkeley, when he wrote:

I thank God there are no free schools or printing, and I hope we shall not have these hundred years, for learning has brought disobedience, and heresy, and sects into the world, and printing has divulged them, and libels against the best government. God keep us from both.

Alongside all this, nevertheless, an enterprise neither Spanish nor English, nor colonial by any way of speaking save in its difficulty and poverty of manner, began widely to form, a new reference by which knowledge and understanding would one day readjust themselves to a changing world. It was America itself which put up its head from the start—to thrive in mode of life, in character of institutions, in household equipment, in the speech, though opposed with might and main everywhere from the official party both at home and abroad. Noah Webster spent a life here building the radically subversive thesis which his dictionary represents. But the same force began pushing its way forward in any number of other forms also. Necessity drove it ahead. Unorthodox, it ran beside the politer usages of the day, never, except in the moment of a threatened national catastrophe, the Revolution, to be given a general sanction.

It was a harsh world the first men had to face. He who has seen the hill coming up from the waterfront at Plymouth, changed though it be from all possible resemblance to the poverty of that day, will have no trouble for all that in imagining the bareness, the savage exposure, of those first isolated buildings regularly laid out either side the one climbing street. Merely to read the stone which commemorates the fifty per cent death rate of that first winter is enough to fasten the picture of tragedy on the mind. But just the bare statement in the chronicles of the necessity the people were under to bury their dead at night so as not to give the natives knowledge of their rapidly diminishing numbers while they waited for the ships to return, fastens the impression of terror and an alien mood toward the land upon the mind indelibly. And these things were repeated north and south in a hundred other instances.

The land was from the first antagonistic. The purpose must have been in major part not to be bound to it but to push back its obstructions before the invading amenities—to drive them before one. To force them back. That these transplanted men were at the same time pushing back a very necessary immediate knowledge of the land to be made theirs and that indeed all that they possessed and should henceforth be able to call their own was just this complexity of environment which killed them, could not become at once apparent.

Even the Revolution would prove anything but a united movement toward self-realization on the part of America. The colonists did not, except in their humbler parts, desire separation from the mother country—not in the beginning, at any rate. It took time for the national consciousness to make itself known, and against heavy odds. The significance of these old conflicts is often lost now, but valuable light arises in them again and again throughout the annals. The conflict existed strongly in the intimate nature of the commander-in-chief himself. He did not for more than a year after the beginning of the Revolution think of his action as anything but the protest of a loyal subject to his king. Not till after bitterest realization of disappointed hopes did the full force of the thing break heavily upon him. It caused Washington a wrench not only of the heart but of the understanding itself to drag himself away from England.

The two divergent forces were steadily at work, one drawing the inhabitants back to the accustomed with its appeals to loyalty and the love of comfort, the other prodding them to face very often the tortures of the damned, working a new way into a doubtful future, calling for faith, courage, and carelessness of spirit. It was, be it noted, an inner tension, a cultural dilemma, which was the cause of this. As corroborating evidence of which, note further that it was Thomas Jefferson, a man of delicate and curiously balanced mentality, not a soldier, who envisioned and drafted the Declaration of Independence. And that it was a practical man of unusual sagacity, Benjamin Franklin, who was the most persistent and successful exponent of the project to take into native hands and to deal directly, by force, if necessary, with the world of their time.

Washington's unique place in the history is that of the blameless leader, the great emblem, almost the unconscious emblazonment of the cause. As a soldier he was merely a servant. The other outstanding figure was John Adams, representing the relic obstinacy of the original Pilgrims.

The war over, the true situation, raised into relief by patriotic fervor, would flatten out as before into the persistent struggle between the raw new and the graciousness of an imposed cultural design. England eliminated, those very ones who opposed her would fast take the leading place in the scheme from which she had been driven, renewing the old struggle at home. The fashionable would still be fashionable, and the unfashionable, unfashionable as before.

In this inevitable conflict of interests Thomas Jefferson stands out as the sole individual who seems to have had a clear understanding of what was taking place. He did appear to see the two trends and to make a conscious effort to embrace them and to draw them together into a whole. But even for him, the disparity remained unbridgeable in his day. It was Jefferson who, when President, would walk to his office in the mud, out of principle, and walk home again as against the others who would, ignoring the mud, ride. And at the same time it was Jefferson who, recognizing the imperious necessity for other loveliness to lay beside his own, such as it was, would inquire whether or not it might be possible, in securing a gardener, to get one who could at the same time play the flute. His home at Monticello, with its originality, good taste, with its distinctive local quality, is one of the few places where the two cultural strains approach in our history, where they consciously draw together. But Jefferson's idea would be sadly snowed under.

While it was destined that Jefferson should directly fail in propagating his cultural insights, it was at the same time the good fortune of Franklin indirectly to succeed.

Franklin, coming down from New England, saw things in a different way from that of Virginia. His talent, primarily technical, with the bearing which all technical matters have upon the immediate, took him quite apart from his will in the right direction. Though there seems always too much of the bumptious provincial in Franklin, he had the luck. For America has approached the cultural plateau from this necessitous technical side.

But with the beginners, facing difficulties, things did not go so well at first. America had to be before it could become effective—even in its own mind. Finding itself, as a democracy, unable to *take up* the moral and economic implications of its new conditions, which Jefferson lived and proposed, America slumped *back to* fashion on the one, favored, side, and, having slighted the difficult real, it fell back at the same time to unrelated, crazy rigidities and imbecilities of formal pattern, later to blossom as Dowieism, Billy-Sundayism, etc., etc., to say nothing of the older schisms over petty ritual of the same sort. Confusion, a leaderless mob, each wandering into a mire of its own—with perfect logic.

All this weight would one day have to be lifted in the final cultural pick-up still waiting—tremendous, neglected; a stone on the neck for the time being at least, it left Jefferson crushed.

When the first courageous drives toward a realistic occupation of America slackened, men like Boone, Crockett, and Houston had to be accounted for. It is not hard to fabricate a melodramatic part for them. The hard thing to do is to make the understanding of what they were appear integral with the history, effective in a direct understanding, of what men have become today. Presented historically because of their picturesqueness or a legendary skill with a gun, actually the cultural place these men occupy is the significant one. And if it seems always easier to romanticize a thing than to understand it, it is so because very often it is more convenient to do so. Especially is this true when to romanticize a thing covers a significance which may be disturbing to a lying conscience.

For Boone, at least, was not a romantic, losing himself in the "mystery" of the forest. He was a technical genius of the woods, enjoying, in that respect, the admiration of the most skillful native craftsmen, who remained actually in awe of his sheer abilities and accomplishments. What more cultured to him than the solitude of the trees? He was fiercely disdainful of the scrambling colonist, and ever more so as time went on.

The significance of Boone and of the others of his time and trade, was that they abandoned touch with those along the coast, and their established references, and made contact with the intrinsic elements of an as yet unrealized material of which the new country was made. It is the actuality of their lives, and its tragic effect on them, which is illuminating.

All of them, when they did come back to the settlements, found themselves strangers. Houston, as late as Lincoln's time, lived apart from his neighbors, wearing a catskin vest, whittling a stick and thinking. But the reason underlying this similarity of action in all of them is not that they were outmoded but rather defeated in a curious way which baffled them. Only Jackson carried the crudeness of his origins successfully up to the top by the luck of battle, and for a short time only. And when he did, as Ezra Pound has recently pointed out, it was Jackson who, because of his basic culture, was able first to smell out the growing fault and attack the evidence of a wrong tack having been taken, the beginning raid on public moneys by private groups, which he turned back for a few years.

Such men, right thinking, but prey to isolation by the forces surrounding them, became themselves foreigners—in their own country. They were disarmed by the success of their softer-living neighbors, a success which can now be marked as the growing influence of the false cultural trend. Actually Boone was a genius, lamed by the gigantic newness which won him but into which he could not penetrate far enough—it was impossible. At least he signalized rightly what was to be done. Such men had no way of making their realizations vocal. They themselves became part of the antagonistic wilderness against which the coastal settlements were battling. Their sadness alone survives. Many of them could hardly read. Their speech became crude. Their manners sometimes offensive. It was the penalty they had to pay.

It was a curious anomaly. They in themselves had achieved a culture, an adjustment to the conditions about them, which was of the first order, and which, at the same time, oddly cut them off from the others.

Even Washington, during a lifetime, was subject to the same torsion, and was extremely backward in adjustment to the growing laxity of his time, by virtue, be it said, of the actuality of this same backwoods training, which in his case did not last long enough to hold him entirely in its narrowing grasp. Another evidence of his great shrewdness. But, at the pinch, it was this which later stood him in good stead, though it caused him, at the same time, endless suffering. It was powerful by its direct relation to actuality but remained heavily opposed by a more fashionable choice. Not he, but Roger Morris got the wealthy Mary Philipse.

It was precisely that which gave them their realistic grasp of situations and things which made these men unacceptable to their world of a rising cultural tide, gone astray, but of the sort which would predominate. Washington had all kinds of luck, quite apart from his character, to get through alive. He did manage to maintain himself intact, but only at the cost of a tremendous isolation, at a time of national stress which required the unique strength of moral base possessed by him, which came from a complexity of events in his birth and bringing up, and in which the others were lacking. But he was generously hated for it. All manner of intrigue dogged his steps in the attempt to break down his difficult standard.

His realization of what he was after came out one night when, on his way to West Point from Hartford, he passed through a small Connecticut town. The women and children came out with torches to cheer him and accompanied him a short distance on his way. This is the army, he said, that they will never conquer. It is easily conceivable that with less luck he could have been destroyed early, and the mud they threw at his carriage during his second term in the Presidency not have been counted among his laurels. He stood out because, like Boone, he stuck fast to facts which enforced his adherence above the glamour of an easier fortune. He was shrewd and powerful in other respects, but it was the unswerving moral integrity by which he clove to the actual conditions of his position which was at the bottom of his courage. It was the strength of a cultural adjustment of the first sort.

One is at liberty to guess what the pure American addition to world culture might have been if it had gone forward singly. But that is merely an academicism. Perhaps Tenochtitlan which Cortez destroyed held the key. That also is beside the point, except that Tenochtitlan with its curious brilliance may still legitimately be kept alive in thought not as something which *could* have been preserved but as something which was actual and was destroyed.

One might go on to develop the point from this that the American addition to world culture will always be the "new," in opposition to an "old" represented by Europe. But that isn't satisfactory. What it is actually is something much deeper: a relation to the immediate conditions of the matter in hand, and a determination to assert them in opposition to all intermediate authority. Deep in the pattern of the newcomers' minds was impressed that conflict between present reliance on the prevalent conditions of place and the overriding of an unrelated authority. It is that which, at its

best, comes like the cut of a knife through old sophistry—but it requires the skillful wielding of a sharp knife. And this requires a trained hand.

Not that this direct drive toward the new is a phenomenon distinctively confined to America: it is the growing edge in every culture. But the difficulties encountered in settling the new ground did make it a clearer necessity in America—or should have done so—clearer than it could have been shown to be otherwise or elsewhere. To Americans the effort to appraise the real through the maze of a cut off and imposed culture from Europe has been a vivid task, if very often too great for their realizations. Thus the new and the real, hard to come at, are synonymous.

The abler spirits among the pioneers cut themselves off from the old at once and set to work with a will directly to know what was about them. America had to be before it could become effective even in its own mind. It set out helter-skelter. And, by God, it was. Besides, it couldn't wait. Crudely authentic, the bulk of a real culture was being built up from that point. The direct attack they instituted, shown in many cases by no other results than the characters of the men and women themselves, was in many cases at least within reach of the magnificent wish expressed in cries of wonder let out by Columbus's men on seeing the new world actually, for the first time, standing and running about before them.

At moments it flashes bewilderingly before people as reflected in the wild cries of the Paris crowds about Woodrow Wilson's carriage when he held up his hope of escape in 1918. But, unrealized in America itself, there too it slipped away again.

It isn't just to say that the acquisition of borrowed European culture was in itself a bad thing. It was, moreover, inevitable that it should be brought here. As inevitable as the buying of legislatures many years later in order that railroads might with the least possible delay be laid across the country. It is only unfortunate that this sort of thing should be taken to be virtue itself, a makeshift, really, in constant opposition to the work of those good minds which had the hardihood to do without it. The appurtenances of Europe came in with their language and habits, more finished than anything native could have been—that is, barring Indian workmanship and manner, which were of slight value in the East. As a matter of fact, these borrowed effects were better in quality than the native.

Samuel Butler's famous witticism, O God, O Montreal! is the sort of jibe the authentic crudeness had to weather at the start.

But while the men working toward the center were inventing their new tools of thought, welding their minds to new conformations with the situation as it existed, the men of the opposing force were in closer and closer touch with the Old World. By improvement of the means of transportation, the slow accumulation of goods, and the coming to the New World of more gentle types, these secured their hold more and more on the American cultural scene.

It was all right to say, as Poe did, speaking of writing, that we should cut ourselves loose from the lead strings of our British grandmama. He did so—to the confusion of critics even to the present day—but few could follow him. And Charles Dickens could well reply by his well-known attack on American manners—his vituperation salted by astonishment before a strangeness he could not explain. Wider and wider the two bands of effort drew apart, the division which must inevitably have taken place signalized by the two more or less definitive parties in American politics. And it was foreordained that the cleverer, more united, and more numerous unrelated element—represented by the cities along the seaboard—should have the ascendency.

After the Revolution there would be a constant gnawing away of the State which, under the powerful influence of Washington and his associates, had been constructed. There would be an accelerated dropping back to style and the unrelated importations. Boone's lands would be stolen away from him by aid of unscrupulous land speculators with influence in Congress, and he would go off to Spanish territory around St. Louis in disgust of his race. It was not "culture" of either sort, to be sure, which drove him out, but it was under the necessities, the conditions, under the skirts of the borrowed lack of attachment, that the agencies throve which were his undoing.

Nor is this solely an American difficulty. It is seen in such things as the steady decay of life in the Shetland Islands, while the Faroes, less favorably situated to the north, too far for exploitation by the London markets, have begun a regeneration under a rediscovered genius of place. A like impetus is behind the bombing by a young and patriotic Breton of the memorial celebrating the absorption of Brittany by a greater France. The attempt of an unrelated culture upon a realistic genius of place is deeply involved in these events, as in the undying movement to free Ireland.

But in America the struggle was brilliant and acute. It was also on a vaster scale.

Many of us, who should know better, are quick to brand Americans with the term "colonial" if in a moment of irritation some Yankee stands up and wants to wipe out, let us say, French painting. In a loud voice he lets go: We can paint as well—or intend shortly to do so—as them demned frogs. We'll show 'em.

But there is a more persuasive phase to the feeling from which such an outburst might arise. It is this: The chief reason for existence cannot be but in the devising of excellence (or in destroying it, for it would be senseless to destroy the worthless) which is in

effect evidence of the approach of equals. And though it is profitable to milk a cow and to use its milk (as well as its manure) it is quite as profitable in another way to talk with a man of sense and novel experience and to propose and carry out with him cultural projects. Especially is this delightful, or of value, when that man's outlook and background are new to us—by that much more in a way to cast a light on old errors of judgment.

In poverty and danger America borrowed, where it could, a culture—or at least the warmth of it ad interim. But this, valuable for the moment and later also as an attribute of fashion and wealth, fixed itself upon the mind until, the realization of the actual, original necessity being largely forgotten, it even went so far that Americans themselves no longer believed in it.

Meanwhile an unrelated Hopi ceremonial—unrelated, that is, except to the sand, the corn, the birds, the beasts, the periodic drought, and the mountain sights and colors—was living in the farther West.

A servile copying of Europe, not Jefferson's, became the rule. And along with it a snobbism from which or from the effects of which very few escaped. The secondary split-off from what, but for fear, had been a single impetus, finally focused itself as personal wealth in America, important since it is wealth that controls the mobility of a nation. But dangerous since by its control it can isolate and so render real values, in effect, impotent.

So, being held as a prerogative, wealth, by the influence it wields, may become the chief cause of cultural stagnation. This has been the case in America. To support its own position it has sought to surround itself with the appurtenances of a finished culture which is of no direct significance in the new sphere. But by this emphasis such a culture of purchase, a culture in effigy, has become predominant. The harm is done. The primary cultural influence, embraced by the unfortunately impoverished native, came to a stop.

Wealth went on. The cities were its seat. By its centralization of money men flocked to them, leaving the already hard pressed and often failing culture of immediate references still farther behind. The small cities and lesser communities involving nine tenths of the population began to waste more and more. In many places life has actually disappeared—buildings being occupied only by chipmunks and porcupines. And these were once sources of energy, drained off by a cause not quite so simple as it has been imagined to be.

Certainly the trend must have been from poor land to good and from cheap lands toward the gold fields, the power sites, navigation centers, and the locations of natural resources of all sorts. Inevitably. One must accept the fact. But the pull exerted by tastes of a secondary order, involved in this rush to the cities, though unstoppable, may nevertheless be traced out and recorded. The cities had at least population and a quickened pulse, but in getting this, as in everything where the secondary culture predominates, the cost was severe. It involved the actual decay of the small community. And the decay of the small community was a primary cultural decay. It would seem as if the city has as its very being the raising of the cultural level, as if it were in the very stream of the great flow. Quite the opposite is true, unless the place of the city, as a sort of turntable and that only, be clearly realized.

The decay of the small community was an actual decay of culture; it was a sack by invisible troops, leaving destruction for which the gains—and they were considerable—did not compensate. It was a loss which degraded, which was compelled by circumstances but which posited a return to sources in some form later on. The inevitable destruction of the South during the Civil War was of this order. It was the overwhelming desire for an immediate realization of wealth, for escape from isolation which made wealth paramount and to be fought for, at any cost. Wealth meant, as it means today, the control of movement, mobility, the power to come and go at will. In small communities being drained of wealth by the demand for it in the cities, men died like rats caught in a trap. And their correctly aimed but crude and narrow beginnings died with them.

Take such a place as H——, Vermont, apart from the difficulties with the water supply—rotten and fallen into decay—inspiration, the full spirit, alone could ever have made it possible for men to live there. It is that something tremendously volatile and important has been withdrawn. Without attachment to an essential reality, nothing could have lived in these closed-off areas. And with it life can spring up in the very sand.

A related culture is a plant of such a sort. It spreads itself everywhere. But an unrelated culture is neither hardy nor prolific.

It was the reality of the small community which settled the territory in the first place, but from behind came the wave which blotted that out. And it was the culture of immediacy, the active strain, which has left every relic of value which survives today. It was a losing battle. Against an overwhelming mass superiority of wealth the struggles of a related culture grew still less and less. The very roots were being dried up.

Note well, that there is a hard law of the world which governs the emergence and disappearance of men as of communities and nations: To the victor belong the spoils. The cultural effects of America are governed by this as everything else is governed. Nothing is good because it is American, as nothing survives merely because it is authentic. The false may and often does supersede it. But the law is operative, like every other law, only under definite conditions. These may be ascertained and measured.

All that is being said is that it must be realized that men are driven to their fates by the quality of their beliefs. And that in America this has been the success of the unrelated, borrowed, the would-be universal culture which the afterwave has run to or imposed on men to impoverish them, if it has not actually disenfranchised their intelligences.

As the force of the crude but related beginnings faded away, for without money to make them mobile they stagnated, it nevertheless had some successes. The most effective drive of local realization came, as mentioned above, in practical inventiveness. Crude, at first, necessitous, immediate, hand-to-mouth, that was the first test. There it could not afford to wait on anything. It had to be cut and go.

And wealth took the scene, representative of a sort of squatter spirit, irresponsible because unrelated to the territory it overran. And wealth, in this temper, grew to be intolerant to the beginning culture it replaced. It seems strange that this mobility should have aligned itself as it did and shown itself antagonistic to the locally related. But being secondary and psychologically inferior to the first, the cause for the antagonism is plainly discernible. This psychological inferiority of position is reflected in the sordidness of much that was tolerated by the rich as time went on, as so well pointed out by Lincoln Steffens, in order to maintain themselves in their position.

It was the new, American phase of that same rule of wealth which "had adapted and converted the vast sources of power in nature to its own use and convenience, and which has exploited and perverted the course of religion and philosophic thought since the dawn of civilization." Particularly vicious was this in a Democracy with the history which had been America's, since it was just that, as the note was set, which the first white men had come here to escape.

And still, men flocked to the cities.

Against this heavy tide, the real cultural forms might take on an unconscious beauty of refinement in the lines of fast ships and, in more conscious form, the carved and painted figureheads of the ships themselves. It might produce glassware, such collectors' items as the wooden marriage chests of Pennsylvania workmanship, an architecture old and new, and many other things as well exemplified as anywhere by the furniture in white pine and other native woods built by the Shakers in their colonies along the New York-Connecticut border. Beautiful examples are these of what could be done by working in a related manner with the materials in hand; they are plastically the most truthful monuments to the sincerity of the motives that produced them that could well be imagined. Here was a sect, isolated by their beliefs, living in small self-sufficient communities, seeking to make what they needed out of what they had for the quiet and disciplined life they sought. It was a bigoted, small life, a closing in of themselves for a purpose, but it was simple and inoffensive. All these qualities appear in the workmanship, a kind of gentle parable to the times. To no purpose. It was vitally necessary that wealth should accumulate. It did. It couldn't help it. The consequences were persistent and unfortunate. And the strategy of fashion, partisans of the colonial spirit, had to be to keep the locally related in a secondary place. They needed art and culture, and the art and culture they fostered, and paid for, major in quantity, overshadowed the often defective and ineffectual new.

And there it was. The insecurity all men felt in the predominance of this purchased culture, unrelated to the new conditions, made them rush for security in money all the more. With these consequences: the abandonment of the primary effort and the further and further concentration of population at the trade centers, the cities, and the steady depletion of the rural districts.

It is in character that Washington with his sense of reality had an instinct away from them to his "vine and fig tree"—though he shared equally with the others, it must be said, the common lust for money and the security it could buy.

Men went to the cities, correctly, not even for the cash directly so much as because of the growing spiritual impoverishment of the outlying districts, a breakdown which brought a moral breakdown in its train. How could it be otherwise? The actual, the necessity for dealing with a condition as it existed, seemed to become unnecessary because of mystical powers represented by money. Decay must, therefore, immediately have got in motion among the faculties which fastened the pioneer to his world.

And the agent serving this colossal appetite for wealth, what has come to be known as "the law," became in fact the index of the moral corruption of the time, actually not the law, but a professional class of law breakers. In Lincoln Steffens's autobiography, the structure of this moral decay is laid bare in its childlike simplicity: the economic, the military, the political masters at the top—all who were in power swept up by the predominant, unrelated culture they had been practising. It grew, a great snowball rolling them up together, minister and financier, Senator and college teacher, woman and man, young and old—fashion and cash. But being unrelated, having no basis in the conditions of the place, it had to have power by other means, and it had to have it quickly.

Museums were founded. Country estates, operas founded. And in the "generosity" of their gifts this series of generations believed they offered an excuse for their actions. The baleful architecture of certain of the years might have made them think, but it appears not to have done so. Religion became a stencil which roused many a man to a pitch of hatred against the form and repetitious stupidity

of it, that would never be eradicated from his nature thereafter.

But those at the top, possessing cash, and so retaining their enviable mobility, relied on the lawyer-politician-officeholder or professional intermediary as the means to keep them there.

It is clear that the racketeer, the hired assassin, the confirmed perjurer, the non-officeholding boss, is the same person as the higher agent of the class holding the money, who by their cash in turn keep the whole range of false cultural agencies in line. Money being power and the power to move at will, it has always been the prime agent of decay in the world. But in America, whose resources made Golconda look like a copper penny, it would run, a fire through the grass, more wildly than anything the world had ever seen before. The organization of the underworld would be exactly the replica, the true picture, of the national government—until finally they fused actually into one in the early years of the century, unabashed.

Incredible, fairy-tale-like, even offensively perverse as it may seem, it is the fear, the cowardice, the inability before the new, which in America whipped the destructive false current on like a forest fire. And, though it is not easily to be believed, it is a sense of their inferior position which drove the early fortunes on to their exorbitant excesses.

A board of directors of a great national corporation which has been using a man's patent illegally for ten years owes him two million dollars in back royalties. He institutes suit against them. He, one man without money. But in this case there are incriminating letters on file in the Department of Justice. Now. These letters may be destroyed if someone in Washington can be fixed. The man may possibly be bluffed out of a realization of his aspirations, or a feeling of futility toward his quest may unhorse him. Or he may be murdered, if possible, "accidentally." There's the set-up. And the law has devised for itself an immunity so that it may with perfect impunity "legally" serve not only the corporate ruler himself but his servants and imitators all down the line to the lowest crook, even to the point of such technical minutiæ of upsetting a verdict as that one of the jurors is slightly hard of hearing.

And such instruments do, very certainly, hold the awed admiration of the sheep en masse, who wish they also could be sure of, be able to pay for, such a friend as the law in time of need.

The influence of a primary culture went on diminishing, save by moments through the work of a Whitman or a Poe; and there were clipper ships leading the race for trade around the world—and in the back yards of their masters and crews, a refined school of literary borrowers looking gracefully askance at Melville.

Andrew Jackson took up his battle with the banks, which by that time had gradually succeeded in diverting every nickel of the government's funds into their private coffers. And three quarters of a century later, Woodrow Wilson would still be making statements relative to the menace to government of a vast and illusive credit power.

And still somewhat later, money was being consciously thrown away to known bankrupts, Brazil, Peru, and the German Reich, for the sole apparent purpose of impoverishing the region in which the bankers happened to maintain their traffic. Dizzily they conceded credits to allied corporate interests, at the same time calling small loans in order to pinch out the individual borrower, thus intrenching themselves in the monopoly and impoverishing the little man more and more till he should leave the field or take less and less in wages.

But this ascendancy of a secondary culture, secure in wealth, was gained not without results that were ludicrous as well as tragic. Wealth established museums, but it could not tell, it had to be told, what was good in them. Nor can it do anything with the treasures of the ages but stand by, while the primary forces employ them with taste, understanding, and, it may be finally, with power. There were the Boni de Castellanes, the Tiara age of American opera, box-holders sleeping through the music or wondering what the hell it was all about, while the American composer, Ives, remained unknown.

And nowhere better than in the case of Ives is shown the typical effects of this neglect: witness phenomenally intelligent and original conceptions, never fully oriented and worked out for lack of the necessary orchestra to work with; recognition first abroad, but a recognition tempered by the palpable deficiencies in finish bred of the inimicable atmosphere in which the work of a lifetime was spent; effects on his character the product of a pitiless isolation, his designation as an eccentric—a typical American retort to the castigations genius ends by applying to its compatriots—and finally a retirement from the encounter with mountains of unfinished and half-finished projects, in which the young of the next generation find "marvelous bits," the work of a man "way ahead of Europe in his time."

At the same time a whole world of successful musicians is carefully quarreled over, as to this or that quality they do or do not possess or would possess—wholly second rate, therefore not dangerous, and so acceptable to the ever present villainy in power. As a postlude Ives's compositions are occasionally performed in cheap auditoriums to the real audiences, potentially at least appreciative —but too late.

It is not to be gathered from this that first-rate work would be set aside for inadequacies merely because of a name. Because a thing is American or related to the immediate conditions it is not therefore to be preferred to the finished product of another culture.

One merely presumes that in a flight of the intelligence the actual body passes through various climates and zones of understanding which are variable. It does not simply arrive at the destination by virtue of wishes and good intentions. And in passing from one place to another it is changed by that which it encounters. It does not just go and encounter nothing. If it did, there would be no use in going, for it would be the same there as here. It is a question of give and take. If there is no equation, no comparable value to be set beside the first, adding or subtracting, multiplying or dividing, the thing stands alone and must stand impotent. America might produce work of value to Europe.

And on the other hand, one does not disguise one's poverty by enhancing one's appearance through the use of another's spiritual favors.

Even an Emerson did not entirely escape, his genius as a poet remaining too often circumscribed by a slightly hackneyed gentility. He did not relate himself so well to the underlying necessity as his style shows him to have been related to the style of the essayists of the older culture—running counter to a world exploding around him. Only at moments did his vigor break through. His formal thought did not set a sufficiently labile mold for his great vigor. It leads one to suspect that, but for this, he might have broken through to an astonishing brilliance actually close to him. He must have written essays of secondary importance, since the correlation of his effort was with the effulgence of other places and times whose direct connection with an actual he could not realize. The wrenchings of fate at his elbow, occupation with which would have put him beside the older efforts on a first-rate, if cruder, basis, he avoided or missed by rising superior to them into a world of thought which he believed to be universal only because he couldn't see whence it had arisen. It had a ground, all must, but it was not his, while his remained neglected.

He was a poet, in the making, lost. His spiritual assertions were intended to be basic, but they had not—and they have not today —the authenticity of Emily Dickinson's unrhymes. And she was of the same school, rebelliously.

It is impressive to experience the reflection of the American dearth in culture among women. Talk to her, to begin with, and see the panorama of her desires. Take the one who is tall, alert, and anonymous. They lead her to incompletions. What is there for her to do outside a pioneer's lot, children, and the sentimentalization of the term "mother"? Loving her and watching her, one sees ghostly figures moving in that curious sexual brilliance. She will listen avidly to the talk of a province, a cultural continent, which men usually think to usurp to themselves. She will love only fully the man who takes her there, where she sees—a life fascinating to her.

They love best where the drink a man offers is of the rarest, and this is the mirror to be used.

But who can blame them for turning to Paris or Britain if they can? Or to someone with at least manners, if only professional manners, Hollywood brand or as it may be. Married, they look, stop, and wish for a paid dance partner. It is one more evidence, though a left-handed one, of the general lack. Is it perhaps a cultural lag in women—or an alertness to the cultural necessity about them by which, for their purposes, they search out the rare men? Mothers wish their sons to be instructed, as fathers that their daughters be beautiful.

On a broker's yacht, as a substitute, drunk in self-defense, what else is there to do but jump overboard?—and be found two days later in the surf—off Coney Island. They have at least experienced what is termed "action," a thorough trial of excitation of a sort. And this may be taken up out of arithmetic into algebra, seldom higher into any very interesting complications. Mostly dullness and the accidents common to all fillgap—the shells and casings to be towed out to sea and dumped.

What have we to offer compared to the effective friendship between Marcel Proust and the Comtesse de Noailles? A few selected suicides.

The ordinary, and I mean extremely ordinary, answer of what would pass for refinement, in the sense that metal is refined out of muck, is inaction with a taste for the draperies of thought. The basis of the impasse is ignored. But without an understanding of the structural difficulties underlying the anticipated pleasure, even poetry might as well be taken in the vulgar sense.

It is seldom realized that what has been borrowed has arisen in a direct necessity, just as the real culture of America must also arise there and that it had a person and a set of circumstances that it was made to fit. It fits the new man under other conditions as any borrowed clothes might fit someone of a different weight or complexion from him for whom they were originally intended.

The burning need of a culture is not a choice to be made or not made, voluntarily, any more than it can be satisfied by loans. It has to be where it arises, or everything related to the life there ceases. It isn't a thing: it's an act. If it stands still, it is dead. It is the realization of the qualities of a place in relation to the life which occupies it; embracing everything involved, climate, geographic position, relative size, history, other cultures—as well as the character of its sands, flowers, minerals, and the condition of knowledge within its borders. It is the act of lifting these things into an ordered and utilized whole, which is culture. It isn't something left over afterward. That is the record only. The act is the thing. It can't be escaped or avoided if life is to go on. It is in the fullest sense that which is fit.

The thing that Americans never seem to see is that French painting, as an example of what is meant, is related to its own definite tradition, in its own environment and general history (which, it is true, we partly share), and which, when they have done with some one moment of it and have moved on to something else, they fatly sell where they can—to us, in short. And that American painting, to be of value, must have comparable relationships in its own tradition, thus *only* to attain classic proportions.

And as for the helpful critics, their cataractous eyes are filled with classic mud.

But you can't quite kill the love of the actual which underlies all American enjoyment. The stage-tricked, waylaid, cheated sucker will yet come to post. When the cheapness of commercial lying is penetrated and something for a moment shows true, grotesque perhaps also, it will always be that which Americans will find amusing: Wintergreen for President; Ben Blue standing indolently and in a storm of wild music making circles in the air with his finger to caricature the violent exertions of Russian dancing. Or as the orchestra plays, to start a fight which ends in the musicians, one and all, smashing their instruments over each other's heads. However, it is the *pathetic* charm of the cowboy which makes him attractive and of use to the movie scenario and the Rodeo.

To many writers the great disappointment of the years just after the war was that Amy Lowell, while sensing the enterprise of a reawakened local consciousness, touched it so half-heartedly and did so little to signal plainly the objective. Much could have been accomplished by aid of what seemed to be her great prestige. Pound, defeated at home, did far better, in reverse, from abroad. The best Amy Lowell had to offer was to say, at ease, that the iron of poverty had better be sunk into the generation's hides, and they'd be the better for it, as witness Villon and some others. Very good. But that is no excuse for a failure fully to realize and to state the project and its conditions.

We have an excellent and highly endowed hospital in the metropolis for dogs and an attractive canine cemetery in the suburbs. There are capital yachts and private vessels for transoceanic travel, airplanes, and flying heroes, de luxe cars, princely estates in the West where liberal barbecues are the fashion, and in the East as well, museums, collections and the patronage of swanky Old Masters, horses, racing—Palm Beach and the abandon of an occasional war for profit; even expensive universities for the propagation of something that passes for the arts. But for the rapid pick-up of clear, immediately related thought (as far as the conscious realization of necessary cultural forms shall go) shove the iron into them.

The slow, foot-weary ascent goes on. And this painstaking construction from the ground up, this Alexander's bridge, does *not* imply lack of appreciation for the French by native artists handling their own materials, but on the contrary, the deepest appreciation for them and the marvels they have performed.

Witness again the extraordinary dullness and sloth of the official preceptors as represented, let's say, by the heads of the cultural departments, the English departments in the lead, in the American universities. The tremendous opportunities under their noses have not attracted them. One would think that the Physics Department alone under the same roof might have given an inkling of the revolutions in theory and practice that had taken place during the last hundred years, the fundamental, immediate nature of the investigations necessary, on the ground, and that this would have started them thinking and into action. Instead, they have continued to mull over the old records, gallivanting back and forth upon the trodden-out tracks of past initiative, in a daze of subserviency and impotence.

Subserviency is the correct term; for the power of wealth, which by endowments makes the university and its faculty possible, at the same time keeps that power, by control of salaries and trustees' votes, in order to dictate what those who teach must and must not say. And the teachers submit to it. And thus the higher is suborned by the lower branch of the cultural split-off, another evidence of how the coercion is applied. The teachers must not venture. Thus they lie, except again in technological branches, the good fortune of those spiritual descendants of Ben Franklin, gelded.

In the same sense, for writers, the official magazines have been a positive plague.

The truly pathetic spectacle of Frank Munsey leaving his money, which he made by capitalizing writers, to the Metropolitan Museum of Art, while the difficulties of a local realization were so patently evident in the difficulty of getting valuable books published, etc., etc., was a gesture to knock 'em cold. Maybe he had an idea that that was the best way to dispose of the stuff, the best way to forward indigenous effort—by his contempt for it. In any case, Stieglitz didn't feel that way—in his sphere. Realizing the fullness and color in French painting—certainly one of the delights of the modern world—he went directly to work, a real act of praise, by striving to push forward something that would be or that was comparable in America.

Over and over again it must be repeated: none can afford to ignore, or to forget, or to fail to have seen, at least for the single glance, the superb wealth of, say, a Morgan collection. Its illuminated manuscripts alone, dating from the fifth century, must make us humble and raise our aspirations to the heights. But neither can a region afford not to have lived. It must be understood, while we are looking, that great art, in all its significance and implications, in all its direct application to our moment, has used great wealth

merely as an instrument, and that the life and vigor of every primary culture is its real reason for being.

Those who appeared to have or did have the opportunity to forward a true cultural effectiveness in America have too often, backed by constituted authority, neglected it—being content, if anything, to push their personal programs exclusively. While these others who had the vision lacked the opportunity, through official neglect, to establish the basic program.

Not Alfred Stieglitz. Using his own art, photography, he still, by writing, by patronage, by propaganda and unstinted friendship, carried the fullest load forward. The photographic camera and what it could do were peculiarly well suited to a place where the immediate and the actual were under official neglect. Stieglitz inaugurated an era based solidly on a correct understanding of the cultural relationships; but the difficulties he encountered both from within and without were colossal. He fought them clear-sightedly.

The effect of his life and work has been to bend together and fuse, against whatever resistance, the split forces of the two necessary cultural groups: (1) the local effort, well understood in defined detail and (2) the forces from the outside.

Lewis Mumford

The Metropolitan Milieu

BEFORE THE CIVIL WAR, New York shared its intellectual distinction with Boston, its industrial place with Philadelphia, and its commercial supremacy with Baltimore and New Orleans. Though it had become the mouth of the continent, thanks to the Erie Canal, it was not yet the maw. After the Civil War, despite the energetic rise of Chicago, New York City became an imperial metropolis, sucking into its own whirlpool the wealth and the wreckage of the rest of the country and of the lands beyond the sea.

When Dickens first visited America, voracious pigs rooted in the streets of Manhattan. Less than a generation later, through the holy transmutation of war, most of them were turned into financiers and industrial enterprisers, and they confined their operations to Wall Street, where the troughs were deep and the wallow good. Poets became stockbrokers; Pan took a flier in railroad securities; satirical humorists hobnobbed with millionaires and turned the lance of their satire against purely legendary kings, instead of driving their steel through the middle of the real kings, the Cooks, the Vanderbilts, the Rogerses, the Rockefellers. New York had become the center of a furious decay, which was called growth and enterprise and greatness. The decay caused foul gases to form; the gases caused the physical body of the city to be distended; the distention was called Progress.

So the city grew. Brownstone mansions, often grotesquely scratched with Eastlike ornament, wheeled into position along Fifth Avenue; and brownstone houses, in solid speculative rows, lined the side streets as the city stumbled rapidly northward. On either side of them, in the cheaper quarters, were the new tenements, with common toilets in the halls, and dusty vestibules where, in the seventies, a row of pitchers would be exposed through the night, to be filled with milk in the morning. The crosstown traffic became less important, as the rivers ceased to provide the main entrances to the city; but the tangle of wheels on the avenues thickened: shafts interlocked, hubs scraped, horses reared, presently a bridge was built over Broadway for the pedestrian. The vivacious dangers of congestion had all appeared: exasperated drivers exchanged oaths as deadly as bullets, and gangsters, lining up for fights on the dingier side streets, exchanged bullets as lightly as oaths. Respectable folk hunched their shoulders, lowered their heads, and hypnotized themselves into somnolence by counting sheep: at all events the population was increasing.

Beer saloons, four to as many corners in most parts of the city, brought together in their more squalid forms the ancient forces of hunger and love and politics: "free lunch," "ladies' entrance," and the political boss and his underlings. The main duty of the latter was to protect vice and crime and to levy a constant tax upon virtue in whatever offensive form it might take—as justice, as public spirit, as intelligence. Whisky and beer ruled the wits and the emotional life of the city: whisky for aggressiveness and beer for good-natured befuddlement. Barber shops specialized, until the present century, in painting out black eyes that did not yield to the cold iron of the lamp-post. The swells of course drank their wine convivially at Martin's or Delmonico's; but that was as far from the beer saloon as Newport or Narragansett were from Coney Island. In the 'nineties Messrs. McKim, Mead, and White began to make over the city for the more polished classes: they designed the Century Club, Gorham's, Tiffany's, Delmonico's, and many mansions in the city for the new Borgias and Sforzas. But these cultured architects of course remained aloof from the principal buildings of the populace, the tenement and the saloon. The dingy brown front of the saloon, with the swinging doors and the sawdust floors and the slate carrying the day's menu and the soap-decorated mirrors, remained unchanged by fashion for two generations or more, obeying the biological law that the lowest organisms tend to remain stable.

In the 'seventies, elevated railroads were built; and for miles and miles, on each side of these ill-designed iron ways, which contrasted so unfavorably with those Berlin built only slightly later, tenement houses were planted. Thousands of people lived under the shadow of the elevated, with the smoke of the old-fashioned locomotives puffing into their windows, with the clank and rattle causing them to shout in daily conversation to overcome the roar outside. The obliviousness to low sounds, the indifference to cacophony which makes the ideal radio listener of present-day America, was part of the original acquisition of Manhattan in the Brown Decades. This torment of noise troubled sleep, lowered waking efficiency, depleted vitality; but it was endured as if it were an irremediable fact of nature. In the lull of the elevated's thunder, the occasional tinkle of the cowbells of the ragman on a side street, or the solemn I—I—I—I *cas' clo's* of the second-hand clothing buyer, would have an almost pastoral touch; while *Carmen,* on an Italian's clanking hand organ, could splash the sky with color.

urban scenes part of landscape

Within the span of a generation, the open spaces and the natural vistas began to disappear. The older beer gardens, like Niblo's Garden, gardens that had frequently preserved the trees and open space of a whole block, were wiped out: only in the further reaches of the city did they remain, like Unter den Linden on upper Broadway, and like the roadhouses which dotted the more or less open country that remained on the West side above 125th Street until the end of the century. The rocky base of Manhattan, always unkind to life, steadily lost its filament of soil. The trees in the streets became more infrequent as the city grew; and their leaves grew sear before autumn came. Even the great Boulevard above Sixty-fifth Street, which the ignoble Tweed had planted along Broadway for his own pecuniary benefit, sacrificed its magnificent trees to the first subway; while only the ailanthus tree, quick growing and lean living, kept the back yards occasionally green, to gladden the lonely young men and women from the country, who faced their first year in the city from hall bedrooms on the top-floor rear of un-amiable boarding houses. And as the city grew, it grew away from its old markets: one of the last of these, to prove more reminiscent of the old than anticipatory of the new, was the Jefferson Market, with its medieval German tower, at Eighth Street. Vanishing from the consciousness of most Manhattanites were the open markets that had once brought the touch of the sea and the country to its streets, connecting farmstead and city home by means of little boats that plied the Hudson and Long Island Sound.

The waterfront kept a hold on the city, modifying its character, longer than the countryside did. The oyster stands remained on South and West streets; and "mast-hemmed Mannahatta" was still an accurate description up to the end of the 'nineties: Alfred Stieglitz has indeed recorded for us the bowsprit of an old sailing vessel, thrust like a proud harpoon into the side of our *Leviathan.* But most of the things that had made life pleasant and sane in the city, the old houses, red brick, with their white doorways and delicate Georgian fanlights, the friendly tree-lined streets, the salty lick and lap of the sea at the end of every crosstown street, as Melville described it in the opening pages of Moby Dick—all these things were disappearing from the eye, from the nose and touch, and so from the mind.

The water and the soil, as the prime environment of life, were becoming "immaterial," that is to say, they were of no use to the canny minds that were promoting the metropolis, unless they could be described in a legal document, appraised quantitatively, and converted ultimately into cash. A farm became for the speculator a place that might be converted into building lots: in that process, indeed, lay the meaning of this feverish growth, this anxious speculation, this reckless transformation of the quick into the dead. People staked out claims on the farther parts of the city in the way that prospectors stake out claims in a gold rush. There was always the chance that some negligible patch of earth might become, in the course of the city's growth, a gold mine. That was magic. In the atmosphere of magic, the desire to get something for nothing, a whole population hoped and breathed and lived. That in reality the environment was becoming unfit for human habitation in the process did not concern the midas-fingered gentlemen who ruled the city, nor did it affect the dull-fingered million who lacked that golden touch: their dreams were framed within the same heaven. Lacking the reality, they fed on the gilded lubricities of Mr. Bennett's, Mr. Pulitzer's, and Mr. Hearst's newspapers.

The ledger and the prospectus, the advertisement and the yellow journal, the world of paper, paper profits, paper achievements, paper hopes, and paper lusts, the world of sudden fortunes on paper and equally grimy paper tragedies, in short, the world of Jay Cook and Boss Tweed and James Gordon Bennett, had unfolded itself everywhere, obliterating under its flimsy tissues all the realities of life that were not exploitable, as either profits or news, on paper. Events happened to fill the paper that described them and to provide the daily titillation that relieved a commercialized routine. When they came reluctantly, they were manufactured, like the Spanish-American War, an event to which Newspaper Row contributed rather more than statesmanship did.

Behold this paper city, buried in its newspapers in the morning, intent through the day on its journals and ledgers and briefs and Dear-sir-in-reply-to-yours-of-even-date, picking at its newly invented typewriters and mimeographs and adding machines, manifolding and filing, watching the ticker tape flow from the glib automatons in Broad Street, piling its soiled paper into deep baskets, burying its dead paper in dusty alphabetical cemeteries, binding fat little dockets with red tape, counting the crisp rolls and bank notes, cutting the coupons of the gilt-edged bonds, redeemable twenty years hence, forty years hence, in paper that might be even more dubious than the original loan issue. At night, when the paper day is over, the city buries itself in paper once more: the Wall Street closing prices, the Five Star Sporting Extra, with the ninth inning scores, the Special Extra, *All-about-the-big-fight,* all about the anarchist assassination in St. Petersburg—or Pittsburgh.

The cult of paper brings with it indifference to sight and sound:

religion replaced

cult of paper

print and arithmetic are the Bible and the incense of this religious ritual. Realities of the world not included in this religion become dim and unreal to both the priests and the worshipers: these pious New Yorkers live in a world of Nature and human tradition, as indifferent to the round of the seasons and to the delights of the awakened senses and the deeper stores of social memory as an early Christian ascetic, occupied with his devotions amid the splendid temples of a Greek Acropolis. They collect pictures as they collect securities; their patronage of learning is merely a premature engraving of their own tombstones. It is not the images or the thoughts, but the reports of their munificence in the newspaper, that justifies their gifts. The whole social fabric is built on a foundation of printed paper; it is cemented together by paper; it is crowned with paper. No wonder the anarchists, with more generous modes of life in mind, have invented the ominous phrase: "Incinerate the documents!" That would wreck this world worse than an earthquake.

Beneath this arid ritual, life itself, attenuated but real, starved but still hungry, goes on. Lovers still become radiant and breathless; honest workers shave wood, rivet steel beams, dig in the earth, or set type with sure hands and quiet satisfaction; scholars incubate ideas, and now and again a poet or an artist broods by himself in some half-shaded city square. In rebellion against this arid and ugly new environment, some country-bred person, a William Cullen Bryant or a Frederick Law Olmsted, would attempt to preserve faltering rural delights: a picnic grove here, a park there. Just before the Civil War the building of Central Park began; and despite the raids of political gangsters, despite the brazen indecent robbery of the Tweed gang—so malodorously like the political gangs of our own day—a stretch of green was carved out, not merely carved out, but actually improved, from barren goat pasture and shantydom into a comely park.

Meanwhile, the city as a whole became progressively more foul. In the late 'seventies the new model tenement design, that for the so-called dumbbell apartment, standardized the habitations of the workers on the lowest possible level, encouraging for twenty years the erection of tenements in which only two rooms in six or seven got direct sunlight or a modicum of air. Even the best residences were grim, dreary, genteelly fusty. If something better was at last achieved for the rich in the eighteen nineties, on Riverside Drive and West End Avenue, it remained in existence scarcely twenty years and was replaced by mass congestion.

During the period we are looking at, the period of Alfred Stieglitz's birth and education and achievement, we are confronted with a city bent on its own annihilation. For New York used its intense energy and its taut, over-quickened life to produce meaner habitations, a more constricted environment, a duller daily routine,

in short, smaller joys, than it had produced during the modest provincial period. By denying itself the essentials of a fine human existence, the city was able to concentrate more intently upon its paper figments. It threw open its doors to the Irish of the 'forties, to the Germans of the 'fifties and 'sixties, later to the Italians, and to the Russians and Jews of eastern Europe: the outside world, contemptuous but hopeful, sneering but credulous, sent many of its finest children to New York. Some of them pushed on, to the cornlands, the wheatlands, the woodlands, the vinelands, to the iron mines, the coal mines, the copper mines; while those that remained were forced to huddle in utmost squalor. But the congested East Side, for all its poverty and dirt, was not the poorest part of the city: it still had its open markets with their color, its narrow streets with their sociability and their vivid common life and neighborly help, its synagogues with at least the dried remnants of a common vision.

This New York produced the elevator apartment house at the end of the 'sixties, and the tall building, called the skyscraper after the topmost sail of its old clipper ships, a little later; and it used these new utilities as a means of defrauding its people of space and light and sun, turning the streets into deep chasms, and obliterating the back yards and gardens that had preserved a humaner environment even when people drank their water, not from the remote Croton River, but from the Tea-water Pump.

The spirit of pecuniary pride was reckless and indiscriminate; it annihilated whatever stood in the path of profit. It ruined the ruling classes as well as their victims. As time went on it became ever more positive in its denial of life; so that in more elegant parts of the East Side today there are splendid "modern" mansions that are practically built back to back, even worse in some respects than the vilest slums on Cherry Street. This negative energy, this suicidal vitality, was the very essence of the new city that raised itself after the Civil War, and came to fullest bloom in the decade after the World War. Beholding it in its final manifestations, a German friend of mine wrote: *Dies ist die Hölle, und der Teufel war der Baumeister.* Men and women, if they survived in this environment, did so at the price of some sort of psychal dismemberment or paralysis. They sought to compensate themselves for their withered members by dwelling on the material satisfactions of this metropolitan life: how fresh fruits and vegetables came from California and Africa, thanks to refrigeration, how bathtubs and sanitary plumbing offset the undiminished dirt and the growing tendency toward constipation, how finally the sun lamps that were bought by the well-to-do overcame the lack of real sunlight in these misplanned domestic quarters. Mechanical apparatus, the refinements of scientific knowledge and of inventive ingenuity, would stay the process of deterioration for a time: when they failed, the jails, the asylums, the hospitals, the clinics, would be multiplied. Were not these thriving institutions too signs of progress, tokens of metropolitan intelligence and philanthropy?

But in the end, the *expectation* of health and wholeness, like the expectation of honesty and justice, tended within the great metropolis to disappear. In the course of its imperialistic expansion the metropolis, as Patrick Geddes put it, becomes a megalopolis, concentrating upon bigness and abstract magnitude and the numerical fictions of finance; megalopolis becomes parasitopolis, dominated by those secondary pecuniary processes that live on the living; and parasitopolis gives way to patholopolis, the city that ceases effectively to function and so becomes the prey of all manner of diseases, physical, social, moral. Within such a town, graft and corruption are normal processes; the greater part of the population shares the animus of the criminal, applauds him when he "gets away with it," and condones his crime when he is caught red-handed. The city that has good words for its Commodore Vanderbilts and Tweeds and Crokers, to say nothing of contemporary gamblers and shysters who have practised on an even larger scale, which multiplied these antisocial types a thousand times, is a city in which a deteriorated social life, without elementary probity or public spirit, has become normalized into the accepted routine.

So every profession has its racket; every man his price. The tonsil snatcher and the ambulance chaser and the insurance fixer and the testimonial writer have their counterparts in the higher reaches of the professions. The more universal forms of dishonor become honorable, and graft and shakedowns, like the private toll exacted for automobile and marriage licenses, become so common that they even escape notice. Those who actively oppose these customary injustices and these systematic perversions of law and decency are looked upon as disappointed men who have set their own price too high. Force, fraud, lying, chicane, become commonplaces; the law is enforced by illegal methods, the constitution protected by unconstitutional practices; vast businesses are conducted in "peace" by judicious connivance with armed thugs—now passive blackmailers, now active strikebreakers—whose work proceeds under the amiable eyes of the very agents supposed to combat it. No one believes that the alternative to living with honor is to die with honor: it is easier, it is more comfortable, to live sordidly, accepting dishonor.

In such a city, an honest man looms high. He is a lighthouse on a low and treacherous coast. To attain even a human level becomes, in this megalopolitan environment, an arduous, almost a superhuman, task.

Any fair picture of New York must confess the underlying sordidness, of a large part of its preoccupations and activities. It is not that manufacture and shipping and the exchange of goods are necessarily antivital or antisocial processes: quite the contrary. But when these activities become central to life, when they are themselves perverted to serve chiefly as instruments in an abstract accountancy of profit and power, the human hierarchy of values is displaced; and, as in some perversion of the physiological functions, the head becomes cretinous, and the subordinate members become gigantic *and useless*. What I have elsewhere called a purposeless materialism became the essential principle of the city's life.

One must not flinch, then, from recognizing the dark elements of the picture. But one would have no true image, in fact, no image at all, if one forgot to add the light that defines and relieves the blackest shape; and even at its worst, these elements were always present. There is, to begin with, the physical magnificence of the scene: the sweep and curve of the bay, the grand spaciousness of the river, the rhythm of the tides that encircle it, the strike of its mica-gleaming schists as they crop out in the park or the temporary excavation, and finally, the proud upthrust of the Palisades themselves. In the very shape of the island is something tight, lean, athletic: a contrast to the glacial till of Long Island, with its fat Dutch landscape, its duckponds, its feathery asparagus beds. The skyscrapers, despite their disorder, have not diminished those positive lines in their stalagmitic upthrust: they are almost as geometric as gypsum crystals. And before the skyscrapers were built, from Brooklyn Heights, from the Palisades, from the Belvedere in Central Park, from Morningside Heights, one could see and feel the hard flanks of Manhattan.

Above all, there is the sky; pervading all these activities is the weather. The sharp crystalline days of early autumn, with intense blue sky and a few curls of cloud, drifting through space like the little jets of steam that were once such characteristic outlets of the older skyscrapers: the splendors of sunset on the waters, over the Palisades, crossing the Brooklyn Ferry, looking toward the Jersey shore from the Brooklyn Bridge; the swift, whiplike changes from heat to cold, from fog to clarity, from the sharp jeweled contours of John Bellini to the soft tones of Whistler and Fuller. Occasionally, too, the sulphurous hell of the dog days, to whip up appetite for the dank clouds in the west and the brave crackle of lightning and the drenching showers. At the other extreme the benignity and quiet of a city quenched by snow: the jingle of sleighbells in the eighteen-nineties, the cold flash of electricity on the elevated tracks twenty years later.

The niggling interests of the day might lead to a neglect of these fundamental beauties; but they could not obliterate them. Nature remained, ready to nourish the first person who opened his eyes and breathed in the air—the clear, slightly salt-laden air, grey wings swooping and circling through it. This clear air and this intense sunlight are no small encouragements to the photographer. And the landscape as a whole has definition, a disciplined line: the rocks run as due north and south as the points of the compass, and the very sides of the island, once scraggly, have been shaped by the hands of man into sharp lines, like the margin of a Dutch canal. No matter how great the confusion on the surface, beneath it all, in the rocks themselves is order: no matter how shifty man's top layer, the foundations are solid. If the streets are dingy, there is the dazzle of the sky itself: if the alleys and streets are foul, heavy with ancient dirt, with the effluvia of the sewers or the factories, there is the sanative taste of salt in the first wind that blows from the Atlantic. The cold sea fog in spring, sweeping inland in the mid-afternoon, calls one to the ocean as imperatively as the proud, deep-throated roar of the steamer, claiming the channel as she passes out to sea. So the ocean and the sky and the rivers hold the city in their grip, even while the people, like busy ants in the cracks and crevices, are unconscious of these more primal presences, save when they read a report in the morning paper, and reach for an umbrella, an overcoat, a fan.

Along with its great landscape, New York has had its men. Even in the worst periods of the city's deterioration, there has always been a saving remnant, that handful of honest souls whose presence might have saved the Biblical cities of the plain.

There was, for one, Walt Whitman himself, "of Mannahatta a son," whose visits to the city, with even occasional public appearances, continued after the Civil War, and whose brief pictures of the city are precious records of its life. Whitman, who had rambled about every part of the city, who knew it coming inward from his native Huntington, from Coney Island when that spot was just a fishing hamlet, from the rocky wilds of the upper part of the island, where he would go walking with Bryant—Whitman knew the city at its best. While he realized the evil significance of so much of its vitality, and the impoverishment of its wealth—see his description of the fashionable parade in Central Park in 'seventy-nine —he was nourished by it and fed steadily on it, opera, theater, bookstalls, libraries, lecture halls; above all, the million-headed throng on the streets.

Drinking at Pfaff's, loafing on the Fifth Avenue stages with the coach drivers, crossing the Brooklyn Ferry, Whitman had caught something in the common life that was dear and permanent. He who really touches the soil of Manhattan and the pavement of New York touches, whether he knows it or not, Walt Whitman. Beneath the snobbery of the commercial élite there was in New York a genuinely cosmopolitan spirit. In those who like Whitman and Melville were well rooted in the provincial soil, this spirit was capable of reaching out for elements that were still foreign to the

new country—the philosophy of Hegel and Schopenhauer, the criticism of Carlyle and Ruskin, the vision of Michelet and Hugo —and transporting them to our unfinished landscape. Melville, who had been a common sailor, and Whitman, a common printer and carpenter, were not caught by the bourgeoisie and debased into accepting their prudent paper routine. Both of them were capable of a passionate aristocracy that reserved for the spirit its primacy in the affairs of men. Whitman's democracy was the prelude to a broader-rooted aristocracy, and none knew that fact better than he.

The Roeblings were in New York, too, during the 'sixties, and Washington remained on, though an invalid, until the Brooklyn Bridge was finally completed in 1883. Not alone did they compose the poem of granite and steel that is the Brooklyn Bridge, one of the first of those grand native works of art that Whitman had demanded of the sayers and delvers, but they brought that arduous habit of intellectual exertion, that capability for heroic sacrifice on behalf of immaterial things, that strict obligation to self-discipline, which came directly from the great Germany of Kant and Goethe and Hegel, a Germany the elder Roebling—who was a pupil of Hegel's—so well knew. It was right for a New Yorker who was interested in science or engineering to seek Berlin during this period; so that even though Stieglitz was unaware of the fact that he was following in the footsteps of the great engineer who built the bridge, it was as natural for him to go to Berlin as it was for Louis Sullivan, a little earlier, to follow the footsteps of Richardson to the Ecole des Beaux Arts in Paris.

Though none of the new buildings in New York could compare in beauty with the High Bridge, in its original stone form, or with the Brooklyn Bridge, there was a stir in architecture in the 'eighties and 'nineties, due chiefly to the work of Richardson, whose influence remained even though he changed his residence from Staten Island to Boston. Beginning with the De Vinne Building on Lafayette Street, an excellent structure created for a scrupulous and craftsmanlike master of printing, the finest works of New York architecture were the series of loft and factory and storage buildings that arose in the 'eighties: buildings whose round arches, solid stone courses, and subtle brickwork set a mark that few later buildings have surpassed. These buildings, moreover, were better than the very best Europe could show in this department at the same period; and contemporary European travelers of discernment noted and admitted this.

Finally, there was Albert Pinkham Ryder, the most sensitive, the most noble mind that appeared in New York after the war, a worthy companion in the spirit to that other post-war recluse, the author of Moby Dick. If the bold sunlight of Broadway made its sheet-iron buildings look flimsy and unreal, the moonlight of Ryder's inner landscape gave body to reality: Ryder with his intuitions of human destiny, Death Riding around a Racetrack, with his wistful melodies of love, the vision of Perette, Siegfried and the Rhine Maidens, with his presentation of fate in the little boats with a tiny sheet of sail on a broad moonlit sea, to which he so often returned, this mystic had a strength and a purpose that the ephemeral activities of the outer world did not possess. A benign figure, ranging up and down the streets after dark, penetrating life in its stillness and peace more bravely than those who flung themselves into the noisiest corners of the battlefield, Ryder also became part of the soil of Manhattan. No one can be aware of the rich vitality of the city who does not know its Ryder as well as its Whitman. He needed little from the city; he gave back much.

The problem for the creative mind in the 'nineties, whether he was a young writer like Stephen Crane or a young man with a passion for photography like Alfred Stieglitz, was to face this New York of boundless misdirected energy and to capture a portion of that wasteful flow for his own purposes, using its force without accepting its habitual channels and its habitual destinations. But there was still another problem: and that was to conquer, with equal resolution, the gentility, the tepid overrefinement, the academic inertness and lack of passionate faith, masquerading as sound judgment, which were characteristic of the stale fugitive culture of the bourgeoisie. The genteel standards that prevailed were worse than no standards at all: dead objects, dead techniques, dead forms of worship, cast a morbid shadow on every enterprise of the mind, making mind itself a sham, causing vitality to seem somehow shameful. To put the choice with the crudest possible emphasis, the problem for the creative mind was how to avoid the gangster without turning into the spinster.

Now, during the nineteenth century, great forces were at work in the world. People who prefer the tight securities of the eighteenth century or the adolescent turbulence of the seventeenth century only prove their own timidity and ineptness when they belittle these forces merely because they destroyed old patterns and worked creatively on unfamiliar lines. But if the artist was to become a force in his own right once more, as confident of his mission as the scientist or the engineer, it was important that he should not identify himself with the senseless acts of imperialist conquest, or with the senseless mechanical negation of life. When I use the word senseless I use it in both its usual meanings—first, foolish and stupid, and on the other hand, without benefit of the senses, shut off from the experiences that come through the eye, the hand, the ear, the nose, the touch of the body. For the weakness of the mechanical ideology that had put itself at the service of capitalism—and that colored even the minds that rejected it—was that it had limited the provinces of the senses, and confined its operations to a blind world of matter and motion.

Following partly from this mechanical philosophy, partly from the new routine of industry, the senses were in fact denied and defeated in all the new industrial centers; not least, certainly, in New York, which concentrated the industry and the finance of the Western continent. To become a force in this society, this city, it was necessary to open up once more all the avenues of human experience: to sharpen the eye, quicken the touch, refine the senses of smell and taste, as a preliminary to restoring to wholeness the dwarfed and amputated personalities that had been produced—the Gradgrinds, the M'Choakumchilds, the Bounderbys. In a world where practical success canceled every other aspiration, this meant a redoubled interest in the goods and methods that challenged the canons of pecuniary success—contemplation and idle reverie, high craftsmanship and patient manipulation, a willing acceptance of the emotions and an enlargement of the erotic ritual, a shift from the specialized masculine interests leading to an exploitation of power to the more generalized, more centrally biological interests symbolized in love: an emphasis on the ecstasy of being rather than a concentration on the pragmatic strain of "getting there."

In the Bhagavad Gita, Krishna says that the way to contemplation may be found through action as well as through exercises that are directly meant to intensify and illuminate the spiritual life. And it was by action, by utilizing one of the fine mechanical instruments that had been produced by the scientist and the inventor, that Stieglitz, on returning to New York in the eighteen-nineties, approached the world around him and helped restore those values that had been left out of the narrow *Weltbild* of his contemporaries. While Stieglitz, through his very use of the camera, allied himself with the new forces at work in the world, he did not, like those who have denied their own humanity, become smaller through his use of the machine. For mark this: only those who live first and who keep alive have earned the right to use the machine. Those who use machinery because they are incapable of facing the stream of life and directing it, those who seek order in automatons because they lack the discipline and courage to achieve order in themselves, become the victims of their instruments and end by becoming mere attachments to a mechanical contrivance. Not so with Stieglitz: from the beginning the machine was as subordinate to his human direction, through his understanding of its potentialities and capacities, as is the breathing of a Hindu guru. When used thus, as part of man's organic equipment rather than as a substitute for a deficient organ, the machine becomes as integral as the original eyes or legs. Assimilating the machine in this fashion, Stieglitz was armed to reconquer the lost human provinces that had been forfeited by the one-sided triumph of the machine.

In the surviving photographs of Stieglitz's early discovery of New York with the camera, one is conscious at first chiefly of his sure and resolute approach to the outward aspects of the city that had been regarded as "unpaintable," and therefore, in a fashion, as unusable. He watches the changing of the horses on a horse car in a snowstorm; he looks at a row of ugly brownstones or hovers above a maze of railroad tracks in a railroad yard, with the locomotives puffing magnificently at the sky. In his interest in these things, he is on a par with another realist, who used paint as his major medium, rather than photography, Thomas Eakins: but his scope is broader, his interests less traditional. Stieglitz does not, like his Parisian contemporary, Atget, range the city from morning to night, deliberately composing a documentary history of its life, after the fashion of Zola. He not merely observes: he waits; he eliminates; he selects. Certain aspects of the city he touches only by implication. Instead of merely mining the pitchblende, he extracts the minute particle of radium, which accounts for the strange behavior of the entire mass.

There are many parts of New York that Stieglitz ignores or leaves no record of, parts of it that have not entered his life or nourished him; there are other parts of his experience, like the grand spectacle of the horse races, which mean much to him and still are preserved only in a print or two. It is not for lack of love or interest that the epic of New York is not caught by his camera, chapter by chapter, as it unfolds from the 'nineties onward; to seize this was indeed part of his conscious intention. But the point is that it is not the document but the life that made it possible that he searches for and holds to: and as Emerson says, the essential fact is unaltered by many or few examples. If one doubts Stieglitz's awareness of the deeper transformations of feeling and thinking and acting that took place in his metropolis one need only examine his photographs more carefully. The external change in the city itself was profound. Within the darkened alleyways of the financial district, people lost their sense of day and night; just as they lost the occasional glimpse of the sky which makes the worst routine bearable. In the new subways they lost even the glimpse of the sun over the roof tops of Manhattan, which had once been theirs from the ramshackle elevated roads. Nature in its most simple form, the wonder of the morning and the night, was missing from the metropolitan routine; and *therefore*—I say "therefore" because such reactions are rarely accidents—these elements establish themselves in Stieglitz's photographs with a new force.

The chief instrument of photography is light; and the fact that Stieglitz always worked by natural light, never by artificial light, with its studied arrangements and its temptations to trickery, is an important one. But all the hours of the days become important to him: so he takes the first night pictures that have esthetic significance. The weather, likewise, is an important element for his vision: hence, too, he takes the first photographs in snow and in rain. He

does not have to escape to the country to find nature, any more than he has to escape to antiquity to find beauty, in the way that the purse-proud art collectors of the period, the Mrs. Jack Gardners and the Pierpont Morgans, were doing. All these necessary elements in life were still present in the city, though they had been excluded from the routine of getting and spending. Just as Ryder continued to be in touch with nature when he had his ailanthus tree and his patch of sky, so Stieglitz found the necessary germs of a living environment even in a metropolis that had lost the most rudimentary sense of the soil, and was turning itself, step by step, block by block, into a stony waste.

During the nineteen hundreds, too, the city was losing its sense of the rivers, despite the extension of Riverside Park. For sewage pollution had driven the North River shad away and made all other kinds of fish that might be caught noxious; so that the old gaffers with their set-lines and bells had disappeared from the Hudson, along with the groups of happy naked swimmers, and another link with nature was broken, even as, because of pollution from the oil-burning steamers, the waters of the Lower Bay lost the bluefish and weakfish that had once been so plentiful there. But Stieglitz, not less than Whitman, preserved the sense of the waters surrounding Manhattan. He photographed the ferry boats coming into their slips, the boatload of immigrants, the skyline of Manhattan from the Jersey shore, with the water establishing a base in the foreground. Water and sky come into his pictures, again and again: the river, the ocean, the bathing beach, the rain, the snow, and finally, dominating the whole landscape in every sense, the clouds. Shut out by the tall buildings, shut out by the dark courts of the new apartment houses, the very stars at night put at a distance by the myriad lights of the city, flaring, as Tennyson said, like a dreary dawn—the sky remains under all conditions the essential reminder of nature and the cosmos. In the course of Stieglitz's own development, the sky becomes a more and more essential part of his pictures; and finally, it becomes the symbol whereby Stieglitz unites his sense of the universal order with the sense of the personality, as developed in the relations of men and women.

In the stoniest pavement of the city there are cracks. And out of the bleakest soil, between these cracks, a few blades of grass will sooner or later show, whose seeds are borne by the birds; here, even, the germ of a tree will take root and spring up, if no foot disturbs it. It is in the cracks between the new buildings that Stieglitz finds the sky; it is in the surviving cracks in the pavement that Stieglitz finds his trees; and in his most characteristic pictures of the city, so far from emphasizing the massiveness and the obduracy of its stones, he emphasizes the presence of life. One of the most moving and impressive pictures he ever made was that of a little tree in

Madison Square Park, young and vernal in the rain, with a street sweeper in the foreground and the dim shape of a building in the background: the promise of life, its perpetual reawakening and renewal, are in that print.

Wherever Stieglitz turns his head in this city, he looks for the touch of life, seizes it, emphasizes it; and by this means he sets himself in opposition to those who would glorify the negation of life and sanction its subordination to metropolitan business, material concentration. Meanwhile, all the forces of urban aggrandizement are on the make: advertising, insurance, and high finance, the divine trinity that rules the world of industry and perverts its honest labors for its own ends, gather together in the city and out of its egotism and self-inflation rose higher and higher skyscrapers, first in the southern end of the island, then, forming a sort of double vertebral column, from Thirty-fourth Street upward, in the new central district. The new office buildings and lofts are flanked by apartment houses as stupidly planned, as extravagantly designed, as crazily and as dishonestly financed as the business buildings themselves. The megalopolitan architects who designed these puerile structures gloated over the prospect of a whole city composed of skyscrapers, with aërial drives for the rich, and in the murky canyons below the working and living quarters for the poor—artificially lighted! artificially ventilated!—a city in which sunlight would be supplied by sunlamps, grass by green tiles, and babies, presumably, by mechanical incubation. (No extravagance of Aldous Huxley's satire was beyond the serious commonplace luncheon conversation of the self-infatuated schoolboys who were financing and planning and building the "city of the future," on paper.)

A generation after his first pictures of New York, Stieglitz surveys the city once more, now from the seventeenth story of an office building at Fifty-third Street, surrounded by the architectural bluff and fraud of the boom period. He ironically portrays these structures with no further hint of nature than the indication of the hour of the day, through the degree of light and shadow that falls on their trivial façades. He shows the skyscraper—the mock city of the future—in the last state of mechanical perfection and human insignificance, devoid at last of even the possibility of earning money: financial liabilities, as well as the social liabilities their reckless misuse had already made them. There, in effect, is the ultimate result of putting nature at a distance and subordinating all the values of living to the paper routine of pseudo-work and profit-pyramiding. These skyscrapers of Stieglitz's last photographs might be the cold exhalations of a depopulated world.

And at the end, with a sardonic gleam in his eyes, he photographs the turning point: the tearing down of a seven-story building at Sixtieth Street and Madison Avenue in order to make way for a new two-story building. The nightmare was over. The human scale had begun to return. Finally, the sterile dream of imperialist conquest externalized itself in that last gesture of the impotent: Rockefeller Center. But this was already an aftermath, which, like an auto rolling backward downhill, continued on its course because the driver preferred the sensation of motion, even if it were motion backwards, to the recognition of his inability to reverse the direction and go forward.

While the tree and the sky are dominating symbols in Stieglitz's work, brought to sharper focus by their steady exclusion from the urban landscape, there are two others that were important, both in his personal life and in his vision: the race horse and the woman. The thoroughbred horse, quivering in every muscle, nostril open, eyes glaring, hooves delicately stamping, ready for the race or the rut: symbol of sheer animal vitality, bred and nurtured with a single eye to that final outburst of speed which carries horse and rider down the home stretch to victory. From the black heavy-flanked Waterboy or the low-slung, short-legged chestnut Sysonby, to the great Man o' War and his present-day successors, these horses represented the pinnacle of animal achievement: proofs of man's skill and intelligence in alliance with the world of life, symbolic of those new strains of wheat, those new hybrids or sports in flowers and fruits, whose conquest was ultimately more important to man than were half the mechanical contrivances on which the metropolitan mind doted.

And if the horse was animal vitality, woman was—if one may combine the words—animal spirituality, that form of spirit which, unlike the lonely ascetic endeavors of man, fulfills itself in the very organs of the body, in the warmth of the arms, in the tenderness that emanates from the breast, in the receptivity of the lap, in the utilization of every physical fiber for the higher ends of life, making the body not the enemy of the mind but the friendly guide and initiator; favoring the warm intellect, touched by the earth, the intellect of Goethe, as contrasted with the cold intellect, the intellect divorced from the earth, the intellect of womanless men like Leonardo. Man tends to overvalue his eyes and his muscles: the organs of definition and of physical conquest. Woman teaches him to use his lips, his sense of touch, and to diffuse some of the fierce tactile sensitiveness that is at first concentrated so exclusively in his generative organ. Here is a vitality even deeper-fibered than that of the thoroughbred horse; for it reaches, through the very structure of woman's body, toward a completer biological fulfillment, never being fully organized or alive except when the relationships lead, through the lover or the baby, to the ultimate breast and womb.

The masculine world, with its strife of markets, with its stultifying ambitions to corner wheat or to cheapen steel, to invent this or that substitute for organic life, to conquer by an equation or a formula this or that territory of the intellect, this masculine world, particularly in our own cultural epoch, has tended toward an asceticism that has left little energy or time for the fundamental biological occupations. The seed was sound and fruitful: the great outburst of vitality marked by the rising birth rate of the nineteenth century proved it: but the soil was too dry and sour and lacking in humus to give the plant itself full growth. So that it was the classes at the periphery of our mechanical civilization, more often the not-serious people, the unbusinesslike, the wastrels and gamblers and sports, the "low" and the "vicious," among the males, who still preserved an alert eye appreciative of the flanks and fetlocks and neck of a horse, or the flanks and belly and buttocks of a woman.

Compare the stock exchange and the race track. Economically, both are mainly gambling devices; and humanly speaking they are both low forms of activity. But one is indoors; it is conducted in a clamorous jumble of noises by means of a series of telegraphic symbols; the realities with which the gamble deals, the automobile factories and packing plants and mail-order houses and banana plantations, are present only as verbal abstractions. The other activity is held outdoors under the sky; the track, heavy or fast, is affected by accidents of the weather; the gamble has to do with visible horseflesh and visible human skill and courage; and in the procession to the post, the suspense of the start, the stretching out of the field, and the final climax of the home stretch, there is a superb esthetic spectacle. The drama itself does not terminate abruptly with the end of the race: the tension is prolonged by the return of the jockey to the judge's stand, where he awaits for an instant, with upraised arm and whip, the nod that gives him the victory in a fairly won race.

Dégas came closer than anyone else among the painters to representing this drama; but there is something, in the four-dimensional continuity of it, that evades even the most skilled of painters; indeed, the impulse to grasp this continuity was responsible for the critical steps in the invention of the motion-picture camera. At the bottom of this interest is the horse himself; and until the automobile usurped this interest, the horse and the gambling connected with the races were ways in which the American, caught in his artful commercial merry-go-round, kept a little of his residual sense of the primitive and the organic. Right down to the end of the first decade of the present century, the Speedway at 155th Street was maintained as a common race track for trotters; and the designer of Central Park, a generation earlier, was forced, in the interests of more general recreation, to plan his horse drives so as to curb racing.

If Stieglitz did not photographically utilize this deep interest of his in the horse races—there is, however, the fine print of Going to the Post—it was only perhaps because its intensity was incompatible with that patient suspended animation which makes photography possible. Stieglitz was too near the race horse, as one is too near the lover in an embrace, to be able to photograph him. And yet the horse symbolized to him, as it did to the author of *St. Mawr* and to the author of *Roan Stallion* in a later generation, something essential in the life of man: that deep animal vitality he had too lightly turned his back on and renounced in his new mechanical preoccupations. So Stieglitz conceived, though he never carried out, a series of photographs of the heads of stallions and mares, of bulls and cows, in the act of mating, hoping to catch in the brute an essential quality that would symbolize the probably unattainable photograph of a passionate human mating.

Just as the old rural interest in animals could enter the city only deviously by way of the race track, so sex itself, despite its endless manifestations, had no central part in the routine of the civilization that had reached a mechanical apex in New York. Where sex was most obvious, in the burlesque houses and musical comedies and in the murky red-light district, it was also most furtive and shame-faced: a grudging admission, not a passionate conviction; an itch, not an intensity; a raw piece of flesh flung to a caged animal, who responded in his reflexes, like a Pavlovian dog, without benefit of mind. Foreign observers noted that women tended to dominate the pioneer society of America, and to hold its males in nominal subservience to ideals of courtesy and chivalry toward womanhood. But although the traditional scarcity of women in a new country gave woman a privileged position and permitted her a freedom of travel and a freedom of choice in mating unknown among similar classes in Europe, the result was to widen the political scope of woman at the expense of her sex life. Instead of ruling with and through her sex, the American woman, despite her studious attention to her own beauty, her figure and her dress, learned to preserve her freedom and power by keeping sex at a distance. It was on the assumption that "nothing could happen" that the sexes came together so easily, and that women in America, up to the second decade of the present century, were given their "freedom."

And in any fundamental sense nothing did happen, even after the American girl extended her flirtations to the length of concluding them in bed. The whole business of sex remained peripheral: sexual expression symbolized freedom or sophistication; indeed, it often sank so low as to justify itself as hygiene. People married and became the parents of children and were driven to seek divorce before they had even scraped the surface of intimacy. This negation of sex was helped, perhaps, rather than hindered by the devices of birth control. Contraceptive devices put between passion and its fulfillment a series of mechanical or chemical obstacles which, though small in themselves, could never be completely routinized into oblivion: the least objectionable device from the standpoint of intercourse was also the most dangerous in the possibilities of serious lesion. If this is still largely true today, a hundred years after the initial movement toward birth control in America, it was even more true a generation ago, when the crudeness and uncertainty of the various devices used added to the clumsiness and anxiety that attended their employment. With sex, the dish often became lukewarm before it could be served; and with the loss of warmth and flavor went a loss of appetite; for why, if the final result were favored by lukewarmness, should people ever bother to reach in the first place a hotter temperature?

Lusty men and passionate women of course remained in this society; but the whole tone of sex remained practically as low as it had been in Victorian days. Although talk about sex, and even possibly physical indulgence, became more common, the actual manifestations often remained placidly anemic: a girl might have a dozen lovers without having known an orgasm, or have a dozen orgasms without having achieved any fundamental intimacy with her lover. On the surface, decorum or the defiance of decorum; beneath it, irritation, frustration, resentment—resentment on the part of the male for the unarousableness of the female, about whom the faint aroma of anxious antisepsis clung like an invisible petticoat; resentment on the part of the female against the male both for his bothersome insistence and his lack of really persuasive aggression. In the course of business, the work in the office and the factory, the activities of the home, the club, the social gathering, men and women saw each other too little on their more primitive levels to overcome all these obstacles and find each other. They sought by the chemical means of drink to reach these levels more quickly—only to lose the sting and sharpness of sex, when what they needed was patience and leisure and sympathy and above all free energy and vitality, for all of which a tumescent animal befuddlement was in no sense a substitute. For what was left for sex but the dreary crowded moments before sleep, when all energy had been spent upon every aspect of living except sex?

One emphasizes the state of sex in American society because here again Stieglitz was to preoccupy himself with symbolic representations of the elements that were lacking in the scene around him. As a young student in Europe, he had found his own sense of manliness and sexual confidence reënforced and cultivated by the great traditions of the arts, above all by Rubens, whose portrait of Hélène de Fourment, an exuberant naked girl wrapped in fur, he had seen on his first visit to Vienna, at a critical moment when it had reëchoed and eloquently justified the impulses he found within himself. The health, the animal vitality, the unashamed lushness of sex in Rubens's paintings, are all as conspicuous as the absence of these qualities in the unhealthy sentimentality that has hung around sex in the Western World, since Christianity attempted to transfer

to heterosexual relations the sick moonlight glamour of unfulfilled yearning that derived ultimately, perhaps, from the romantic homosexual love of the Greeks. Rubens was a long step back to reality from the misty mid-regions inhabited by Poe's pallid maidens, girls who were reproduced in paint in the adolescent sweetness of George Fuller's paintings in the 'seventies, and still further attenuated in the popular Dewing ladies who ruled the 'nineties. The ideal maiden of adolescent America was a sort of inverted pariah: untouchable by reason of her elevation. In defiance of Nature, her womanliness and her untouchability were supposed to be one. But what was sex, how could it exist, how could it nourish the personality, if it were not in fact the most essential demonstration of touchability—if the intercourse of lovers, at all its levels, from the intuitions at a distance to the final stages of union, were not accompanied at every moment by that direct sense of touch, that tact, which removes the need for words and signs and breaks down the formidable distance between object and subject, between thine and mine?

In all the manifold meanings of the adjective, sex was primarily the realm of tactile values. Stieglitz was to discover these values and intensify them in his photography even before Berenson had used them, too narrowly, as a key to the great painting of the Italian Renaissance. The blindness of love, debased as a mere figure of speech, is indeed one of the most characteristic of its attributes. It is blind in the fact that it reaches deeper levels of consciousness, below the open-eyed rationality of practical achievement. It is blind in the way that it often shuts out the outer world in order to concentrate upon the inner stimulus, blind as in terror, blind as in prayer; and finally, it has the beautiful compensation of blindness, for it learns to see with its fingertips, and to offset the closed eyes, reacts more quickly with the other available senses in every region of the body.

It was Stieglitz's endeavor, at first mainly instinctive, finally, through a better self-knowledge, with a fuller awareness of his actions, to translate the unseen world of tactile values as they develop between lovers not merely in the sexual act but in the entire relationship of two personalities—to translate this world of blind touch into sight, so that those who felt could more clearly see what they felt, and so those who could merely see might reach, through the eye, the level of feeling. Observe the work of Stieglitz's contemporaries in photography, moved perhaps by the same desires but deeply inhibited. See, in the many reproductions in *Camera Work*—which doubtless helped pave the way to the sun-bathing and easier nudity of a later day—see how they portray the nude body. However honest their efforts, they nevertheless surround the body with a halo of arcadian romanticism; note how resolutely they equip their naked models with glass bubbles; how they compel these naked girls painfully, for the first time in their lives, to pour water out of narrow-necked jugs; how they lash them to tree stumps or make them shiver at the edge of icy pools. Sex must be disguised as art —that is, as artiness—before one may peep at it without blushing. Undisguised, the girl averts her face from the camera, so that the self-conscious and self-righteous face shall not acknowledge the powers of the body. The efforts of these earlier photographers are not to be despised; but the tantalizing fear of sex, a fear of its heady realities, is written over their pictures, with their dutiful aversions, their prescribed degrees of dimness, their overarch poses.

It was his manly sense of the realities of sex, developing out of his own renewed ecstasy in love, that resulted in some of Stieglitz's best photographs. In a part by part revelation of a woman's body, in the isolated presentation of a hand, a breast, a neck, a thigh, a leg, Stieglitz achieved the exact visual equivalent of the report of the hand or the face as it travels over the body of the beloved. Incidentally, this is one of the few aspects of photography that had not been anticipated in one fashion or another by the painter, since the dismembered anatomical studies of the Renaissance, which casually resemble these photographs, are purely instruments of factual knowledge: they make no appeal to sentiments and feelings. In more abstract, yet not in less intimate form, Stieglitz sought to symbolize the complete range of expression between man and woman in his cloud pictures, relying upon delicacies and depths of tone, and upon subtle formal relationships, to represent his own experiences. Earth and sky, root and topmost branch, animal intimacy and spiritual expression—these things, which were so remote from the routine of the metropolitan world, or which there existed in such loud disharmony, were restored to their natural integrity in Stieglitz's life and work. What was central became central again; what was deep was respected for its profundity, instead of being ignored; what was superficial was thrust behind the essential.

Stieglitz was never a better son of the city he loved and identified himself with than when he turned his back on her desiccated triumphs and recalled, in word, in photography, in the tenacious act of existence, the precious elements that the city had excluded. With Whitman, with Ryder, with the handful of other men that each generation has produced in New York, Stieglitz has served his city, not by acquiescing in its grandiose decay, nor yet by furthering its creeping paralysis: he has served it by nurturing in himself, and in those who have witnessed his work, the living germs that may reanimate it, quickening the growth of the higher forms of life it has excluded. For, as Whitman said, the place where the great city stands is not the place of markets and stretched wharves and multiplying population and ships bringing goods from the ends of the earth: it is the city of the faithfulest lovers and friends.

Paul Rosenfeld

The Boy in the Dark Room

JULY, 1873. Guests of the Fort William Henry Hotel at Lake George are drifting to a corner of the hotel piazza to watch a knot of small boys at their sports. On a parchesi board perched on the arms of a couple of chairs they have laid out a miniature race course, and are playing a game of races with tiny leaden horses on it. Upon certain of their little toys they have bestowed the names of historic race horses; on others, those of girls; and on a few select groups of them, the names of very favorite girls. All have been divided, for the sake of the fun, to represent the constituents of imaginary stables managed by the several contestants, and carry their personal colors. To the tune of dice shaken from a cup, they advance about the little field, reënacting famous turf events and enacting new ones. From time to time, the eldest of the boys, a dark-haired, deep-eyed youngster occasionally deserving the nickname "Hamlet," teasingly given him by his mother's Edwin Booth-adoring friends, proposes a change of rules, reviving the excitement.

It is he made up the game. The intelligent observers, whose numbers include the Governor of New York, perceive it represents the contents of a unique, child's world.

The youngsters carry their toys to the stall of the village tintyper to have them photographed. The play leader insists on arraying his horses on the artist's stand in an order satisfactory to himself. And when at length the man retires behind the curtain in the booth to develop the tintypes, an obscure interest in what is going on there inside the primitive dark room spurs the boy to get permission to enter it. The rest of the children remain without. Fascinatedly he observes the photographic process.

On several later occasions he returns to the booth, and on each he reënters the laboratory. One day he asks the tintyper the reason for his application of carmine to the cheeks of his human images. "Makes 'em look more natural!" the man insists. The nine-year-old ventures stubbornly to disagree with him.

At two years of age this boy had gotten hold of the photograph of a beautiful child, a boy cousin, and refused to allow himself to be parted from it. At present he treasures a collection of English racing journals carrying pictures of famous race horses.

The home from which he springs loves life and believes in the enjoyment of its gifts and has a genuine, if slightly soft and sentimental, feeling of beauty and a great friendliness for the human being.

His father, Mr. Edward Stieglitz, is a woolen merchant. At first, after his migration from Hanover-Münden to New York City in 1850, Edward Stieglitz manufactured mathematical instruments. At the outbreak of the Civil War he enlisted in the army and became a first lieutenant. In 1863 he retired from it in order to marry; and engaging in the woolen trade, promptly attained commercial success. Solid and honorable, he contrived at a very early period in his business career, to persuade the president of the Chemical National Bank, at this epoch the most conservative and desirable fiduciary in New York City, to advance him a relatively large sum of money over a period of days without collateral other than his personal word. At present, in 1873, he can count A. T. Stewart and Marshall Field among his constant customers. Two years ago, he brought his family from Hoboken, N. J., to live in a brownstone house which he had built in East Sixtieth Street, in New York, and equipped with such ultramodern conveniences as steam-heating and special piping for refrigerated water. Still, commerce has never been anything but a means, and one not highly interesting, for him. Edward Stieglitz is a great child of nature, liberal, loving life, fond of sport, of art, of good company, of fine wines and cheer. Slender, moderately tall, always well groomed and very much the cavalier, he appears, with his proud carriage, his fine head and luxuriant mustaches, much less the business-man than a cross between an Hungarian *magnat* and a gypsy violinist, and he is a patient and by no means talentless amateur painter. He also owns horses and is a member, the only Jewish member, of the New York Jockey Club; and he infinitely prefers the society of sportsmen and artists, painters, musicians, and actors, to that of his commercial associates. At the regular Sunday-afternoon assemblages at his home, no word of business is exchanged by the company. The shutters of the dining room are closed early in the afternoon, the gas is lit, and the group of gentlemen segregated there are informed that the outside world no longer exists, and that time is infinite and theirs to enjoy. These pleasant gatherings are frequently attended by his eldest son, Alfred, the small boy of the dark room: indeed, the lad has to perform a function connected with them. The keys of the well-stocked wine cellar have been confided to him by a father proud of a son able to assume responsibilities; and it is the boy's business to bring bottles from below when they are called for.

And some years hence Edward Stieglitz will retire from business. He will have amassed the sum of $400,000 and perceived that its interest, considerable for the period, has provided him with the means of raising his brood of six, supporting sundry dependent relatives, and devoting himself to those joys of life which appear to him its end: painting, esthetic study, horseback, billiards, sporting events, and picture auctions, the protection of artists and the cultivation and embellishment of the extensive grounds of the summer home which he has built himself on the shores of his beloved Lake George. In time, Wall Street will regain some of his attention, but again only as a means to the end of keeping open house at the Lake: as many as thirty persons will at times sit down to table there. Luckily, his liberal ideas of life are as agreeable to his wife, Hedwig Werner, as to himself. Cultured, soft, hospitable, generous, in nothing the bourgeoise, and basically as simple, as innocent and childlike as her leonine spouse, she is witty, fond of bright society, of the company of her family and friends, and is an insatiable devourer of novels. She reads as many as a hundred of them every year; and what is even more remarkable and indicative of an extraordinary capacity for the concentration of attention about these fictions and an extraordinary memory, she can recollect their plots, characters, and situations distinctly many years after she has read them; and will continue to be able to do so up to the very time of her death.

2

May, 1881. EDWARD STIEGLITZ has decided to remove his family for a few years to Europe, to the end of giving all his children the advantages of a Continental education, and his son Alfred in particular the opportunity of studying engineering at one of the great polytechnics.

Alfred, in the meantime, has grown up an active ingenious boy; fond of sport. He has taught himself to play billiards on the paternal table and beaten his father at the game. At nine he has figured in a public billiard contest in Boston; but competition interests him less than the perfection of difficult shots.

At thirteen years, he ran a twenty-five-mile race against himself in about three and a half hours around the furnace-heated cellar of his home. The event was conceived in the style of the record-breaking contests of the period. There was an attendance of other boys and younger brothers holding stop-watches, pails, and sponges, and periodically mopping the athlete's face.

And he has all unconsciously gained a great friend: the singer of the ultimate salvation flowing from unflagging, disinterested endeavor, and attraction toward a hidden goal symbolized first by the figure of a simple girl, later by that of Helen of Troy, and last by the feminine principle in Creation. Never held by fairy tales, Alfred has wonderingly, stretched full length on the back-parlor floor, turned the pages of Goethe's masterpiece. It contained for him chiefly at first the curious business of the juxtaposition of Gretchen and the devil. He found the intrigue pathetic and mysterious. And he has already returned, and will hereafter return, to the poem innumerable times. He has even grown conscious of the searching passion lodged in Faust's own bosom.

And, quite as unquestioningly as most American children, perhaps more reverently than the majority of them, he has honored the claims to the love and loyalty of its constituents which American society bases on the value it appears to lay upon the human being and on the opportunities for human development that its "democratic" institutions seem to provide. And out of the American epic, the saga of the revolutionary birth of this most noble, humane, and free of lands, the figure of a hero has beautifully risen before the lad. This figure is not the immortal George's, but that of General Nathanael Greene, sometimes styled the American Turenne because of the rapidity of his maneuvers, sometimes the American Scipio Africanus for the reason of his successful attack upon the enemy on his own ground. Greene's merit, in the boy's eyes, flows from the fact that he had broken the British strength down there in the South, and had lost few men doing so; from the fact that he had broken the British strength precisely because he had sacrificed so few lives in his own army. Greene indeed had won no signal victories or their shining glories. He was too poor in men and munitions to risk decisive encounters. But he had invariably retired from unequal engagements with his resources intact, allowing Cornwallis and the rest of his opponents to exhaust their powers in futile, extended efforts to force the issue. Like Goethe's *Faust,* the image of democratic victory gained by the patient conservation of resources over a long period, and the willingness to let the enemy purchase Pyrrhic triumphs dearly, proves endlessly gratifying.

And, since 1877, Alfred Stieglitz and his brothers have not been pupils at the Charlier Institute. For reasons of democracy as well as economy, they were withdrawn from it and sent to public school, with the consequence that Alfred has lost his habits of study. His excellent grounding at the private institution has enabled him to keep abreast of his grade without doing much school work; and billiards and baseball and the piano, all played with characteristic intensity, have occupied the large number of hours at his disposal. During the last year, he has been attending the City College; and it is, chiefly, Professor Werner of that school, one of his relatives, who has persuaded Edward Stieglitz that the future of the country lies in the hands of engineers and chemists, and that it might be advisable, in view of the fact that Alfred appeared to have a good mathematical head, to make an engineer of him.

Before sailing, Alfred explains to the Italian organ grinder that he is going to Europe with his family for five years. The old man nods. For four years, now, he has been bringing his hand organ and monkey before the Stieglitz house regularly every Saturday evening at seven sharp, and playing first the Marseillaise, and then the Miserere from *Il Trovatore*. On the first evening he appeared, Alfred had risen from the dinner table and its hedge of parents, aunts, brothers, and sisters; gone into the kitchen and gotten the cook to give him a sandwich and a cup of coffee, and taken the food and a dime out into the street. He found a little monkey huddling on a hand organ, and behind it, turning the crank, an old gray-bearded Italian. The man courteously thanked him and made the monkey doff his hat: and after carefully putting the sandwich in his pocket, continued grinding. And every Saturday evening since, as soon as the hurdy-gurdy has begun playing, Alfred has gone to the cook, who has learned to have the sandwich and the hot drink ready for him, and taken the food and the bit of money out to the man. This custom has drawn a comment from the elders on only one occasion. The night was cold and snowy, and Alfred, who had gained his man's stature in a year's time and was very thin besides, happened to wear an acute variant of the cadaverous look which periodically frightened his mother into supposing him tubercular. The soup had just been served; and, as he rose, his father and mother, neither of whom frequently made requests of him, simultaneously said, "It's terribly cold out-of-doors. Won't you please drink your soup while it is hot?" Alfred had not appeared to hear them, continuing on his way. When he returned, his parents were silent. Nothing further was said. Nor will anything further about the incident be said by either of them for many years to come: not until Alfred is in the fifties. Then, one afternoon in the course of a half-serious conversation between himself and his mother, during which she will, maternally, remark on the frequent incomprehensibility of his motives and on the infrequency of his response to requests dictated by the feeling of his best interests, she will suddenly, out of a clear sky, ask him, "Do you remem-

ber the night long ago, when it was so cold, and your father and I asked you for your own sake to take your soup hot, and you insisted on first going out to the organ grinder? I'd like to know why you did that."

Half jocosely, Alfred will reply, "Ma, do you really want to know why? Well, then, I'll let you in on the great secret. Do you know who the organ grinder *really* was?"

She will respond, "I'm glad your brother the doctor is coming. I think I may have him examine your head."

"I'm going to *tell* you who the organ grinder really was. *I* was the organ grinder!"

"There you go again. I think you must really be insane!"

"But, Ma, I'm always the organ grinder! I've never given to anybody but Myself!"

Mrs. Stieglitz will lay her sewing in her lap. "How long have you known this?" she will inquire.

Alfred will smile and answer, "I've *always* known it!"

3

WINTER OF 1882–83. BERLIN. After a year spent as a guest at the Karlsruhe Realgymnasium, Alfred has registered for a couse in mechanical engineering at the Berlin Polytechnic, then under the rectorship of the famous Professor Reuleaux.

Edward Stieglitz has chosen the Berlin Polytechnic for his son in preference to the Zurich one, for the reason that though both schools are equally well provided with laboratories and scientific teachers, the Swiss is dangerously full of cigarette-smoking Russian women-students. Still, his parental advice to his son has always confined itself to two admonitions. One, a counsel fairly regular among upper-class fathers, is "Always live within your income!" The other, less regular, is "Don't ever be afraid to tell the truth!"

On his way to Berlin, Alfred has stopped off with his traveling companion, a painter, at Weimar: colored, still, by the setting sun of romanticism. Princess Sayn-Wittgenstein lives at one of the hotels, and Liszt goes to her rooms daily to play the piano for her. At the Erbprinz the travelers encountered an old friend of the painter's, another artist, who had just returned from Bayreuth where he has heard all the first performances of *Parsifal*; and for three hours that evening Alfred heard him render the new *Bühnenweihfestspiel* on the piano. At midnight, all repaired to the dwelling of another old friend, an intimate member of the Liszt-Wagner circle. The young American was struck by the fact that each of the rooms in the house contained a bed draped like an altar and surrounded by different feminine mementos. The host solemnly informed him that each of these couches had been consecrated by himself to the imperishable memory of that particular one of his various sublime experiences in which it, individually, figured.

Now, in Berlin, Alfred is having a great time playing billiards, chess, and, sometimes, cards, at the Café Bauer; and playing the piano, seeing something of mixed society, and attending the races, the theaters, concerts, and the opera. At German universities at this period, students are not obliged to attend the courses for which they have registered, or to stand examinations and take their degrees until they feel inclined to do so. And, in Berlin, an ordinance places all those tickets for performances at state theaters which have not been taken up by the public an hour in advance of the curtain, at the disposal of university students. The tickets cost the scholars from 50 *pfennigs* to M1.50. Alfred assists at innumerable performances of plays by Shakespeare, Calderón, Goethe, Lessing, and Schiller, and by such moderns as Ibsen and Echegaray. At the opera, he hears his favorites *Tristan* and *Carmen* over a hundred times apiece.

He is already managing to assist persons less fortunate than himself with his modest allowance.

And he has discovered the Russian story tellers for himself: first Lermontov, then Gogol, then Pushkin; last, Turgenev and Tolstoy. The realists at first interest him less than do their more romantic predecessors; before long, however, he is going to chance upon a novel of Zola's; then, naturalism will stir his depths. The particular novel of Zola's which will so profoundly move him is *Madeleine Férat,* and, after finishing it, Alfred will sit up all night reading it aloud to his friends. And he will immediately procure others of the works of the Frenchman who is employing fiction experimentally as a means of penetrating to the laws underlying the phenomena of life, and will read in rapid succession *La Faute de l'abbé Mouret, Une Page d'Amour, L'Œuvre,* and others of the Rougon-Macquart series. Among American novels, only those of Mark Twain are going to interest him for a time. Among German, it is Scheffel's *Ekkehard,* that song of the dignity of woman that auspiciously still remains his preference.

On a day about four months after his matriculation at the Polytechnic, the glimpse of an object resting on a tripod in the window of a shop in the Klosterstrasse gives him a peculiar little thrill. It is a small black box, a camera with a single lens. Impelled to enter the shop, he promptly purchases the simple apparatus.

The sports of life have acquired a small brother. Young Stieglitz takes a few photographs of the views from his window, of the contents of his room, and of some photographs of himself. During the following winter he registers for and attends a course in photochemistry under Prof. H. W. Vogel and appears a dull pupil, largely for the reason that he takes the instructor's prescriptions quite literally. He continues desperately laboring at the chemical cleansing of glass for the preparation of wet plates while the rest of the class has long since advanced to other problems, unaware that he has long since learned to clean his glass to the requisite degree. One of the exercises of the course consists in the photography, for the purpose of accurately reproducing the contrasting values, of a plaster Juno draped with a black cloth that stands in the studio. Stieglitz struggles despondently to solve the problem, dissatisfied with each one of his solutions of it. To his surprise, the professor explains to him that the faithful reproduction of the values of the white bust and black velvet is impossible; that, as in all things, in photography, too, compromises are inevitable.

Photographic dry plates have recently appeared in the market, vastly facilitating photography; and, realizing that he has familiarized himself with the wet process, Stieglitz acquires a modern camera and takes up the dry plate. Suddenly his energies release themselves through the instruments. He sets zealously to work solving self-appointed photographic problems, photographing commonplaces of the homely city, walls, *Litfassäulen,* many, in cases as often as a hundred times; till the characteristics of the objects translate themselves satisfactorily into the terms of his medium. He takes university courses in chemistry with photography in view; he diligently utilizes the laboratory of the Polytechnic for photographic experiments. In consequence of his protest, the regulations limiting the hours during which the laboratories are open to the student body are altered to permit the scholars access to them at all hours of the day and night: Stieglitz having assumed complete responsibility for the safety of the workshops. In his bedroom, he improvises a dark room by swinging a door backwards towards the wall and covering the interjacent space with a blanket. Again, he drapes the blanket over his table and crouches underneath the little tent with his developer bath and lamp. (These dark rooms are typical of the ones whose use he will enjoy during most of his life. He will rarely have the privilege of a well-equipped laboratory, and never until 1930 possess one of his own that has even the semblance of completeness. Empty farm kitchens, or bathrooms, will have to content him.)

The small brother of the other games has swiftly become the king of them all. The pleasures of photography are curiously deeply satisfactory. When the enthusiastic young photographer looks at the image on the plate of his camera, he sees not only the image which his eye beholds, but the image also of what the object, the fine human being, the lovely woman or child, makes him feel: something that is life itself in its wonder, laughter, and pathos. And not even expression at the piano gratifies him as deeply as the act and process of photography. All about him there now extends an infinite region favorable to photography; gloriously filled with beauty that has never hitherto been seen or expressed by others, and that the black box and the chemical bath and the printing paper can catch and hold.

And he is possessed by a curious certainty that his instruments will record to his satisfaction everything he now feels, and afterwards will feel, about the world. The limits which professors and wiseacres assign to it drive him to demonstrations of the fact that these limits are arbitrary. He is told that the camera can photograph only in daylight; and promptly he shuts himself and his camera into a cellar lit by a weak electric lamp and occupied by a disused dynamo. He focuses the camera, uncaps the lens; and, after an exposure lasting over twenty-four hours, finds that he has secured a perfect negative of the machine. Again, he is filled with the desire to find out how rapidly he can make a photograph; and photographs, develops, and prints a picture in thirty-four minutes. The amazed professor nevertheless shrugs his shoulders: what point has the demonstration of speed, he inquires? The American impulsively replies that the medium's demonstrable speediness may in time make it valuable to the newspapers.

Deliberately, in other ways, he is pushing the camera beyond its accredited frontiers; obliging it to attack complex problems of plastic representation. Now already, as later, each of his prints is the result of a complete consideration of what exposure, developing, and the quality of the paper can do toward solving the problem presented to him by feeling. Each is an experiment, the result of the application of the power and wisdom gained in past experiences, to the end of the solution of the new problem. He is already beginning to make, if necessary, ten, fifty, even a hundred prints of a negative, for the sake of capturing the vitality he pursues. Like an inventor, he sometimes works for years on a single problem till it is solved; and after having gotten a satisfactory print from his negative, sometimes sets to making it render a feeling latent in it but unregistered by the earlier proof, and gets as many as ten or twelve different sensations out of it.

4

A GOOD INNER FEELING has gradually been suffusing young Stieglitz. Since he has set earnestly to work with the camera, he has come to feel for the first time that he has a right to life, and a right to be living here in Berlin.

It is the unconscious, the integral self, that is declaring its satisfaction to him. In the camera, the boy of the dark room has finally

secured a means almost perfectly fitted to enable him to gain the ends towards which he is naturally directed.

Because of the currency, at this very late hour, of much mischievous misunderstanding of the subject, perhaps it will not be futile or presumptuous of us to point to what appears to us to be the evident reason for the affinitiveness of the man and the machine.

Let us commence by indicating to ourselves once more the nature and constitution of the genius. The genius is one in whom the intuition, directed towards the inward realm of life itself, the region of the truth, and present to some degree in all men, is powerful, pure, and constant to an heroic degree. This intuition is instinct become disinterested. It is active sympathy. It is the æsthetic, suspended touch that asks nothing for itself alone, and desires life for its object and the conditions making for that object's persistence. It is selfless love; in the words of Schopenhauer: "Perfect objectivity; an objective direction of the spirit as opposed to a subjective one directed towards one's own person and its will." Or in Goethe's (*Maxims and Reflections*): "the capacity to give up our own [selfish and limited] existence, so that we may truly exist." Since this intuition spontaneously "places itself back in the object, breaking down the intervening space" (Bergson) and "achieving a sympathetic communication between its possessor and the rest of the living, and widening consciousness," it penetrates the region closed to intelligence unperfected by intuition: the region of life, of the inwardness of matter itself—sometimes that of a single individual, sometimes that of all individuals in general—the region where "all is reciprocal penetration and continual creation." This is what Goethe signified in another of his Maxims "Antagonism and hatred limit the spectator to superficialities, even when they are coupled with intelligence; but if intelligence unites with fraternity and love, it can penetrate the world and humanity; indeed, it can attain the sublime." For, there, at the living heart of matter, intuition finds something that is both distinct and universal, momentary and eternal, of the many and the one: a kind of culmination of the entire universe onto one of its parts and moments—events past or approaching—that, for all their instantaneity, share the infinity and eternity of the whole. And with the tactile, visual or auditory, rhythmical symbols instantaneously communicated to it there, "Ideas"—which, for the reason that intuition itself is love, it suffuses with "wondrous beauty and inexpressible worth," and "consecrates and illumines and turns into forms of Joy" (Santayana)—it reveals that ever changing and still permanent harmony, order, and law of nature: that deeper truth without which there can be no sympathetic communication between individuals; nor can human life persist. That is what Beethoven indicated when he declared the *Missa Solemnis* directed to hearts from the heart; what Moussorgsky meant when he asserted that music was the speech of Man with Man.

Now, with the photographic means—so the lesson of Stieglitz has taught us—events had placed in the path of the species of genius which sees that which it feels and perceives the object's essence, its inward nature, and the harmony of forces that maintain its life and position, through the object's form, seeing the Idea as it were with the eye, and seeing and feeling with flashlike quickness and exquisite sensitivity and subtlety: in the pathway of this species of genius, we say, events had placed, in the camera, an instrument capable of being made to record its exquisite visions accurately in all their original complexity, and with the dew, the bloom, the intense gleam of the natal moment, still fresh upon them. Because of its capacity for exceedingly rapid reactions, the camera can reproduce significant, revelatory shapes in a permanent if monochromatic form; the appearances of visible and mobile objects, as temporary conditions of light model them, with a fidelity to subtle, ephemeral, complex detail beyond memory's capacity to hold or the hand's to achieve. It can immediately follow a complex conception with its expression, fixing the intricate Idea through the momentary forms which actually reveal it. Veritable attempts to "photograph" with the means of painting had indeed long anteceded the invention of the machine itself—notably those of those genial revealers through the patient record of visible appearances, the brothers Van Eyck, and Memling. And shortly after the invention of the camera, a partial actualization of its peculiar potentiality occurred, at the hands of the Scots academician David Octavius Hill, in collaboration with the chemist Robert Adamson. To secure the likeness of notabilities for a vast historical painting of the founding of the Free Church of Scotland projected by him, Hill, in the 1840's, set up a photographic atelier, and during several years made magnificent camera portraits of Edinburgh intellectuals, dominies, professors, scientists, artists, critics, and the ladies of their world. In these portraits, this veritable "old master" of photography recorded not only the appearances of these personages in moments of revelatory expression but revealed their interior life—the qualities, characters, forces of temperament which he had sounded—through pattern and the contrast and relationship of pictorial forms. Some of his photographs, which belong not only among the triumphs of the medium but among the world's fine character studies, were exhibited at the Crystal Palace Exhibition in 1851 and attracted great attention; but before the exhibition Hill had already dropped photography to return to his dull historical canvas; and though he temporarily had a successor in Mrs. Margaret Cameron, the veritable exploitation of the individual means of the camera

ceased around 1870. Nor was the fact observed. The potentiality of the camera was not really felt and understood. Hill's portraits were scattered. Indeed, the obituary notices of his decease made no mention of his photographic work; and it was only about 1900 that his negatives were rediscovered by the photographer Craig Annan, who circulated new and handsome prints of them among Whistler, Sargent, Leighton, and other artists. As for the work of the photographers of the immediately succeeding period, it either, like that of Nadar, is interesting almost exclusively because of its subject matter, or constitutes the results of unnecessary attempts to imitate painting.

At length the new means encountered its liberator in the keenly humorous young student developed from the small boy curious about what went on inside the tintyper's dark room. The coincidence of many forces, apparently, predestined Stieglitz to the work demonstrating the photographic medium's parity with all other mediums through which man has expressed his feeling of life. He not only was a genius, gifted with an extraordinarily fine capacity for the sympathetic penetration of the true nature of things, and the laws of being, deriving a living sense of order from his intuitions, disinterested, playing the game beautifully for the love of it, and equipped with an exquisite sensitivity to material. He also had the capacity for feeling and seeing and acting with extreme swiftness and certainty: a trait very possibly intensified by the American milieu in which he grew; Americans as a people having a tendency to rapid motory and mental reactions, to the development of sprinters in all fields, to the discovery that the processes of other peoples "come by freight." It is the remarkable fact that, technically speaking alone, the soundest work with the quick medium of photography has up to the present writing been done by Americans: besides Stieglitz, Steichen, White, Eugene, Sheeler, Keiley, Strand, Coburn, Käsebier, Man Ray, Weston, and others. Their prints alone combine tactility with strict authenticity of vision. It is also remarkable that another medium requiring extremely rapid decisions, water color, has most brilliantly been exploited by "the nervous, swift American."

Again, Stieglitz's natural bent toward the camera was probably augmented by the circumstance of the inclusion of knack with machinery, the ability to control natural forces through mechanical means unassisted by the heavy exercise of the humaan organs, in the national temperament; and by the fact that the pioneer initiative, the bold disregard for precedent, the perfect respect for the identity of an unconsecrated medium, which the camera demanded of its liberator and which he beautifully brought to it, lie in the high national tradition. Finally: it is possible that the man's native democracy, the conviction of the divinity immanent in every individual, and the willingness patiently to await the moment of its spontaneous selfconsciousness, and all that made him take the American faith so very seriously as a boy, added another subconscious dynamic to the photographic impulse. The medium was supremely capable not only of demonstrating the eternal in the fleeting expressions of the moment, in every leaf of grass, and verifying the democratic intuition of the ubiquity of divinity. Its apparent capacity for multiple products could render it, in the hands of an artist, an immensely potent agent of truthful communication with vast numbers of people flung over a continent: thus, an incomparable means of symbiosis. And it is possible that the young Stieglitz in some way inferred this fact in the Berlin of the 'eighties. Certainly, at times he cherished dreams of large, widely distributed printings.

But to the actual evolution.

5

SPRING OF 1887. ITALY. Alfred Stieglitz is in Lombardy and the Veneto on one of his regular spring and autumn excursions from Berlin, accompanied as is usual by his large camera, living as is usual at modest inns, and taking photographs. He photographs in Bellagio, in the country around Mantua, and in Venice, working as if possessed. Twelve prints of his new negatives are sent by him to the London *Amateur Photographer's* competition. He receives first prize, a medal, and a purse. The award was made by Dr. H. P. Emerson, an American resident in England, the future author of the revolutionary book *Naturalistic Photography,* and himself an amateur photographer whose work will shortly win the praises of another American, J. McNeill Whistler.

These prints, and prints of some of the other negatives Stieglitz has just made, are fortunately going to be preserved by the members of his family to whom he presents them, and will constitute the earliest known specimens of his work extant in 1934. They are perfect, originally realistic little genre pictures, taken in streets and fields, and in the courtyards and passages of Venice. Their symbolic references are largely the beautifully felt shapes of a common completely unromanticized and undecorated humanity that, anticipating most of the photographer's future human subjects, has yielded itself in open truthfulness to his camera's eye. The photographs themselves are excellent, straight, original exploitations of the photographic medium; rich and subtle and correct in their dispositions of light and dark; bare of "artfully" blurred effects or other consequences of manual manipulation; firm and sharp and in some instances fluent in their drawing. They have form, the

characteristically Stieglitzian form; even though it is a relatively simple one, a thing more of composition and of balance than of rhythmic order. In each, the shapes, lines, and tones constitute two great major complexes, one wedgelike, the other complementary to it. These balance the picture by their gentle but firm counterposition. Their points of deepest conjunction generally lie in the center of the picture: in several cases, however, they lie very high in it, inducing the perceptive eye to rise, as it were, not only toward something which lies in the inner depths, but also in the heights. And with their constituent symbolic delicately tactile references, the shapes of smiling children assembled by the fountainside, of women drawing water from the well-heads, of a young lazzarone stretched comfortably asleep on the sunny pedestal of the column of the Lion, the forms reticently, tenderly, clearly communicate what was being felt by the alert and sensitive young male while he photographed. It is the beautiful spirit of the homely, the earthbound reality, itself one of the persistent master themes of the Stieglitzian photography; here, in especial, that of the warm soil, the natural life, and its simple, uncerebrating, untheoretical children; and the peace and gayety that greet the gentle, living touch. But it also is the magnetism of the inner, spiritual dimension of things, its mysterious appeal and summons toward the ideal depths. These prints are love poems. And they have the directness and firmness that flow from passion and utterly unquestioning conviction in the artist.

Lenbach, who sees some of them in a photographic exhibition held that winter in Munich, inquires of a common friend where the photographer learned the laws of composition. Young Stieglitz is amused by the reported inquiry: he knows nothing about these laws. Analysis of the work of painters has never interested him (nor will it ever do so). If he adores Rubens, it is entirely for the master's puissant feeling through flesh of the beauty of life. As for himself, he has merely striven to secure a balance among the constituents of photographic forms that lie in what his eye sees, and are placed in his power by the crude drawing of the camera.

For a few months that summer, he revisits America and then returns to Berlin for three more years of intensive experimentation; definitely decided that he is going to spend his life fighting for the recognition of photography as an additional means of expression: for the sake of something of importance which, he feels, it has to give to the world. The prejudices of the artists against the work of the camera do not disturb him. What if the photographic process does exclude the direct introduction of the human organs? He will not for an instant grant that products made by a largely mentally controlled apparatus cannot have the quality of works of art. Does literature require the introduction of the human organs, as the plastic arts and music do? And if literature does not, why need photography be misprized for the reason it is not "done by hand"? Besides, most of the artists' manipulations of their sacrosanct media are "dead."

He photographs in the Black Forest and in the Tyrol. Again, it is something that the simple human being gives him, the feeling of the spirit of the clay, that he sings.

He begins sending his work to competitions and exhibitions the world over.

Once, he declares, "I would rather be a first-class photographer in a community of first-class photographers, than the greatest photographer in a community of nonentities."

Suddenly, recalled by the death of one of his sisters, he goes home to America.

6

1895. NEW YORK. It is now five years since Stieglitz has lived in America; five years since he has been in business, and two years since he married Miss Emmeline Obermeyer, the sister of one of his friends.

During the first period of his repatriation, disgust at the rankness of the civilization in which he found himself assailed him almost physically from the gilded and the naked squalor of the city and its nasty streets. But, walking down Broadway one evening shortly after his return, his eye fell on a theater-sign reading, "Roman Actress—Camille." He had seen Bernhardt play the rôle; he thoroughly disliked Dumas fils's claptrap; but he entered the theater and took a front-row seat. There were perhaps fifty persons in the audience. The curtain rose, the play commenced; at length the leading lady, an unknown to himself, appeared. From the moment of her entrance he sat in a spell. At the close of the performance he bought front-row seats on the aisle for every one of her subsequent appearances. And on the way home that night he reflected that, could he but occasionally in New York see something with a quality of life and beauty comparable to that of the performance just given by the unknown actress, he might very well be able to endure his native land.

He had just discovered Eleonora Duse for himself.

A year before his return, his father had posted a bond assuring Alfred of the option on a photo-engraving and printing concern called the Heliochrome Engraving Company. Attracted by the apparent opportunity for craftsmanlike work, young Stieglitz, together with two of his future brothers-in-law, took over the little

plant and for the first time entered into direct relations with the American workingman. The Heliochrome Company had been acquired from Mr. John Foord, the editor of *Harper's Weekly,* under the agreement that all existing contracts with the workmen be assumed by the new owners; and there was no business for the company. Times were hard; other concerns in the field were putting their men on half pay or laying them off altogether; the three young business novices secured no orders. Still, they kept paying their staff their regular wages irrespective of the number of hours the men actually put in or the absences caused by sickness. For a year, their employees made samples, oiled the machinery, and sat about reading newspapers. At last, when the small capital the three young men had raised between them had practically been exhausted, the company procured a large order for color prints to be done by the three-color process which it was among the first to utilize. Joyfully, Stieglitz showed the order to the workmen.

Scarcely a half hour after, the foreman entered the office and announced that he had been delegated by the men to say that unless they received an immediate ten-percent increase in their wages, they would refuse to go to work.

Dumbfounded, Stieglitz demanded, "But aren't you willing to give us a chance to get on our feet? You know we haven't drawn a cent of salary ourselves, or any other money out of the business."

The foreman expressed regrets. He merely represented the workers, he said.

Stieglitz had to dampen his partners' immediate impulse to discharge the men. A new agreement was reached. It assured the ten-percent increase on the basis of the hours actually put in.

The employees had indicated their disability to understand the functioning and interests of the concern as a whole. Still, it was not merely the interests of the concern itself they evidently could not grasp. The new arrangement later proved actually less to their own advantage than the former one, reducing their wages instead of increasing them.

The entire incident, born of an emphasis on the clichés of a unionism whose principles were not truly understood, at the expense of emphasis on the execution of work and matters of craftsmanship equally vital to all involved, was symptomatic of a spirit Stieglitz was to encounter all during his life, and by no means only in the persons of workingmen.

Fresh capital was raised. But during the last four years of its life the concern has never thoroughly prospered. It has done good and original work, and some of its methods, which will be taken to Germany by Stieglitz's friend Fritz Goetz, will be put to profitable uses there by the Bruckmann Verlag. But here in New York, conditions have not been favorable to success; like the workmen, the business people have little intelligence. The inexperienced partners began in perfect trustfulness, and, reports of their innocence having spread through the business world, they have again and again been victimized by concerns famous to the trade for their dishonesty. Only the warning of one of its own competitors has saved the Heliochrome Company from executing a large order for a theatrical company which has swindled various other engraving concerns. Indeed, up to the present hour, the partners have found only two customers willing to pay promptly what they owe. One of them is that eyesore to the virtuous, the *Police Gazette.* The rest chronically, after their orders have been executed, strive to lower, by innumerable artifices and extortions, the prices they have originally agreed to pay.

Meanwhile, Edward Stieglitz, under the pressure of financial cares, has, after a period of thirteen years, reëngaged in the woolen trade. But during the course of a single year, he loses a quarter of his fortune. Again he retires from affairs. And, in the panic of 1907, about a half of the sum left in his possession will finally slip from his hands.

Now, in 1895, Alfred Stieglitz is ailing. A kidney colic has developed; he has been prostrated by pneumonia; he is nervously worn down. Like many other normally fearless and confident individuals, he is subject to periodic fits of discouragement; and he has been disillusioned about the workers, the business world, and their provision of opportunities for work of the quality and in the spirit that will draw his best energies from him. Yielding to universal advice that he drop affairs and go with his wife to Europe for a couple of years, he too decides to retire from business.

All this while he has not neglected photography. He has been editing the *American Amateur Photographer;* he has found time to photograph even during business hours; he has almost regularly spent his evenings developing and printing his negatives at the Camera Club. Marriage has only brought about this change, that his evening trips to and from the clubhouse have been made in the company of his young wife. And he has produced a few great photographs, sober, pellucid little prints that like The Terminal fit into no preëxistent category of work; and with them has entered the ranks of the American artists who have expressed the American reality. The Terminal, Winter—Fifth Avenue, Five Points, South Street, and some of the others incidentally are uniquely beautiful little representations of New York and the common metropolitan scene; and as successful photographs of snowy streets they are going to provide photography and art too with a new motive. City snow scenes are going to make their appearance in numbers after their exhibition, precisely as city night scenes are going to

follow in numbers the exhibition of Stieglitz's pioneer photographic nocturne, the Icy Night, of 1896. What however concerns us here is their indication of the fact of a decided development of the feeling and the art of their maker. The character of the feeling has not changed since the European days: it is still as marvelously gentle and firm, warm and penetrating as before; nor will it ever in the years to come change its essential character. And the form is the Stieglitzian one, though perhaps more rhythmic and dynamic than it was. The feeling has merely broadened and deepened and struck a more robust and tragic stratum of life than previously, and the expression has, together with the old delicacy, a new power, roundness, and intricacy. And the forms render not only the superficial "feel" of New York, the snap, the sharpness, the hardness and brightness. They convey the lives of the sturdy, responsible, earth-fast common men whom Stieglitz to his joy has discovered at their work in the pretentious city. The broad, humble, and earthy rhythm and shapes of The Terminal give us the whole world of the sturdy, responsible little horse-car driver there on the firm ground with the elements and his horses: its ruggedness, its peacefulness, its healthy lowness. The dynamic form of the stagecoach advancing under the guidance of a weather-beaten driver between the recessive bluish shapes of the sleety Avenue communicates the dogged endurance of the men who really battle things. And all the prints of the period unconsciously convey another world: that of the photographer himself. That too is real. He too is on the earth, the individual struggling with life; touching it, receiving its buffets, tasting the salt of its breath, seeing its strange darkness and its stranger beauty; detecting, understanding, appreciating the other embattled individuals; and speaking to their kind.

7

1899. WHAT HISTORICALLY will be known as "American Photography" has broadly been making its appearance in the world. American Photography is pictorial photography, by a group of American camera artists: photography nonimitative in spirit, the live exploitation of an individual means; a reënforcement of the artist's perennial demonstration that labor with tools can be a joy with the novel demonstration of the truth that labor with the machine can be one, too; and a proof that the mechanical apparatus is at least quite as capable as is the hand or the implement of producing objects with the quality of life and not considerable upon valid grounds as secondary. Thus, American Photography is an instrument and an incentive toward "the humanization of society, the furtherance of the cause of social justice, the creation of a democracy of the spirit." Such an instrument and such an incentive art has always provided; since the esthetic, selfless, sympathetic touch of man upon his fellows, masculine as well as feminine, subhuman and inanimate as well as human, which it organizes, and the sense of life itself, and the intense respect for it in all its forms, and the feeling of its wonder communicated by it, provide a basis for relationships and a commonwealth of responsible, self-regulatory individuals, and democracy. And to communicate the esthetic touch and its findings through objects clearly demonstrative of the machine's perfect ability to transmit them is particularly to awaken in the industrialist, the mechanic, the sense of the potential fraternity of his machines, and with that feeling, to make him an agent like the artists of eld, of social relationships.

For a century, the general misuse of the machine, in the interests of cheap, quick mass-production, has helped weaken the feeling of life and isolate and depotentiate the human being. To this general misuse, "democratic" America, with its original weakness of feeling, its indifference for quality in things, has, curiously enough, even more than England with its "cheap merchandise," been contributing a preponderant incentive, and helping fill the world it meant to unite, with insane, destructive little egoists. And it is out of America that the demonstration of the possibility of fraternity between man and the machine, so fraught with importance for society, has come.

In 1896, the New York Society of Amateur Photographers was considering the project of transforming itself into a bicycle club. The flare of interest in photography had died away. As a nation, we have always mounted some steed or other, whether horse, bicycle, ocean liner, or theory, and used its motion as a means of escaping from ourselves, and the expressions that bring us into living relationship with one another.

Stieglitz, who had been devoting all his energies to photography, had offered to help rebuild the club, to organize its exhibitions, and to publish a photographic magazine, *Camera Notes,* that would be issued gratis to club members. The members were won over by his proposal and offered him the presidency of the association. He preferred the position of vice president: it gave him greater freedom for action.

In the rooms of the club, and in *Camera Notes,* Steiglitz began demonstrating the human friendliness of the machine. The demonstration rapidly took form in exhibitions all over the world, and continued to do so. Prints of others were shown far more frequently by himself than any of his own, for with characteristic sportsmanship he again was playing for the sake of the game,

working in the interests of the idea, giving the work of others wherever possible the *pas* over his own. In the course of years he has and will continue to receive medals from all over the world, a hundred and fifty of them; from London, Paris, Brussels, Turin, Hamburg, Berlin, New York, Boston, Philadelphia, Munich, Toronto, and other centers; and groups of his prints will find their way into the museums at Dresden, Brussels, Berlin, Boston, and Buffalo; into many private collections; and finally into the Metropolitan Museum of Art in New York. But in the American Photography campaign it is Steichen who carries the banner. Stieglitz, who in Icy Night, and The Flatiron and The Hand of Man, has been producing the first of his prophetic prints stands behind as the director.

Let it here be stated that the moralist in Stieglitz neither now is, nor ever in the future will be, separate from the artist. In him, as in every great artist, the moralist and the esthete are coördinate, unified by the total impulse of the artist embracing them both. If, therefore, in his various laboratories he shows pictures, his own and others', in consciousness of an ethical end, and will continue so to show them, he is not shaping his own or others' works to an end not their own, but merely helping the whole spirit of the artist to realize itself in the world.

And let here also be stated that his forty-year-long prodigious General Nathanael Greene campaigns for democracy are going to be conducted altogether on subsidies amounting to $37,000.

In the meanwhile: the leaders of American Photography have formed an inner group which, adopting the name of the modern art movement in Munich, calls itself the Photo-Secession. Its London correspondent calls itself the Linked Ring, and Stieglitz, who is one of the active members of both groups, generally is considered the international leader. The founders of the Photo-Secession are, besides himself, Clarence H. White, Edmund Stirling, and John Francis Strauss; while among its fellows it includes the photographers Frank Eugene, Gertrude Käsebier, Joseph T. Keiley, Eva Watson-Schütze, Eduard J. Steichen, Alvin Langdon Coburn, and Wm. B. Post. In 1903, after resigning from *Camera Notes,* Stieglitz begins the publication of the group's quarterly organ, *Camera Work,* itself another magnificent demonstration of the potentialities of the machine and of what the feeling of life can create through it and its products in the way of printed publications. *Camera Work* is perhaps the handsomest, most esthetically presented of all periodicals, outdistancing even its closest rival, the shortlived *Pan* of Bruno Cassirer. It is itself a work of art: the lover's touch having been lavished on every aspect of its form and content. Spacing, printing, the quality of the paper, the format of the pages, the format of the advertisements, even, are simple and magnificent.

Many of the reproductions are actual pulls from photogravure plates made directly from the original negatives; and all are printed in the spirit of the original pictures and retain their intrinsic qualities. They are actually original stamps. In 1904, for instance, when the Photo-Secession exhibit contributed to the show of the Société l'Effort in Brussels happens to go astray, the exhibition committee takes thirty of the gravures of *Camera Work,* mounts and frames and hangs them to represent America in the exhibition. And according to the criticisms, the little American section makes the show a success; and it is not until it is over that the fact that the American section has consisted entirely of the plates of *Camera Work* becomes generally known. Later, in making an address before the Royal Photographic Society on the development of photography, the president illustrates his talk with photogravures from the American quarterly.

It is a constantly progressive, steadily cumulative work of art. In the course of its fifty splendid numbers, *Camera Work* will come to give the complete record not only of the evolution of pictorial photography, but of modern art in America up to the time of America's entrance into the World War. It presents, to begin with, numerous significantly arranged specimens of the experiments in the new photography, the coloristic as well as the monochromatic, representing the work of the most important American photographers as late as Paul Haviland and Paul Strand, and that of their European collaborators Demachy, De Meyer, the Hofmeisters, Hinton, Annan, Evans, Henneberg, Kühn, Watzek, Puyo; and plates by Hill and Mrs. Cameron. (The unfortunate, unavoidable omissions are few: principally Emerson and the then entirely unknown Atget.) Besides, it carries important critical articles on photography and art specially written for it by Bernard Shaw, Maeterlinck, Charles Caffin, R. Child Bayley, Annan, Sadakichi Hartmann, John B. Kerfoot, Ernst Juhl, Roland Rood, Virginia Sharp, Stieglitz, Marius de Zayas, Mabel Dodge, Benjamin de Casseres, Demachy, Keiley, Oscar Bluemner, Francis and Gabrielle Picabia, and others. From the beginning of 1906 onward, shortly after Stieglitz and his friend Steichen open the little experimental Photo-Secession gallery in the attic of No. 291 Fifth Avenue, its issues begin recording the public reception of the exhibits by reprinting the press notices of the leading New York critics, Caffin, Huneker, McBride, down to the very divinatory *chefs d'œuvre* of Cortissoz and Elisabeth Luther Cary. After 1908, when Stieglitz discovers the complementariness of modern art to photography and begins reënforcing his idea by showing the new coloristic work of the modern painters at 291, its issues contain, together with a citation of Plato's early salutation of cubism in the *Philebus,* magnificent colored and black-and-white reproductions of the work of the painters and sculptors the gallery exhibits; sometimes for the first time in New York, sometimes for the first time in the world. They contain superb colored reproductions of the washes, till then ridiculously neglected, of Rodin; of water colors of John Marin; and paintings by Steichen; and black-and-white reproductions of Cézanne, whose water colors Stieglitz was the first to show in America; and reproductions of those other introductions of his, the paintings, drawings, and sculpture of Picasso and Matisse, the paintings of Picabia, the drawings of Manolo and Walkowitz, the "characatures" of De Zayas; and photographs recording the disposition of the exhibits in the Brancusi shows. And in *Camera Work's* letterpress, there appears some of the first work of Gertrude Stein, Mina Loy, Max Weber, John Marin, and Leonard van Noppen to be published.

The annual subscription rate is five dollars, later six. Like the attic-gallery and the deeply critical spirit of *its* demonstrations, *Camera Work* creates a climate in which life and art can thrive at a high level. In 1917 it suspends publication, with a subscription list of thirty-six.

8

FEBRUARY, 1921. Up in the daylit galleries of the Anderson Galleries in New York City, the shabby walls are supporting a show of a hundred and forty-odd major works of art representing the life work of the boy in the dark room: a life work not yet complete. Let us examine these majestic little harmonies of gorgeous shadows and burning lights effectively centered in their mats of white.

They are optical and tactile images surpassingly possessive of at least three of the values that everywhere to some degree have been considered those of the creations of great pictorial artists. They conform, first of all, to the appearances of the actual world; in certain respects with matchless accuracy. Though they are monochromatic—their colors lying within strangely pungent tonalities of black and white, gray, silver, bronze, fawn and pearl—their distribution and interdependence of lights and darks drawn from a wonderfully clear and gradual scale, ranging from deepest shadow to brightest light, and including a fabulous variety of intermediary qualities of lustrousness, precisely corresponds to Nature's. It renders the differences of distance correctly, and in some measure distinguishes the variety of color. The photographic textures are as continuous and unbroken as those of the visible scene; and as subtly, if not more subtly so than those of any other pictorialist. The drawing is sensitive and fluent, in many instances prodigiously delicate and swift, vigorous and powerful. Besides, these photographs' conformity with appearances is invariably extraordinarily bold and inclusive; for it is a conformity with appearances hitherto unrecorded. The prints bring wonderfully clearly before the eye virgin day and night-time aspects of the city, of the countryside and humanity. They represent skyscrapers, windowpanes filigreed with frost and dust, glistening wheel rims, car horses, smudged snow, brick walls, cement walls, wooden barn walls, steel girders, smoke, cloudlands, steel rails and wires. They portray the folk of the American streets in moments of intense expressiveness: workmen, business people, professional people, artists, the women of the kitchens, the little West Side apartments, the shining limousines. They bring the eye close to the human epidermis, to the pores, the fine hairs on the shin bone, the veins of the wrist, the moisture on the lips. They draw motives beautifully from every portion of the person of the woman, from naked feet and feet stockinged and shod, to ears and nostrils, breasts, bellies, hips, buttocks, navels, armpits, and the bones underneath the skin of throat and chest.

But these accurate and novel representations are also complete abstract, individually dynamic, forms. Each is a total three-dimensional form made up of formal units. The rectangular surface of every one of the prints is divided into two or more rhythmically disposed, intrinsically interesting primary units, which in turn are made up of aggregations of smaller units, some of them fine hair lines, some of them gamuts and rhythms of light. These primary units compose pairs or groups of antitheses, intricately, subtly complementary in point of tone and of shape and balance; for they are predominantly triangular and oval, beak-shaped and bell-shaped. And these pairs of antitheses define dynamic pyramidal and concave volumes: a prodigy potential in the medium of chiaroscuro for the reason that, when juxtaposed, different qualities of light recede, and fall from, and advance toward, and ascend from the eye at various degrees of speed. The volumes equilibrate each other in weight and direction of movement: and what the student of the photographs actually had before him is one hundred and forty-odd simulacræ of spaces coextensive with dynamically counter-pressing, interpenetrating, and mutually equilibrating volumes or forces in motion. The character of this counterpressure and interpenetration varies from picture to picture, quite like the character and disposition of the formal units. Invariably firm, in instances it is gentle, in others strenuous, in still others violent, suggesting struggle and conflict. But in all the pictures, the aspiring tendency of movement predominates, despite the earthward declension of the blacks: possibly for the reason that vertical pyramids seem to dominate the other forms, possibly for the reason that small masses of ascensive burning white by virtue of their intensity balance superior masses of shadow. Held though

they are by their complements, the pyramids and whites still appear to tend and shoot infinitely upward. The whole space seems to float aloft.

And again: these accurate representations and forms enchanting the eye as patterns, unities, complete and balanced living objects, are immensely symbolical. The shapes transmit deep, broad experiences of life: deep large draughts of American nature, American life in particular: the restless reaching and overreaching soul of this country today; in all the tensity of the terrific psychic and sexual conflicts following the multiple appearance of the determinately individual woman; in all its rapid tempo and rhythm and the struggle of the forces underlying the individual and society; in all the novel beauty of their momentary harmonies and ordinations. The transmissions are direct. The images are spontaneous, complete transpositions into the visual and tactile field of the ineffable sensuous unities, ordinations, wholes, and worlds that have constituted the content of the photographer's experience; the ideas that, like all their sort, appear to lie eternally behind the material existence in which they have momentarily incorporated themselves. Thus in the form of relationships of shape and line and color they symbolize the harmonies of living matter, restlessly yearning, aspiring, struggling to reach beyond itself, the cosmic order concurrent with those yearnings, insurgences, ecstatic leaps; and the eternity and infinity that seem to lie magnetically at the apex of their roads of progress. They also symbolize relationships the most subtle and intricate; relationships of nervous refined moderns giving life to each other, fortifying each other by their free counter pressure and interpenetration; relationships of whole groups and communities of nervous refined moderns making life possible by their free mutual oppositions and complementariness; whole democracies; "anarchist communes." They actually are symbols of the Most High.

The photograph's individually dynamic "abstract" form is actually a spontaneous, uninduced photographic representation of material harmonies and cosmic ordinations, produced in profound sympathy with these relationships. And their superfine "conformity with nature" is a conformity either with the objective forms whose relationships actually excited the photographer's imagination, or with an equivalent of some vision excited by a previous experience and carried about in his head against the discovery of objective circumstances propitious to their expression.

The Sublime! Before these hundred and forty-odd somberly, deeply glowing representatives of a life work still far from culmination we are facing one of the grandest consequences of the emergence of spirit from the American soil. We face symbols of a Life, a Law our very own affirmed by the beauty and worth with

⌐ aspiring tendency of movement ⌐

which the photographer has suffused them. Before these revelatory forms, second in beauty, inclusivity, and significance to none of those of the present period, and to very few of past ones, we know, as for a first time, our very Self in its depth and height and possibility; know it in the myriad surrounding human forms once strange, now plainly kindred to us, and in the soil we tread.

A slender, medium-sized man in a business suit, with a shock of iron-gray hair and intensely bright eyes glowing through iron-rimmed spectacles, stands in a corner of the gallery, talking humorously, passionately, debonairly to the people, battling for the Ideas; letting them generate in many heads, his own and others, in their own time; letting them form the basis of relationships. He is the author of the prints.

We know: at some time this man recognized not only that he was seeing symbols of the order and law of things, but knew that their beauty and worth, and all the floating "higher, purer, more unknown" Thing perpetually attracting him and moving him to give himself "freely, gratefully" to itself, were inextricably connected with his own person's unity of function and active health and love; and that that spirituality and its fruits in life and art and leadership themselves were born of and were portions of the vast harmony of an infinite substance sometimes called God.

That evidently was the light in the dark room.

R. Child Bayley

Photography Before Stieglitz

A NOTABILITY IN THE CAMERA WORLD once said, "Photography would be a fine thing if it were not for the pictures." At that date, three quarters of a century ago, it might well be true. The known processes offered little temptation as a means to artistic expression. Essentials to success were a leaning towards chemistry and physics, a liking for the manipulations they entailed, and—for work away from a studio—good muscular development. Enlarging was not practical, even if negatives could have been made which would stand it; so that a large camera was needed. The process which was then mostly used made it necessary for the glass to be coated, sensitized, and developed where the photograph was made; for the exposure had to be given while the freshly prepared plate was still wet, so that some sort of dark room must accompany the camera. A photographer's outfit often weighed fifty or even a hundred times what we now use. Moreover, making a negative called for manual dexterity and skill, only acquired with much practice and many failures.

When, in spite of all these obstacles, the photographs were made, they had defects, apparently inherent, of just the kind to deter an artist. Exposures had to be so long that in portrait and figure work stiffness and camera consciousness were rampant. To the same cause must be attributed the blurs which represented leaves in landscapes. In many cases there was a queer falsity in the perspective which was ascribed to the lens, although actually due only to its misuse. A very serious imperfection was the way in which the tone values of the original subject seemed in the photograph to be falsified, not only in the reproduction of colored subjects, but even where color did not obtrude. Little was then known on the subject of gradation; in fact, it was not until some time after the dry plate had displaced the wet plate that we learned how incorrect had been our notions and how limited our control over tone relationship.

Photography, when first known, was expected to follow respectfully upon the lines followed by painters, and that epoch was the very heyday of the painting which told a story or taught a lesson. So, almost without exception, photographers tried to make their prints dramatic or even didactic, which, as we now see plainly

enough, is precisely what photography is least fitted to do. If subjects of this kind are worth doing, at any rate they are not worth attempting with a camera; but they were attempted; and for a long period of years these photographs which when they were exhibited received the most applause appear to us now as melancholy examples of misapplied skill and wasted labor. There was this excuse for the pioneers, that, while they were only attempting work of the kind which was to the front in the other graphic arts, even if they had had other aims, the materials and knowledge then at their disposal were not enough to enable them to achieve them.

Bernard Shaw later on (1901) summarized the period when he wrote:

. . . the process was not quite ready for the ordinary artist, because (1) it could not touch colour or even give colours their proper light values; (2) the impressionist movement had not then re-discovered and popularised the great range of art that lies outside colours; (3) the eyes of artists had been so long educated to accept the most grossly fictitious conventions as truths of representation that many of the truths of the focussing-screen were at first repudiated as grotesque falsehoods; (4) the wide angled lens did in effect lie almost as outrageously as a Royal Academician, whilst the anastigmat was revoltingly prosaic, and the silver print, though so exquisite that the best will, if they last, be one day prized by collectors, was cloying, and only suitable to a narrow range of subjects; (5) above all, the vestries would cheerfully pay £50 for a villainous oil-painting of a hospitable chairman, whilst they considered a guinea a first-rate price for a dozen cabinets, and two pound ten a noble bid for an enlargement, even when the said enlargement had been manipulated so as to be as nearly as possible as bad as the £50 painting. But all that is changed nowadays.

What follows is an outline of the period from the first photography to the end of the nineteenth century, by which time both the processes and those who used them had progressed, so that in the eyes of many best qualified to judge, photography had become a medium capable of use by the artist, and was so being used more and more each year. The change was necessarily gradual, depending upon many factors, but for at least the last fifteen years of the century it was plain enough. It is at that period that we first encounter the name of Alfred Stieglitz, so this sketch may be taken as a background against which other writers will set their record of what he did and what he has been in photography during the last thirty years or more. While not dealing in detail with the technical side of photography, we must have some outline of its development if the progress of its use as art is to be traced, since the one acted directly upon the other.

2

PHOTOGRAPHS IN THE SENSE in which the word is generally understood today were first made almost exactly a hundred years ago; for although 1839 is accepted as the date of the birth of photography, since in that year both Daguerre and Fox Talbot published their methods, both of those experimenters must have obtained some kind of photographs before they felt their process to be ripe for publication. Talbot we know did so, for a view of his home at Lacock Abbey exists dated 1835. In fact, it was under some form of gentle pressure that in January, 1839, a fortnight later than Daguerre, he announced what he had already done.

The photographs which Daguerre exhibited were delineations of outdoor scenes in the neighborhood of Paris made on highly polished plates of silvered copper. At first, the exposures required were too long to make human portraiture possible; but later the sensitiveness of the metal plates was increased, and for about a dozen years daguerreotype portraits were made in large numbers. Many are still in existence, and form the only photographic record we have of those they portray. The process held out little hope of any application to art. The pictures were on metal and had to be held at one particular angle to the light to be seen at all, the high lights being then formed by a kind of graying over of the polished surface, and the shadows being a reflection of some dark mass by that surface. At another angle the image appeared as a negative, with its light and shade reversed. There was no satisfactory way of duplicating daguerreotypes, each one being the result of a separate exposure. Their outstanding quality was their fine detail; and this enabled them to hold their own for portraits, until the wet plate gave us paper prints which might show as much detail as the daguerreotype itself. Daguerreotypes then ceased to be made, and were not followed by anything which could be said to derive from them, photography today having developed from the process invented by Fox Talbot.

Talbot's process gave negative images on paper: images, that is to say, in which the shadows were the more transparent parts and the lights the more opaque; but by what may be regarded as a repetition of the process, these paper negatives would yield positive prints, prints in which the lights and shades were no longer reversed. The process required much longer exposures than that of Daguerre, and owing to the negatives being on paper and not on glass, prints from them had a granular appearance, which could not be entirely prevented by waxing the paper of the negative. In those days, and for long afterwards, clean-cut definition was demanded so insistently that any process which did not yield it was thought little of; so that although "Talbotype," or "Calotype," as its more sensitive modification was named, was used with great pictorial effect by one worker, Hill, his pictures were disregarded and allowed to drop quite out of sight for nearly half a century.

For about a dozen years there was no other photography than these two methods. Then, in 1851, Scott Archer announced the wet collodion process, which gave negatives on glass from which prints could be made on paper; and although at intervals in the next thirty years other methods were evolved, some of which came into use to a limited extent, they had no great significance or lasting quality. From its introduction in 1851 wet-plate photography was supreme, until it was finally displaced during the 'eighties by gelatino-bromide emulsions, first with glass as the support, and then with celluloid film. These are the materials we use today. The gelatine-silver emulsion has been greatly improved since it first became available, in its sensitiveness, in the way in which it renders tone values, and in its power of dealing with colored subjects; but in all its essentials it is today the process which between 1878 and 1888 supplanted wet collodion, except for certain special purposes.

From the time when the first negatives on glass were made, processes for giving paper prints from these negatives became of importance. At first plain paper was used, sized, it is true, but not so as to impart any glaze to the surface. The sensitive material was silver chloride, salts of gold subsequently giving a purple color to the image. Then this "silver paper" was coated with either one or two layers of albumen, which gave a gloss enabling it to reproduce all the fine detail in the glass negative. Most of the old faded portraits in family albums were printed on this albumenized paper, which was also very largely used for exhibition work. That the fading was avoidable is plain, since many of these exhibition prints still exist without any great signs of change, demonstrating that with the care more likely to be used with a print for exhibition, the results gave fair promise of permanence.

Photographers wanted something more than fair promise, though; and in 1864 this was found in the carbon process of Swan. Carbon prints can have an image of any desired color whatsoever; almost any pigment which can be used by the painter can be made the basis of a carbon print. This enabled the worker to get away from the "photographic purple" and red-brown silver prints. Moreover, there was a wide choice in the papers which were its basis, and the surface could be glossy or mat at will. A few years later the platinum process was introduced; and platinum and carbon prints figured very largely in the exhibitions, although never displacing the earlier methods entirely. Bromide paper followed, giving a pure black image, unless toned, and not involving a glossy surface, this paper being sensitive enough to allow enlargements to be made upon it. Modern photographs are more frequently made on bromide paper, or on modifications known as chloro-bromide; but other methods, such as "gum-bichromate," "oil-printing," and "bromoil," may be mentioned.

Such in outline are the principal processes which have been at the disposal of the photographer. Their later progress has been on two lines, one giving greater powers by increased sensitiveness and more faithful tone rendering, the other by simplifying the manipulations to such an extent that they no longer demand almost the monopoly of a photographer's attention. He can concentrate upon those quite different problems which are concerned with picture-making itself.

Limiting what follows to British workers almost exclusively has not been voluntary on my part; but attempts to discover parallel instances in Europe or America, at any rate until about 1890, have ended in failure. Great attention was given to the technique of photography wherever it was practised, as is shown by the contents of the photographic journals; nor were the commercial aspects of studio portraiture overlooked. Landscape subjects seem always to have been almost a British preserve; but although exhibitions were held from time to time, most of the recorded criticisms indicate that professional portraiture was their backbone. Certainly I have failed to find traces in other countries of workers such as Hill and Mrs. Cameron—except perhaps Adam Salomon in France. This may be due to the fact that we have had in London regular annual exhibitions organized by what is now the Royal Photographic Society, going back for sixty years or more without a break, when in other countries exhibitions have only been held irregularly and at longer intervals. My failure is to some extent confirmed by a book by Bossert and Guttmann, *"Les Premiers Temps de la Photographie, 1840–1870,* published in Paris in 1930 by Flammarion. The authors seem to have been at great pains to collect early photographs from all over the world; but out of two hundred which they reproduce almost all are either portraits of the usual professional kind, mostly complete with painted studio background, or else rely upon the intrinsic interest of the subjects photographed. Almost the only exceptions to this are the British contingent, pictures by men who are now to be mentioned. If I have overlooked pictorial workers who should have been considered, I can only plead Dr. Johnson's excuse of "pure ignorance."

The first name we meet, and that at the very earliest stages of

photography, is that of David Octavius Hill. Hill was a Scottish painter who was inspired by the disruption of the Church of Scotland in 1843 to paint a picture commemorating the event. He proposed to include likenesses of all those most concerned; and as this meant several hundred portraits, he called in the aid of Calotype. Wisely Hill decided not to embarrass himself more than need be with the manipulations, so he engaged Robert Adamson, a skillful chemist, as his collaborator. In his studio on the Calton Hill, Edinburgh, he photographed many of the ministers, and in addition a number of the celebrities who then made Edinburgh their home or who came to that city. Some of his pictures, faithfully reproduced in photogravure by Craig Annan, a name of note in the world of pictorial photography, appeared at different times in *Camera Work*—the magnum opus of Stieglitz.

Many are surprised when they learn that some of the finest and strongest portraiture ever done by photography goes back to 1843–1846, years before negatives on glass were practicable at all. It may not have occurred to them that success in photography is not a matter of modern appliances and inventions—these only extend the sphere within which successes may be made—but is concerned with the artist using the camera. Besides, while Hill had many handicaps, he was not without some counterbalancing aids. In his day there were at least no photographic conventions to trammel him. He had not to please a public which had its own notion of what a photograph should look like. To the vast majority of those who then saw his portraits, they must have been the first photographs on paper they had ever seen. The long exposures (three minutes is said to have been usual), the imperfections of the only lenses then to be had, together with the granularity of the paper on which his negatives had to be made, combined to free him from any fear of that excessive and unnecessary detail which is one of the bugbears of the modern photographer. Again, work in any light weaker than direct sunshine was most difficult, and this also helped to give the breadth and vigor which characterize all his prints. But these may be taken merely as some offset to his difficulties; and the merit of the work which we have by this old master of photography is Hill's alone. Craig Annan writes:

He had an absolute genius for seeing his sitters in a grand and impressive manner. His spacing is always perfect, his masses of light and shade are always broad and simple, and his pictures possess that power and distinction so difficult to describe or explain, but which is always apparent in the work of a master, and distinguishes it from that of an earnest conscientious practitioner of less capacity.

J. T. Keiley, writing in *Camera Work* of the Buffalo Exhibition of 1911, described the Hill Collection shown there as:

. . . splendid, vital, virile, and by comparison, some of the finest of the modern portraiture shown in this collection seems thin, anaemic and over-conscious.

Hill's photography ceased in 1846, and the remaining twenty-four years of his life were occupied with painting. For the best part of half a century after he ceased to photograph, his work was lost sight of. No one could read of it; for all that photographers knew, he might never have existed. A volume of his prints was in the possession of the Royal Photographic Society; but it was not until Mr. Craig Annan drew attention to him at a time when the academic influence upon photography was passing away, that it began to be realized that in the Scottish painter the use of the camera had found a great pioneer. Then David Octavius Hill began to take his proper place in its history. By great good fortune not only many of his prints, but his negatives, all upon paper, of course, waxed to give it greater translucency, had been preserved; some of them have been printed by modern methods and now have a permanence which will enable future workers to see them as they should be seen. Most of Hill's pictures were portraits, single figures or groups of two or three, although there were a few exceptions. Landscape apparently he did not attempt.

The next outstanding photographer in order of date was Mrs. Julia Margaret Cameron, who also restricted herself to portraiture. At her home at Freshwater, in the Isle of Wight, she enjoyed the friendship of many of the notable men and women of the day. Carlyle, Darwin, Sir John Herschel, Holman Hunt, Tennyson, Ellen Terry, and G. F. Watts are only a few of the celebrities whom this ardent amateur persuaded to sit to her; and some persuasion must have been necessary, for although she used the wet collodion process, far more sensitive than the Calotype to which Hill was limited, we read of exposures of two, three, or even five minutes. She was the pioneer in the movement against the belief in the necessity for pin-sharp definition in a photograph, though a protest had been made against it ten years before, at the very first meeting of the Royal Photographic Society, by its vice president, the painter Sir W. J. Newton.

Mrs. Cameron did not so much verbally preach as visibly practise. She used large-size plates—many measured 12 x 15 inches; she worked with very imperfectly corrected lenses, although later on special lenses for soft definition were made for her; the long exposures almost inevitably entailed movement on the part of her sitters, which in itself destroyed fine definition; it is reported also that she did not hesitate to put sheets of glass between the negative and the paper when printing. All contributed towards securing soft results. Her work was first publicly shown at the exhibition of 1864, where it was highly praised by some of the lay press, notably the *Athenæum*. Its critic remarked that her pictures, "although sadly unconventional in the eyes of the photographers, give us hope that something higher than mechanical success is attainable by the camera." Not so the photographic journals. These grant that her portraits "have a very distinctive character of their own," as indeed they have, but "as one of the especial charms of photography consists in its completeness, detail, and finish, we can scarcely commend works in which the aim appears to have been to avoid these qualities"; while another refers to Mrs. Cameron as "one of the very few ladies whose works adorn (?) the walls of the room." Owing to its reception by photographers, Mrs. Cameron subsequently held a separate exhibition, where the pictures received appreciation from some of the critics; but among photographers she proved to be altogether before her time. At her death in 1879 it was grudgingly admitted that she had exerted a beneficial influence upon the disciples of the camera—which few now will deny. Some of her negatives still exist, and a few were reproduced in *Camera Work* in 1913.

If we look to see who were enjoying a general acceptance when Mrs. Cameron was passed over, we find two names outstanding in the exhibitions for some thirty years, Rejlander and Robinson. Both of them, with a host of followers, trod in the footsteps of the popular painters of the day to the fullest extent photography would allow. They even attempted allegory, as, for instance, Rejlander in The Two Ways of Life, and drama, e.g., Robinson's Fading Away. The mere technical difficulties were immense; but, great as they were, they were exceeded by the artistic difficulty that the camera's supreme merit is precisely that it cannot do the one thing or the other. It depicts far too faithfully. Nevertheless, these workers had a great vogue.

Rejlander, a Swede, spent some of his early years at Rome and in Spain, studying painting, and came to England as a portrait painter. Much of his photography was done in the dingy Black Country, at Wolverhampton, but in 1860 he moved to London, where he lived until his death in 1875. Beginning with prints made from a single negative, many of which enjoyed a popularity far beyond photographic circles, he took up combination printing. His best known picture of this sort was The Two Ways of Life, already mentioned, exhibited in 1857. It combines in one print parts of more than twenty different negatives; and in a succession of tableaux symbolizes the careers of two youths who follow much the same diverse paths as were followed by Hogarth's apprentices. As a *tour de force* it is indeed remarkable; but even at the time when it was made, it was viewed by some as marking out a limitation of photography which is plain enough to us today. Rejlander himself realized this, and abandoned combination printing soon after. A few, but very few, of his photographs remain, though a great many persist in the form of woodcuts in popular magazines. He was intensely enthusiastic in his photography and made a host of friends, but his worldly position suffered from his enthusiasm.

Mention has been made of Adam Salomon, and what need be written of him may be interpolated here. He was a sculptor in France who turned to photography in 1861; but his portraiture was first brought into prominence at the Paris International Exhibition in 1867, when the Paris representative of *The Times* gave so glowing an account of it that English photographers went across "in hundreds" to see it. After reading this, we are not surprised to learn that it had "a greatly beneficial effect upon the practice of professional photographers." A contemporary review describes his portraits as possessing—

. . . a far more extended scale of tones than photographs generally, and as the arrangement and juxtaposition of these tones is skilfully managed, the result is extreme brilliancy. On a closer examination we find that there is as much delicacy as brilliancy, the utmost gradation of half-tone prevailing throughout the whole picture.

Probably some of Salomon's portraits still exist in old albums in French provincial homes, but we have no means now of judging work which undoubtedly impressed his contemporaries. We are told that he did not hesitate to use brushwork on both negatives and prints, and that while his pictures were not as sharp as the lens could make them, there is nothing he was so intolerant of as anything out of focus. Salomon lived just long enough to use gelatino-bromide plates, dying in 1881. As far as one can learn, he limited himself to portraiture.

To resume, in exhibition history between 1858 and 1890 the name which looms largest of all is that of Henry Peach Robinson. His first important picture, exhibited in 1858, was Fading Away, depicting the deathbed of a girl, with three other figures introduced. This print was obtained by combination printing from several negatives. A long series of pictures followed, some of them having a similar origin, but most being simple straightforward prints from a single negative. Robinson had the reputation of a "combiner," and many of his pictures which were alleged to be combination prints actually were not. For many years he led the way, imitated by a host of disciples who did not find him at all easy to follow. His name will always be coupled with work of a particular style, but actually he was very far from hidebound; and the photographer whose pictures were made on wet plates at a time when, as he told me once, he not only had to coat his plates, but actually to

make the collodion with which he did so, at the end of his career was enthusiastically using a hand camera and exhibiting work done with it. He died in 1901.

3

FOR MANY YEARS, more than a quarter of a century at least, photography as recorded in the exhibitions went its way, following at a respectful distance the example given by the painters whose names were most in evidence, academic workers expounded and praised by academic critics. Towards the end of the 'eighties the movements which had stirred the art world began to affect that of the camera. Amateurs no longer concentrated their attention upon technical problems; improvements in material made this much less of a necessity. Attempts at picture-making by photography became more plentiful, and societies and clubs were formed at which, although processes and appliances were not ignored, the results of using those processes and appliances took a more prominent place. Both in New York and in London, Camera Clubs were started, and the old-established professional and scientific journals found themselves confronted by publications which concentrated on subjects which previously had received only casual attention.

Throughout the period then coming to an end, writing on art for photographers had been almost exclusively limited to the subject of composition. Burnet's *Art Essays,* published half a century before, had been long out of print; but later, books designed avowedly to meet the needs of photographers, in which the same material had been used, and rules formulated on generalizations from the works of great painters, illustrated with sketches demonstrating pyramidal construction, balance, and kindred matters, had enjoyed a large sale. Among their authors Robinson attained an easy preëminence. By his books and countless magazine articles, he took and kept the first place for over twenty years. He wrote interestingly and fluently, and had also, of course, a great advantage in being known not merely, or even primarily, as a writer but as a worker, teaching as much by example as by precept, although his teaching was accepted after his picture-making had become a little less outstanding. People began to realize that combination printing, even in hands as skillful as his own, was not justified in the result. Not only were its ideals wrong, they were out of reach by photographic means.

It was at this stage that the picture-making photographers received three very great helps. The gelatino-bromide dry plate did away at a stroke with three fourths of the trouble and messiness of negative making. Its great sensitiveness at once enlarged the scope of the camera, making many subjects available which until then had been quite impossible, and leading ultimately to instantaneous work and the hand camera—the greatest change of all. It was followed by the introduction of orthochromatic emulsions, the first step towards correct color reproduction in monochrome; although it took another thirty years or more for this to reach perfect accuracy in the panchromatic plates and films as we have them today. The early 'eighties saw also the perfection of Willis's "hot-bath" platinotype, followed a few years later by the "cold-bath" process, a further simplification. These methods gave prints of a quality which surpassed altogether everything that had preceded them. Now that the cost of platinum has almost made the process obsolete, the platinum print is still the criterion by which other printing methods are judged; and modern chloro-bromide papers can have no higher praise than that they yield results "equal to platinum." We may note in passing that the process was worked out with no such object. Its inventor was not a photographer at all, but an engineer, who was led by some experiments to devise a paper which would give an image consisting simply of metallic platinum on plain paper, thus yielding a print which it might be assumed was as permanent as a print could be. That these prints should be ideal for pictorial work just happened.

Such was the state of things in the middle 'eighties: not so very different from what it had been twenty years before, but ripe for change. In Great Britain the pioneer in the revolution then beginning was Dr. P. H. Emerson, whose landscapes had begun to attract attention—and denunciation. He seems to have been quite prepared for both; his powers as a picture maker being at least equaled by his vigor as a controversialist. When I say that one single letter to the press from his pen contains among its expressions "ignorance unbelievable"—"wilfully and stupidly malicious" —"another sweeping lie"—"doubly dishonest as a critic and a man" —"I brand him as a coward and a liar," the letter itself being written to "contradict a few of the lies"; it will be admitted that as a denunciator Dr. Emerson had little to fear. The cause of all this, and a great deal more, was the publication of his book, *Naturalistic Photography,* which first appeared in 1889 and was followed almost at once by a second edition.

In any history of pictorial photography this is an outstanding event. It marks the coming of photography as we know it today; of that photography which is enshrined in the pages of *Camera Work.* It is true Hill and Mrs. Cameron had lived and died: but when *Naturalistic Photography* was published, photographers knew just as much of Hill's portraits as they did of the contents of the tomb of Tutankhamen; and Mrs. Cameron's, if not quite lost to sight, had at least never had photographic appreciation. In a paper read in 1886 before the Camera Club of London, Emerson had

sketched out his position; three years later he gave the finished picture.

He describes his aim in *Naturalistic Photography* as to "give enough science to lead to a comprehension of the principles which we adduce for our arguments for naturalistic photography, and we shall give such little instruction in art as is possible by written matter, for art we hold is to be learned by practice alone." The need for it is described by saying that "nearly all the text-books teach how to cultivate the scientific side of photography, and they are so diffuse that we find photo-micrography, spectrum analysis and art all mixed up together."

The author's object was accomplished in three sections. The first contained the "terminology and argument" with an account of naturalism in pictorial and glyptic art, and a chapter on the phenomena of sight and art principles deduced therefrom. The second section on technique and practice is sufficiently described by those words. The third, entitled "Pictorial Art," included in its scope the education of the eye, composition—which criticizes Burnet's *Treatise on Painting*—suggestions on picture-making both in the studio and out-of-doors, and general "hints on art." In "L'Envoi" Emerson puts the case for photography as one of the pictorial arts, claiming for it "a technique more perfect than any of the arts yet treated of," "standing at the top of the tone class of methods of expression; so nearly perfect is its technique that in some respects it may be compared with the colour class." He claims that while its scale of tones is limited "it is less so than that of any other black and white method. Its drawing is all but absolutely correct, that is if the lenses are properly used." "It renders the values relatively correct if orthochromatic plates are used, and it renders texture perfectly."

Such is this book in outline; but description cannot give its supreme freshness, free from any trace of an echo of the textbooks which had preceded it. Copies of the first or second editions are still to be picked up second hand. To complete its history: the second edition was withdrawn, and some years later a third edition was published in America and in England in 1899, much inferior in typography, and largely altered. The cause of the changed contents was that Dr. Emerson had become acquainted with the scientific work of Hurter & Driffield; and, from what I believe to be an entirely mistaken view of its bearing on the subject, had come to the conclusion that photography could not be an art. This, however, is not very material. The book had done its work; and the author's published "Retractation" was about as effective as a captain's "retractation" of a discharged torpedo. The book had been compared to a "bomb," so such a simile may pass.

The reception given to *Naturalistic Photography* was a mixed one. In quarters which it made no attempt to assail it was favorably if mildly reviewed; in the strongholds of amateur photography, where all that it denounced was rampant, it was received with vituperation inferior to its author's only because its opponents carried fewer literary guns. The discussion which at first raged around *Naturalistic Photography* and its champion passed gradually to the subject of definition in photographs, on which even now it bubbles up from time to time. The old type photographer, actively encouraged by the lens maker, regarded the most pin-sharp definition and the clearest possible details as essential. As all his life he had been confronted with the difficulty of getting such photographs, it was only natural that he should consider any that had not these qualities as defective, made because those who produced them could do no better. It was then that the phrase "the cult of the spoiled print" was coined. Many of these critics never did realize that some of the workers who used such means for the suppression of unwanted detail were perfect technicians.

The last decade of the nineteenth century may therefore properly be regarded as marking the birth of photography as a means of artistic expression. We have seen how the technicians and the manufacturers had cleared the way; and this having been done, there was consequently an immense accession to the ranks of photographers. Among these thousands were a few who saw in it a power they had not hitherto possessed, and endeavored to use it. They began also to demand recognition, and to claim a place among those who had hitherto been supreme. It was a time of struggle. In England, the technicians were strongly entrenched in the old-established Society; its hanging committees and boards of judges had hitherto been their preserve, and they were not prepared at first to admit any of the newcomers if they could help it. They could not help it, however, and pictorial photography in the modern sense was accepted.

We have now come down to the time which bounds my subject. Stieglitz was known in England as an occasional exhibitor. At the Royal, in 1894, we find him showing a New York subject, Winter, which was favorably criticized but none too well hung. There was an impression that he was inspiring work in America which went far beyond anything which had been done in Europe; but it was not until the Royal Photographic Society in October, 1900, opened its house to "An Exhibition of Prints by the New School of American Photography" that this was much more than an impression. Although the collection then shown was far from complete, it was known that the very possibility of such a show was largely his, and that in the movement which that show demonstrated he was the leader. One critic then wrote that this was "without question the most interesting photographic exhibition it has ever been our lot to see. Its influence on British work is bound to be a great one."

It was.

Herbert J. Seligmann

291: A Vision Through Photography

STIEGLITZ MADE PHOTOGRAPHY something more universal than the draftsmanship of light, controlled through use of lenses, darkened enclosures, sensitive surfaces, and chemical processes. In him it became the act of vision, of life itself, by which all things, all relationships might be focused at a timeless moment in their flux, held as the artist holds his picture: a vision of the world serving as a challenge, a guide, a corrective, and an incentive. In this second phase—of photography as method, as philosophy of truth—the materials on which Stieglitz worked became human beings, and their relations to one another, the abstract and timeless constantly emerging from the most personal, the most deeply intimate.

The history of this evolution, as a public demonstration in America, falls roughly in two periods. The first extends from 1890, when, aged twenty-seven, Stieglitz returned to America from Europe, where he had absorbed with passion the contemporary culture and had become famous in his use of the camera. His first international competition medal—one of 150 he won in capitals of the world from Paris to Calcutta—had been awarded to him by P. H. Emerson, author of the revolutionary *Naturalistic Photography*.

During this first period here, Stieglitz encountered the stale cultural barbarism that this country then was: business ethics, those of the criminal thinly veneered with social complacence, guiding machine industrialism; labor unions fighting a battle in which the true craftsman and workman were threatened with extinction.

In the midst of such a society Stieglitz conducted his world-wide battle to achieve the recognition of photography as an art equivalent to the other accepted arts. To this end he shaped and led a succession of groups. The Camera Club of New York, the Photo-Secession, and the international Linked Ring. The foremost art museums in America and in the capitals of the world were opened to receive photography on a parity with painting and sculpture. In America, the serious, devoted, and accomplished workers whom Stieglitz inspired and led, fought and broke the exhibition system that then prevailed, with its emphasis on medals, awards, and wire-pulling, and established standards of workmanship that were acknowledged to be without equal anywhere.

As an individual worker Stieglitz had from the outset deepened and enriched the resources of the medium. Independently, and simultaneously with Paul Martin in 1895, he was the first to introduce figures in night photography. His exposures in snowstorms and rainstorms, until then never achieved, on city streets and in railroad yards, became famous both for their pioneering and for their wistful and sensitive revelations of beauty.

As part of the organized activity, Stieglitz published a complete record of the cultural history he was making. In the six volumes of *Camera Notes* and the fifty numbers of *Camera Work*, both quarterly magazines, is contained the clear vision of an idea in evolution, an immediate projection in definite form of elements in human relations which would otherwise not have been recorded. Aside from the marvels of printing and reproductive invention and sensibility which these periodicals are, they represent the photographic method applied to historical record, even to reprints of newspaper criticisms on the exhibits and demonstrations held.

The battle to have photography officially and publicly recognized as a medium of intimate, profoundly personal and lyrical expression was decisively won. Its summation and the summation of what had been achieved in the history of the medium as art was presented, November, 1910, at the Albright Museum of Art, Buffalo, N. Y., in what was acknowledged to be an epochal demonstration, organized under the leadership of Stieglitz and contributed to by distinguished workers in all parts of the world.

The force which guided the entire development was manifest to Joseph T. Keiley, the one encyclopedic historian of the movement, and I cannot do better than quote from what he wrote of the Buffalo exhibition:

Largely to one man does the success of the Buffalo Exhibition, with all that that implies, belong. Over twenty-five years ago he recognised the possibility of photography. He realised that there were many persons who, if they came to regard photography seriously as a possible means of original pictorial expression, would give to the world individual conceptions of the beautiful that could be produced through no other method and for which the race would be richer; and that through a medium with which the general public was more intimately familiar than with any other, the public taste could through understanding be trained to a keener and truer and more catholic perception of beauty in all fields of artistic expression; and, furthermore, through such education of artistic perceptions to emphasise the principle that a large class of paintings—many of which are even housed in art galleries—will be superseded by works produced more beautifully and less mechanically through the medium of photography. This was the germination of the Secessionistic idea. Through writings and exhibitions that battle was begun and tirelessly waged with this end in view; and so it has gone on tirelessly for a quarter of a century, to be finally crowned with this splendid achievement—the Buffalo Exhibition.

Keiley gives us a picture of himself, sitting dreaming, in the museum that housed "such an exhibition as will never again be gotten together."

Visible to me were the creative forces behind all of these pictures—the lives that had gone into their making. Many of these forces were warring with themselves, warring with each other, seeking violently to rend the whole asunder. Many of them, apparently, if left to themselves, would have destroyed their own work. Clouds of jealousies from time to time obscured the whole. But all the while some central force held the mass together, drawing out and sometimes shaping the best work, helping those who stumbled and uniting all the complex, imaginative energy into one purposeful whole towards a definite end. This central observing, guiding mind appeared to see and understand the evolving minds about him, and to be endeavoring to evoke for each that which was finest and best, to be endeavoring to make each bigger and finer and immortal. And as he worked and planned a great structure seemed to be growing under his building—and all the while his eyes were fixed on a distant horizon which showed a beautiful light, which was the glow of Beauty.

Official recognition of what Stieglitz had contributed to this evolution came on January 7, 1924, when the Royal Photographic Society of Great Britain conferred on him·its highest honor, the Progress Medal, for

. . . services rendered in founding and fostering Pictorial Photography in America, and particularly for your initiation and publication of *Camera Work,* the most artistic record of Photography ever attempted.

2

A MEDIUM, PHOTOGRAPHY ITSELF, could not circumscribe what Stieglitz was creating. From the outset he had undertaken to establish photography, not exclusively, but in the comity of the arts, among other forms of utterance. Photographers could not understand the evolution of the Little Galleries of the Photo-Secession, at 291 Fifth Avenue, into "291," where new and unknown painters, sculptors, writers, were shown in exhibitions that seemed to be superseding and crowding out photographic exhibitions.

Photographer as he was and remained, Stieglitz found himself championing the living insurgent against routine, institutional deadness, political inertia, whether in the Metropolitan Museum of Art under Sir Purdon Clarke, or in the ranks of the photographers seemingly close to him. What he came to be fighting for was the spirit animating true explorers and creators in the arts, without which photography itself, however accepted in museums, could not exist. A living consciousness, expressed in relations, perceptions, not dead pictures in whatever medium recorded, was the basic issue.

It has occurred to me that, lavishly as he spent himself on people, Stieglitz's deepest friendship was reserved for a living principle that transcended any individual. At various times it was named photography, the truth, a spirit, Woman, even America. To champion that element of life he had to contend, at times, with every individual he ever knew. The choices involved in his public demonstration—and no life was ever less private than his—were dictated seemingly by chance and unconscious impulse. Yet the entire scheme fitted into what may be seen later as a conscious purpose, a definite, deepening selection.

So, when 291, as its first nonphotographic exhibition, showed the work of Pamela Colman Smith, a woman unknown, ranked by such a casual commentator as Huneker as being among "the choir of mystics" of William Blake, it was the quality of imagination in her work, of direct feeling as against the "autocracy of convention," that determined her being shown.

A succession of exhibitions followed, with Steichen, who had photographed Rodin, sending Rodin's drawings from Paris, and the paintings of Matisse, a leader of the *fauves,* the "wild animals." The sequence led quite naturally into a further series of demonstrations that included the salients of living contemporary painting and sculpture. Taken individually, the exhibitions, given the public in a setting of exquisite taste, designed to liberate the character and quality of each artist or group shown, were bright, pulsating events in the dead sea of New York commercialism. Taken together, they gave to New York, and to America—tens of thousands of people from all parts of the country attended these exhibitions—an opportunity to see the organic evolution of contemporary European expression.

The roster of artists and work first shown in America at 291, many of the one-man shows being world premières, included all those forces which were later to be emphasized as the basic impulses in the revolt from academicism: Cézanne, Matisse, both as painter and sculptor, Picasso, Braque, Toulouse-Lautrec, Henri Rousseau, Severini, Picabia. Moreover, the relationship of these workers and tendencies to other racial sources was documented in

effect of impressionism on photography

the first exhibition anywhere as art and not as anthropology, of Negro sculpture. On the other hand, the inquest into the expressiveness of the race and the effect of what is known as art education, brought about the pioneer exhibitions of the work of young, untaught children.

The world grouped the tendencies being unfolded and gave them names—"Post-Impressionism"; "Modern Art," which was later to become a commercial label. But what was being exhibited at 291 was a series of liberating and questing experiences. These included the return to freedom in the use of, and respect for, media—a freshness of gesture and intonation breaking the molds of the buckeye painting, of Meissonier, Rosa Bonheur, Greuze, then favored by the Metropolitan Museum of Art and academic circles generally. In the aggregate, too, the exhibitions served as a prophetic notation on the ferment then stirring in the souls of those most finely attuned to the psychic life of humanity. It was a ferment presaging the era of violence and insanity into which the world was to plunge.

Moreover, conducted with scrupulous exactitude and respect for the individuality of the workers and the work shown, in a truly photographic spirit, the series of exhibitions continued to explore and basically affirm the legitimate claims of Photography as a medium founded in vision, capable of exact record, responsive to any depth or subtlety of feeling and potentially a challenge to the entire assumption that human culture and concepts were primarily a verbal logic.

The attitude of the opposed and reactionary New York surrounding this oasis of vital experience and inquiry was well represented in an interview with Sir Purdon Clarke, director of the Metropolitan Museum, who had been appointed through the friendship of J. P. Morgan. This museum director, in an interview reprinted by *Camera Work,* declared:

There is a state of unrest all over the world in art as in all other things. It is the same in literature, as in music, in painting and in sculpture. And I dislike unrest.

His dislike of unrest had a wide scope and included the poet Browning, the music of Richard Wagner. As for Blake, "a Blake drawing is not worth the paper it is printed on."

It was with such forces as this, dominant in the American scene, that the vital American creative spirit had to contend. For out of the series of exhibitions at 291 came a group of young workers, some of them, like Alfred Maurer and Arthur Dove, admittedly and powerfully redirected in their painting by the influence of Matisse; others, like John Marin, emerging from the chrysalis of Whistler influence and building upon the organic experience demonstrated in the inner movement of Cézanne water colors.

291 served to give these and other Americans, Weber, Walkowitz, Marsden Hartley, Nadelman, their first comprehensive exhibitions. Here they were tested against the best and most vital that Europe had to offer. The test affirmed a basic growth from the roots, of something distinctively national, a potential flowering akin to those utterances in which nations of the past had come to their own timeless and essential character.

Insensibly, almost, Stieglitz found himself fighting for the very existence of the living spirit in America. The personalities that emerged from his tests were not lightly accepted. They had to be judged by standards derived from the most exalted expression the world knew. Their sincerity, stamina, vitality, and power to grow were tested in successive yearly exhibitions attended by hosts of the most enlightened and critical people in New York—for the 291 series of demonstrations were the very spark of life in the New York art season, a center of discussions and rages, a source of lengthy controversy in the press, of which *Camera Work* preserves a full and detailed record.

Whatever of life and vital impulse came to America, or out of America, was fatally and inevitably attracted to the small exhibition rooms and the burning spirit that centered there. So it was that drawings sent from Texas by a young woman to a friend in New York, with the injunction to show them to no one, came to Stieglitz because the friend felt he must see them. "Finally, a woman on paper," Stieglitz exclaimed, recognizing at once their profound significance. In this way, after he had examined the drawings daily for months, and shown them to many sensitive people, to make sure they really contained what he felt was there, came about the first exhibition of Georgia O'Keeffe.

And in the course of the entire demonstration, at 291, all those forces and movements emerging in Europe, futurism, dadaism, vorticism, cubism, surréalism, found their primary impulses registered. In the field of letters *Camera Work* published the earliest work of Gertrude Stein, essays interpreting in her peculiar prose the work of Picasso and Matisse.

Continuing its photographic evolution, 291 showed in its concluding years the photography of Paul Strand, to whom two numbers of *Camera Work* were given, the only young American photographer then felt to be contributing something vital in that medium, aside from Stieglitz. It is characteristic of the rigorous self-suppression of Stieglitz that his work alone, of all the many photographers whose work is preserved in the *Camera Work* reproductions, is not adequately represented, none of his later work being reproduced.

As the war of 1914 approached, and the disruptive forces of the world were expressed and reflected in the group represented by and surrounding 291, Stieglitz gathered a consensus of expression concerning the spirit animating its work and essence. He asked twenty or thirty people—and more volunteered until the total reached sixty-eight—to write what 291 meant to them, eliminating if possible reference to himself The resulting *Camera Work* 47, dated July, 1914, and published in January, 1915, entitled "What is 291?" constitutes as comprehensive and penetrating a cross-section of spiritual America as can be found. It was testimony to the free and inquiring spirit, the liberation from dominant commercialism, the reality of art, the fellowship and tolerance, the undeviating direction that people had found there in brilliant, vital, pioneering years. The individual contributors to the symposium are shown in their varying grasp of the central idea, international, multi-racial in its scope. The book, opening with Mabel Dodge, ranged from the Negro elevator boy at 291, Hodge Kirnon, whose contribution is one of the clearest and most perceptive the volume contains, to J. P. Morgan's librarian, Belle Greene; from a banker, Eugene Meyer, Jr., later a governor of the Federal Reserve system, to a man in jail on Blackwell's Island, for political "crime." Artists, writers, photographers, teachers and engineers, anarchists and journalists, merchants, lecturers, soldiers of fortune, clergymen, chess experts, radicals and conservatives, Frenchmen, Englishmen, South Americans, Germans, all testified to the reality and vitality of the living spirit of freedom, tolerance, vital experiment which had found a home at 291.

3

I MET STIEGLITZ in 1917. Paul Strand took me to 291 Fifth Avenue, where, in a long dingy room fronting on Fifth Avenue, stood rows of pictures stacked on the floor leaning against the wall. Outside and below roared the traffic of Fifth Avenue, along which massed and armed men were soon to march to and from war. Stieglitz stood in the wreckage—for the exhibition place of 291 had been dismantled—his coat collar turned up, meeting all comers.

As the disintegration of wartime progressed, there were many evenings on which Stieglitz took Strand and myself on walks, long walks in the city streets, often terminating in some small restaurant, where we sat entranced as this man unfolded by the hour stories out of his life, the substance of his experience of men, of women, of art, and of life.

Once I accompanied him to his home, a long walk at night up Fifth Avenue, to the apartment where he lived, isolated from his family, in a single room, every available inch of wall space crowded with pictures. There he drew out the drawings of Georgia O'Keeffe and with passion pointed out the new language in which the course of a woman's life was being unfolded.

Later I knew that he was living in a small studio belonging to his niece, and that O'Keeffe was with him, painting. Their life in the small rooms had the quality of the brilliant whiteness of the walls. Writers, painters, photographers, people of all sorts still sought him out. Privacy in the ordinary sense seemed hardly to exist for Stieglitz. He was on call, seemingly at any hour, any day, for anyone who chose to participate in the experience he was having.

Then, and when he and O'Keeffe had moved into rooms put at their disposal on the top floors of his brother's house in East 65th Street, Stieglitz continued his demonstration. People of all kinds came from all parts of the world to the red-carpeted room on the top floor of the East 65th Street house, people known and unknown: Sherwood Anderson, Gilbert Cannan, Carl Sandburg, John Marin, Arthur Dove, the composer Ernest Bloch, Walter Lippmann, David Liebovitz, Gaston and Madame Lachaise, the orchestral conductor Leopold Stokowski. All the activities of men were represented, and many races of men. Stieglitz was photographing; O'Keeffe was painting.

Stieglitz would talk for hours, for entire days, and his talk would be directed in various planes of exposition to two or ten or twenty people, draped on the couch, occupying what chairs there were, sitting in ranks on the floor. People came, departed, stayed till the early morning hours.

When he went to supper, as for a time he did regularly at the Chinese restaurant on Columbus Circle, there would be from two to a dozen people accompanying him. There had been ruptures of friendship, people had gone out of his life never to return. Some did turn up out of the past.

A nucleus of workers was again building. There were the photography of Stieglitz and the painting of O'Keeffe as a rallying point, and the austere simplicity of their life. For some reason those who wrote, painted, photographed, and many who did none of these things, felt impelled to bring their works, or if not their works then their human problems, to Stieglitz. Perhaps it was because they felt he was the only person in America, if not in the world, who would receive them in a disinterested—a photographic—spirit, for very nearly exactly what they actually were.

He released forces for O'Keeffe that found expression in her paintings, and in him she released the pent-up torments of years. She served as his model, and in the series of photographs that began to issue from the relationship was a minute, almost a slow-motion documentation, using all the resources of a mastery of photographic means, of the psychic states whose forms O'Keeffe was committing to canvas.

Meanwhile, the group of Americans who had emerged from the sixteen years' evolution of the Photo-Secession-291 experiments, formed a responsibility that rested on Stieglitz. Of them, John

photography seen as disinterested

Marin and Georgia O'Keeffe may be held representative. Stieglitz faced the self-imposed task of continuing his demonstration by keeping these and other free and creative artists alive in America.

Marin's work had been shown every year since his first 291 exhibition. In the absence of an exhibition place of his own, and feeling the impulsion to discover whether some dealer could not undertake the responsibility for which several professed themselves eager, of enabling Marin to live and work, Stieglitz arranged a series of Marin exhibitions at what was then one of the foremost galleries in the city, the Montross Gallery. Invariably Stieglitz and O'Keeffe and a varying group of their friends hung these exhibitions, building up the rhythmic sequence of pictures, balancing the wall spaces, the shapes and colors, scrutinizing every detail with exhaustive and exhausting acuity, adjourning to a restaurant for lunch or supper, and returning to work till late at night or through the following day, until the exhibition was as perfect and self-contained a production as the individual pictures constituting it. For those who took part in these occasions it was experience of an unique character in the interaction of various personalities and in the subtle effect upon each other of pictures and colors and forms.

The successive Marin exhibitions were one of the foremost events in the New York art season. It was recognized that in him America had produced a master of water color, one to be ranked with its supreme adepts, the Chinese. For Stieglitz, Marin, as he grew, became more and more a symbol. In himself, Marin was the true, free, joyous, and simple human being, whom it became a necessity to enable to live, as a flower is cared for, or a tree bearing fruit. He represented, too, all artists, purity of spirit and mastery itself, in America. The logic of his situation was clear. If this supreme instance of creative genius and integrity could not survive in America, freed from the degrading and destructive exactions of business, then what chance could there be for lesser strength or for any honest workman?

The successive exhibitions proved that only Stieglitz could cope with the spiritual and the material problems that must be dealt with in Marin's behalf. Just as he alone could inspire and protect O'Keeffe, who became the song of liberation for all women. Something was being kept alive by Stieglitz and around him, in the years that followed the World War, that seemingly found small support or tolerance elsewhere.

The accumulating pictures, his own, those of O'Keeffe and Marin, of Hartley, Dove, and others, formed an increasing pressure upon Stieglitz to find a new place where the public could adequately see the work being done and help the workers to live. Mitchell Kennerley, then president of the Anderson Galleries, at Park Avenue and Fifty-ninth Street, spoke the decisive word. He offered Stieglitz two large rooms on the top floor of the building for a summing up of his photographic work. Here, on February 7, 1921, was opened "An Exhibition of Photography by Alfred Stieglitz—145 prints, over 128 of which have never been publicly shown, dating from 1886–1921."

The catalogue was prefaced with a "Statement," which is so characteristic, that it follows:

This exhibition is the sharp focussing of an idea. . . .

The Exhibition is photographic throughout. My teachers have been life—work—continuous experiment. Incidentally a great deal of hard thinking. Any one can build on this experience with means available to all.

Many of my prints exist in one example only. Negatives of the early work have nearly all been lost or destroyed. There are but few of my early prints still in existence. Every print I make, even from one negative, is a new experience, a new problem. For, unless I am able to vary—add—I am not interested. There is no mechanicalisation, but always photography.

My ideal is to achieve the ability to produce numberless prints from each negative, prints all significantly alive, yet indistinguishably alike, and to be able to circulate them at a price not higher than that of a popular magazine, or even a daily paper. To gain that ability there has been no choice but to follow the road I have chosen.

I was born in Hoboken. I am an American. Photography is my passion. The search for Truth my obsession.

ALFRED STIEGLITZ

The exhibition covered the entire career of Stieglitz. Beginning with the European prints made in his student years, it included portraits of friends, family, vistas of Victorian bourgeois rooms, scenes from the windows of places in which he had lived. It documented the first photographic mastery of modern cities and industrialism. One entire section was devoted to the personalities who had been in one way or other part of 291, another to those who had been close to Stieglitz momentarily or over long periods.

Undoubtedly that part of the exhibition, comprehended under the general title, "A Demonstration of Portraiture," in which a single portrait was shown to consist of at least two and in some cases twenty-five or forty-five prints, emerged as preëminent. Hands, feet, hands and breasts, torsos, all parts and attitudes of the human body seen with a passion of revelation, produced an astonishing effect on the multitudes who wandered in and out of the rooms. A few prints were withheld from public view, because certain parts of the human body, in the strange tribal morality which still prevails, are judged unfit to be publicly represented.

What was being demonstrated here was, primarily, craftsmanship carried by rigorous will and native endowment to the point where many visitors forgot that it was pictures or photography they were looking at and felt themselves in the presence of Life itself. It was a revelation of vision in which all things could exist in their peculiar character and essential beauty. It showed that the very contour of the animate and inanimate world carried its story of essence, that the hidden was revealed, and that the tangible, real, and visible bore on its face the symbol of the invisible and inexpressible.

As for portraiture, traditional conceptions of it were shattered at one blow. The Stieglitz portraits evoked characters comparable only to the studies in the unconscious of the great psychological novelists and of the Freudian school of psychoanalysis. These portraits, and those that Stieglitz was to make in the succeeding years, further demolished the thin, conceptual, intellectual notion of human experience. Some, who were brought face to face with themselves in these notations, felt and suddenly recognized their hidden selves made visible, a perfectly clear presentation in terms no words had reached or could reach. The relativity of this work was plain to be seen. Of a series of prints constituting a portrait, no one could be said to be more final, more characteristic, than any other. Nor was the portrait confined to the face. Any part of the body was seen in its revelation of the characteristic, timeless, essential being that the individual was, and the moment chosen, the psychic state of the subject, the light of the month, the day and the hour, the very tonality and intensity of the print played their parts in this arrestation of the fluid elements of experience. Clearly here was something no other medium could even attempt and something no other photographer had ever dreamed of.

The exhibition created a sensation in New York. Kennerley had arranged an exhibition and auction of "old master" drawings in an adjoining room, and the highly selected group of visitors to this showing augmented the crowds who flocked wondering into the Stieglitz hall of miracles. Articles and interviews in the press, and eventually in books, testified to the profound effect of this demonstration.

The second Stieglitz exhibition, also held in the Anderson Galleries, contained 116 prints, of which 115 had never been publicly shown. It included an entire section, a large one, devoted to portraits (four to twenty-five prints in a portrait) of women, notably those of Georgia O'Keeffe, a section devoted to men, among them John Marin, Sherwood Anderson, Marcel Duchamp, and Charles Demuth, a miscellaneous section, one devoted to small prints and, most significant of all, "Music—A Sequence of Ten Cloud Photographs."

The significance of the title and the genesis of the cloud entities is set forth in a letter which Stieglitz wrote to R. Child Bayley,

editor of *The Amateur Photographer* (London) and published in that magazine September 19, 1923. Stieglitz stresses two motives which led to the cloud photographs: first, a written statement by one of his friends to the effect that much of the power of his photography consisted in his influence over his sitters: second, a remark by his brother-in-law, asking how one so musical as Stieglitz could do without a piano:

Thirty-five or more years ago I spent a few days in Murren [Switzerland] and I was experimenting with ortho plates. Clouds and their relationship to the rest of the world, and clouds for themselves, interested me, and clouds which were most difficult to photograph—nearly impossible. Ever since then clouds have been in my mind most powerfully at times, and I always knew I'd follow up the experiment made over 35 years ago. I always watched clouds. Studied them. Had unusual opportunities up here on this hillside. [Lake George.]

My mother was dying. Our place was going to pieces. The old horse of 37 was being kept alive by the 70-year-old coachman. I, full of the feeling of today: all about me disintegration—slow but sure: dying chestnut trees—all the chestnuts in this country have been dying for years: the pines doomed too—diseased: I, poor but at work: the world in a great mess: the human being a queer animal—not as dignified as our giant chestnut tree on the hill.

So I made up my mind I'd answer Mr. Frank and my brother-in-law. I'd finally do something I had in mind for years. I'd make a series of cloud pictures. I told Miss O'Keeffe of my ideas. I wanted to photograph clouds to find out what I had learned in 40 years about photography. Through clouds to put down my philosophy of life—to show that my photographs were not due to subject matter—not to special trees, or faces, or interiors, to special privileges, clouds were there for everyone—no tax as yet on them—free.

So I began to work with the clouds—and it was great excitement—daily for weeks. Every time I developed I was so wrought up, always believing I had nearly gotten what I was after—but had failed. A most tantalising sequence of days and weeks. I knew exactly what I was after. I had told Miss O'Keeffe I wanted a series of photographs which when seen by Ernest Bloch (the great composer) he would exclaim: Music! music! Man, why that is music! How did you ever do that? And he would point to violins, and flutes, and oboes, and brass, full of enthusiasm, and would say he'd have to write a symphony called "Clouds." Not like Debussy's but *much, much more*. And when finally I had my series of ten photographs printed, and Bloch saw them—what I said I wanted to happen happened *verbatim*.

People meanwhile were asking that the work of O'Keeffe be exhibited. Stieglitz, on January 29, 1923, in the Anderson Galleries, presented "One hundred pictures, oils, water colors, pastels and drawings," by Georgia O'Keeffe, American. There was no catalogue, the pictures had no titles, but the announcement republished

emphasis on nationality

the masterly essay on O'Keeffe from Marsden Hartley's *Adventures in the Arts,* a book published in 1921, assembled out of Hartley's published and unpublished essays at the instance of Stieglitz.

As O'Keeffe herself wrote in the announcement, she had found first that, though she was restrained from living where she wanted to, saying what she wanted to, doing what she wanted to, she could at least paint as she wanted to; and as she did so, she found she could "say things with color and shapes that I couldn't say any other way—things that I had no words for."

To Hartley the pictures were "probably as living and shameless private documents as exist, in painting certainly, and probably in any other art. By shamelessness I mean unqualified nakedness of statement." He found O'Keeffe nearer St. Theresa's version of life as experience than to that of Catherine the Great or Lucrezia Borgia, adding:

Georgia O'Keeffe wears no poisoned emeralds. She wears too much white; she is impaled with a white consciousness. . . . She has wished too large and finds the world altogether too small in comparison.

The recurrent intensities of this and the subsequent O'Keeffe exhibitions established her as the essential reality which the so-called feminist movement—now partially at least historic—was groping for and about. Woman's experience, as biologically and spiritually distinct from man's, was set down, boldly, exquisitely, clearly. Oscar Bluemner, himself a painter, wrote that she had

. . . the classical conception of Life—the Dionysian cult—beyond the confines of the human body. . . . The human form and face as motifs avoided yet presented in every flower, tree, pebble, cloud, wall, hill, wave, thing. . . . The Feminine Principle has only occasionally stepped out from its retreat behind the scenes to lighten up an age, a race. . . .

The third exhibition of photography by Stieglitz, like its predecessors held in the Anderson Galleries, beginning March 3, 1924, added a miraculous series of tiny "Songs of the Sky—Secrets of the Skies as Revealed by My Camera and Other Prints," to the Cloud Music. Included in this exhibition was a print named Spiritual America, which showed in uncanny detail the coat, the individual hairs, the traces and harness of the thirty-seven-year-old gelded horse at Lake George—a hauntingly perfect statement.

The catalogue announced an event of significance in connection with the basic advancement of photography: that one of the most conservative museums of art in the United States, the Boston Museum of Fine Arts, had acquired a comprehensive collection of 27 photographs by Stieglitz—given by Stieglitz in response to the enthusiasm of Ananda Coomaraswamy, curator of Oriental art.

4

THE NEEDS AND PRESSURES accumulating out of the successive Stieglitz and O'Keeffe and Marin exhibitions, the focus of American spiritual intensity and psychic life which they had become, led Stieglitz to present his problem to Kennerley, who offered a small corner room on the third floor of the Anderson Galleries, giving Stieglitz the privilege of terminating the occupancy at any time. The opening of this center was preceded in March, 1925, with a presentation by Stieglitz of "Seven Americans—159 Paintings, Photographs and Things, recent and never before publicly shown," the work of Arthur Dove, Marsden Hartley, John Marin, Charles Demuth, Paul Strand, Georgia O'Keeffe, and Stieglitz.

The exhibition summed up the exploration extending through the long years of the Photo-Secession and 291; it demonstrated that the creative Americans discovered and evolved during that international search conducted in a photographic spirit were alive, growing in maturity and power, and voicing on American soil something not to be found elsewhere in the world. This aspect of it was stressed by Arnold Rönnebeck, sculptor, later director of the Denver Museum of Art, who wrote of it:

These Seven Americans are explorers. . . . I believe their creative self-discovery means nothing less than the discovery of America's independent rôle in the History of Art.

The spirit in which the work was done and shown is reflected in what Arthur Dove, one of the Seven, wrote for the catalogue:

A WAY TO LOOK AT THINGS

We have not yet made shoes that fit like sand
Nor clothes that fit like water
Nor thoughts that fit like air.
There is much to be done—
Works of nature are abstract.
They do not lean on other things for meanings.
The sea-gull is not like the sea
Nor the sun like the moon.
The sun draws water from the sea.
The clouds are not like either one—
They do not keep one form forever.
That the mountainside looks like a face is accidental.

In the "Equivalents," by which name Stieglitz designated the small prints he showed in this exhibition, he extended the concept of his photography. The prints included pictures of natural objects, clouds, a poplar tree, its leaves shimmering in wind and sunlight, which were recognized as portraits. The translation of experience through photography, the storing up of energy, feeling, memory, impulse, will, which could find release through subject matter later presenting itself to the photographer, were thus made evident. This should have ended for all time the silly and unthinking talk to the effect that the photographer was limited to a literal transcript of what was before him.

Stieglitz's statement in the catalogue of the "Seven Americans" exhibition read:

These photographs continue the search for my Truth—Photography.

5

THE NEW CENTER, Room 303 in the Anderson Galleries, was opened to the public on December 7, 1925, with a John Marin exhibition, under the name, "The Intimate Gallery." The intimate, the private, the personal—as always with Stieglitz—and the public, were brought into direct juxtaposition.

The announcement stated that the gallery would be used more particularly for the study of Seven Americans: Marin, O'Keeffe, Dove, Hartley, Strand, Stieglitz, and Number Seven.

It will be in the Intimate Gallery only that the complete evolution and the more important examples of these American workers can be seen and studied.

Intimacy and Concentration, we believe, in this instance, will breed a broader appreciation. This may lead to a wider distribution of the work.

The Intimate Gallery will be a Direct Point of Contact between Public and Artist. It is the Artists' Room.

It was stressed that the Intimate Gallery was not a business nor a "social" (in the narrow sense) function, nor was it competing with anything or anyone.

The choice of Marin as the first, the typical and representative creative spirit for presentation in this new center of radiation lay in the inevitable line of the entire evolution. Marin was being more and more widely acclaimed as a water colorist. He was compared more and more frequently with the greatest known masters of wash, the Chinese; moreover, he was rehabilitating a medium which in the hands of Sargent had been impurely used as ancillary to oil painting; which in the best of the Americans, Winslow Homer, had been more largely a vehicle of illustration.

Marin, who had elected to fight out in America the life of an artist and a creator, was identifying himself forever with that rocky, sea-swept Yankee bit of American coast in Maine and with the soaring, turbulent, chaotic, steel-pinnacled New York. Utilizing the unitary emotional structure that made a Cézanne water color, Marin had infused his work with higher tensions, characteristic American shocks of shape and color, derived from speed, the

various stresses of the American psyche. By common consent and recognition, Marin had become a master, one whose complete evolution had been shown by Stieglitz in yearly exhibitions, one who by right represented the spirit Stieglitz had been fostering and championing.

The Intimate Gallery enlarged the scope, more fiercely directed the focus of the 291 experimentation and exposition. In this room, perhaps twelve feet by twenty in dimension, was being tested the possibility of the life of the spirit in America. Situated as it was, in the very heart of New York, in a building devoted to auctions of pictures, furniture, jewelry, and other articles of luxury, it had a quality of the surgical operating room and of a sanctuary. Clusters of electric lights glittered overhead throughout the day. The windows looked out on Park Avenue, whose traffic roar could be heard, even as buildings were torn down and skyscrapers erected in plain view. And at intervals the room could be entirely silent with a silvery magic in which the pictures or sculpture being shown lived the life of reality and imagination.

It was part of the spirit of photography, animating and guiding this place, that it became a confessional, a resort of many who came, they knew not why, and, suddenly, without reserve, would find themselves unfolding such a story of themselves, of their intimate struggles, despairs, loves, frustrations, of the sum and substance of their persons, as people rarely confess to themselves, never to another. On one occasion, the Rumanian sculptor, Brancusi, his head like that of a peasant Christ, talking with Stieglitz, said quietly: *"Avec vous, je suis libre."*

Even as the Intimate Gallery was fighting for the very lives of the artists, and for a value in the lives of multitudes who depended on these artists whether they knew it or not, there was time always for the moment, the crystallization and revelation of life. The problem might become acute, whether America, richest nation of the world, whether New York, most lavish and luxurious city flaunting its wealth in the very building in which the Intimate Gallery was situated, would give the creative spirit bread. However the pressures accumulated, and they became intense sometimes beyond the breaking point, this living focus was maintained.

For it was not mere economic sustenance that the Intimate Gallery was standing for, it was the relationship of the divinity in men and women as represented by the creative artist, with the entire nation and the life of the world. In this room the painters, sculptors, and others of all arts and professions who gathered about it, were submitting themselves and their productions to the test of truth. Stieglitz alone was there to receive and to preserve. It was his spirit—photographic—that enabled the picture to live its own life in relation to other works, that evoked from those with whom he came in contact aspects of themselves of which they had never become aware. In the succession of exhibitions held during the six years of the Intimate Gallery, in which others besides the primary six were shown—Lachaise, Peggy Bacon, Oscar Bluemner, Francis Picabia, a European link with 291—the primary idea manifest in all its variants took on a stern note of warning.

The civilization that could neglect or refuse its best, yield its choicest spirits to ostracism, exclusion, starvation, and extinction, was in that degree signing its own doom, its own death warrant.

In Stieglitz and the work he was doing centered the hope of youth. And youth has rallied to him, as it did always. Now that the Intimate Gallery has passed into the sequence of forms that have constituted the published private life of Stieglitz, it is succeeded by another, appropriately known by the simple name, An American Place. There, in a setting austere as a cell, overlooking the serried architectural anarchy of midtown New York from the seventeenth floor of an office building at 509 Madison Avenue, the theme is sustained. The exhibitions go on, exhibitions not alone of pictures but of human beings, essential relations, of publications, such as the "Letters of John Marin," the "Dualities" of Dorothy Norman. And by its very serene contrast with the surrounding chaos, this place affirms the polarity, the fiery stillness of its Americanness.

On the stage known as the world of nations, its peoples racked and torn by mass movements of hope and terror, of strife and impending collapse, it was becoming more and more clear that material progress alone could not supplant or replace that sustenance fed into the life of a people by the spirit of selfless inquiry, of resolute giving, of the essential humanity by which alone nations and peoples and races have come to life. Gathered and conserved in and about Stieglitz were and are those ancient elements of the spirit that cannot with impunity be denied; that make history and that press forward into the future.

Stieglitz / O'Keefe as androgynous

Dorothy Norman

An American Place

WHEN YOU ENTER An American Place the first thing you feel is the quality of light. It cannot be because it is high up in an office building, for you have been elsewhere high up in office buildings, and there was not that particular kind of light you find when you enter An American Place.

You notice that the bare undecorated structure of the building is the bare structure of the Place. The space itself is divided into well-proportioned rooms of varying sizes, each almost square in shape. There are thresholds without doors, the rooms leading one into the other without barrier. The walls in the different rooms are painted from varying pale luminous grays to white, which reflect the light coming in through large windows, so that with the white ceilings and bare, uncovered light gray painted stone floors, there pervades the space a clear and subtly fluid ever varying glow of light. Light and room are as one.

A single threshold with door leads out of the larger rooms, separating them from a smaller section. In this section there is space, small, enclosed, windowless, painted black, with two openings: a small aperture in the wall and a double threshold also without doors, both equipped to be tightly sealed so that no light may enter, none may be reflected. Here, darkness and room are one.

At times there are pictures on the walls of the larger rooms, and on shelves in some of the smaller rooms there are books and more pictures, sometimes covered, sometimes visible. The door leading into this specific enclosed space—in simplest terms, space in America, "An American Place"—is open to all. It might be a commercial art gallery, but one overhears this: One day when there are pictures on the walls, a woman who has been walking about looking at them suddenly addresses Stieglitz, who stands there as usual, seemingly as integral a part of the Place as the walls themselves: "This is a very exciting show. What else ought I to see in New York?" Stieglitz replies: "I have no idea what else you ought to see in New York." Woman: "Could you tell me, by any chance, where Mr. Stieglitz's gallery is? I hear that he has the finest things in New York, but I cannot find his gallery listed anywhere." "Mr. Stieglitz has no gallery." "You are mistaken. I was distinctly told

that he has, and that I must surely go there when I came to New York." Stieglitz finally raises his voice: "Well, I ought to know. I am Mr. Stieglitz, and I tell you he has no gallery." Mystified, the woman departs, no further information forthcoming from Mr. Stieglitz. Someone standing there, amid the laughter after she has gone, asks why he has allowed her to walk out without explaining what he meant; that she looked well-dressed besides and might have bought something. To which Stieglitz replies: "Something more was at stake than her knowing where she was for the moment. And I am not in business. I am not interested in exhibitions and pictures. I am not a salesman, nor are the pictures here for sale, although under certain circumstances certain pictures may be acquired. But if people really seek something, really need a thing, and there is something here that they actually seek and need, then they will find it in time. The rest does not interest me." An American Place is not listed in the telephone directory, one learns, for the identical reason: only if it is really needed, deeply needed, will it be found . . . there is no attempt made to advertise, to publicize.

Standing before one of the large windows one day, looking out upon the world stretched forth before him, Stieglitz remarked: "If what is in here cannot stand up against what is out there, then what is in here has no right to exist. But if what is out there can stand up against what is in here, then what is in here does not need to exist."

You begin to wonder what the out there, the in here, signify; what is the test of what is within, functioning as a force in relationship to what is without. You begin to wonder what this space actually is, so apportioned and so spoken of by a man: Stieglitz. What brings people here besides the pictures, and what was at stake? Why does the quality of the light seem significant, as if it had some special meaning, the way light in a cathedral with its unearthly, strange, concentrated quality seems to have a special meaning? The dark room with its aperture and mystery might be a confessional, and you hear people as they come in talking to Stieglitz as if he were a father confessor. The bare clean walls might be, save for the pictures, laboratory, hospital, model workshop walls. Or again, the light rooms might be a photographic studio, for there are cameras standing in a kind of vault, and the dark room might be a photographic workroom. True, there are some photographs standing about and hanging on the walls at times, and there are on the shelves some volumes called *Camera Work*. Or is it possible that the books and the workshop atmosphere signify that Stieglitz is a teacher and An American Place an educational institution? In some of the books on the shelves there is mention of Stieglitz as a great teacher, a great educator. Or, with the emphasis not put upon selling pictures, perhaps this is a museum and Stieglitz the curator. If the Place is not *his,* surely, then, it must be *he* who guards and directs it.

But strangely enough, even when there are no books, no pictures, no cameras, no people; when, in short, nothing whatsoever seems to be happening, somehow the character of the Place does not seem to be in any way limited or changed by that fact.

One has but to ask Stieglitz what An American Place is, to be told, "What is life itself? What does life mean?"

And so in the heart of every man who enters An American Place there remains the question: What is it? And each will give his own answer as before a work of art, or before life itself—uncategorizable in so far as they are art and life.

Founded in 1929, when Stieglitz himself was nearly seventy, An American Place must, however, surely bear close relationship to the foregoing activity of his life; must represent a most mature, most significant expression of that life. And An American Place can be but precisely that: the most complete embodiment of the manifold aspects of a tradition, created by and identical with the work and the dream that have been Stieglitz's; that have been Stieglitz. . . . In this tradition, laboratory, cathedral, museum, workshop, and all of the countless other meanings as well, must play their rôle—each as an integral part of the whole.

But let us first, for a moment, examine the forces behind An American Place: what is the essential meaning of what lives within for that which lies outside the large windows; for America itself? How is it identical with Stieglitz, and he with its essential meaning?

2

"WHAT DOES LIFE MEAN? What does life itself mean?" Stieglitz replies.

And then suddenly you stop asking. You begin to listen to Stieglitz ever more intently and not to waste time asking any more questions. You begin quietly to look at the things at the Place and at the Place itself and to absorb them without asking anything about them. You begin to realize that it will take time. You begin

to realize that this is exactly what Stieglitz is telling the people to do when they come to the Place and begin to ask him their questions. He tells them how you cannot ask what life is, but you must taste it, feel it, live it. You realize that he never answers the questions but is always telling instead some story out of his life: that is, out of his own experience, to illustrate what he cannot otherwise tell them in answer to their questions, to which in turn they will have to find their own answers, out of their own lives.

Someone will ask what a picture means, as one has oneself asked what the Place means. "You will find as you go through life that if you ask what a thing means, a picture, or music, or whatever, you may learn something about the people you ask, but as for learning *about* the thing you seek to *know,* you will have to sense it in the end through your own experience, so that you had better save your energy and not go through the world asking what cannot be communicated in words. If the artist could describe in words what he does, then he would never have created it."

You begin to identify what Stieglitz is saying with what you yourself are feeling through the Place and about the Place. You begin to realize that if you will only listen hard enough, look hard enough, you will begin to know something that you cannot know *about* through asking. You begin to sense that knowing the Place is in itself a living experience and not a knowing about something. It is like probing life itself. You begin to see how, unless the Place is part of your life, you cannot know anything about it, and that to make it part of your life is not to talk about what it is but to give yourself to it, even as you absorb it. You begin to realize that as Stieglitz tells stories or parables or discoveries out of his own life to illustrate what he cannot generalize about, since the abstract is dead, like telling something that does not come out of your own body, he is creating life itself or art or whatever it is one wishes to call it, which in turn must be understood and felt and experienced as deeply as the thing he nevertheless illuminates indirectly through his challenge to one to see for oneself, experience for oneself.

You cannot, for example, be told about such phenomena as sunsets or love. You have to experience them with your own being. And while you watch and feel, it is not the words and their meaning which are the abc that you are preoccupied with, but with the xyz which is their essence, and about which one cannot learn save through oneself. Even the experiences of others, communicated through their creating an equivalent of what they have felt, which we call art, or the art of living, we cannot absorb until we have ourselves experienced the spirit of what they have recreated. "It takes two to make a truth," we hear Stieglitz say. "A Yes to one's Yes, a No to one's No, that is one's truth. But one cannot find corroboration for one's Yes, for one's No, until one is clear within oneself as to what one's own feeling is."

You begin to feel Stieglitz's words become living experiences. They preoccupy you. They beat within you. They are added to you, the way a sunset is added to you, or the way something that moves you in people is added to you. It becomes part of you so that if you are cut off from it you are hurt, the way you are hurt if part of your body is cut off, and so you know definitely it is part of your body, the way it is added to you when you are with it and you feel cut off from it when it is not there. You know that the world would not be the same without it, for you are not the same as you were before you found it and you find others corroborating your feeling and so you know that it is not just a personal feeling, but a true feeling. You find yourself using the word "true" now in Stieglitz's sense, and understanding what he means by saying it takes two to make a truth and "For me, all true things are equal to one another," because you understand about the corroboration making a thing stand on its own feet outside your personal feeling like a third thing, and you understand the predictableness of the effect this third thing will have upon others, so that your truth will be equal to their truth, in the sense that it will be the same truth, as the sunset you see is incontrovertibly there for all and not merely in you. You begin to feel that this thing that has been added to you is like all created work, an addition to the world as something that did not exist before; and you know that the world will be both greater for its presence and less if it is allowed to disappear. And you want to make certain it will remain in the world. You begin to feel new life beating within you through this thing you feel. You sense that the new life must be born. All criticism, all that we call art, is like that—is born of a desire to recreate what you have been given—and it is this, too, that the Place is saying and doing and making you feel you must do.

It is as if An American Place were fertilizing people to say the thing that it is saying, but each must say it anew—each in his own way. It is like a church where you give yourself to the thing that frees you—and you can give forth its spirit again only by continuing to build it in whatever form is your form. It is the spirit and not the letter that is the church and its name is of no consequence. For what else is a church if it is not this?

You cannot keep that surge of new added life inside you, without giving it to the world anew. It is like a law of life at work in you. It is the counterpart of what people feel when they come in and feel that they can tell all to Stieglitz, which is what makes him a father confessor without ever seeking to be it. You can tell all to him because he gives all of himself to each. "You do to another as another does to you" is one of Stieglitz's laws. The telling will be

the bearing of it. But you find telling *about* it abortive. It leaves you unsatisfied and sterile to tell *about* it. You have to *tell it,* and the telling has to be part of your own life, the form your own life.

It is all very well to try to tell what the Place is like, but what it is like is as solid, as concrete as the walls before you or the man before you or the things on the walls. You realize you have to prepare yourself. You have to be able to recreate the original touch of the object itself that you wish to reproduce. You have to train yourself as for any other work. You have to give the magic that you have felt. To reproduce is one step removed from creating the original. There must be a sense of responsibility towards the creator, towards the original. You begin to understand that Stieglitz must mean this when he says that exhibitions and pictures do not interest him. Graven images are graven images when they are pictures that make you remember that they are pictures and do not carry you beyond to that throbbing essence which is the original—which is God. The medium must disappear, you yourself must disappear. And you will have to prepare yourself. The Place itself teaches how the true artist in reality always has a sense of responsibility towards his materials and towards what he communicates the spirit of. You will hear Stieglitz tell about how they cannot reproduce his photographs in America because they have no feeling about the actual touch of things. It isn't part of life the way it is lived today in America. You begin to realize that Stieglitz tells about his photographs not because he is thinking about himself, but because his own experience is all he knows at first hand, and his own experience is but a corroboration of what he senses going on everywhere. These stories he tells about his own experiences and about America, for that is where he lives and what he knows, you begin to feel as concrete expressions of the man and you want to get these stories down, for you feel that through them you are seeing not a man and not a country but some universal eternal thing. He has said, "Beauty is the universal seen."

Yet all the while you feel the urge to get things down, you feel that short of being thoroughly prepared, you will, with your own lack of preparation, but increase the mess of dilettantism to which the Place is a challenge. But as there is a challenge against dilettantism and picture-making and against not being prepared, so there is a counter challenge: "If you really care about a thing, you *do* something about it. You don't sit around talking about it, you act. The act came first and then the word." "All of my life I have been trying to find out what people mean when they speak, what they feel when they say a thing and then do not act in accordance with the feeling they claim they have."

And although you know that you can do nothing until you are ready, still you feel sick at heart that, paradoxically, the while you sit spellbound by what Stieglitz is saying and by what is happening at the Place, you should actually be communicating the man and the Place to the world at large. It is a strange feeling to feel guilty about absorbing the very center of the thing you want to communicate. But that is what happens. You love the inevitability of Stieglitz's replies to people who, when he challenges their avowals of caring about something, by pointing out to them that they do not care in reality, or they would do something about the thing they claim to care about, ask, "But our lives are complicated. What are we to do?" He will say, "You must do exactly as you are doing. There is nothing else to do save what you are doing." He never has a feeling that a person is good or evil because he has or has not done a thing, but what he always challenges is the self-deception involved in people's saying one thing and doing another and not realizing that what they say about what they want to do is not doing it.

You love the inevitability until you find the knowledge that you are not deceiving yourself and that you really know that you want to do what you say you want to do is small recompense for not doing what surges within you to be done. You wonder, "Have I it straight within me, the subtlety of the line of what Stieglitz is saying? Can I remember it clearly? Can I recommunicate the spirit—the communication of the spirit of a thing being the very essence of the spirit of the Place?" The challenge comes back: "If you are clear within yourself, you can communicate clearly what you have to say. If you are not clear within yourself you can communicate nothing with clarity."

While Stieglitz is challenging he is not thinking of you but of a point where all people meet—and then of the point even beyond that. It is this point beyond that you yourself wish to communicate . . . He never means a challenge personally, but when you are with him the meaningfulness of his challenge strikes home, for in being universal in implication it must touch all men, even himself, through whom alone he must know the essence of what he says or it will automatically be a baseless formulation, and short of being as relentless as it is inspiring, the challenge will scarcely reveal the core of life, will scarcely be that solid concrete reality: beauty.

There is something in a challenge impersonally given that will liberate where a sweeter personal promise of salvation would paralyze. "To show the moment to itself is to liberate the moment."

You listen and listen while you are at the Place. People come. You hear the people as they talk in front of the pictures and when they are not in front of the pictures. You listen to Stieglitz. You hear what is said, but when you try to retell it later, something is missing. Perhaps you do not quite know enough yet to include that point beyond. You will have to wait until you have seen it under all conditions and know the entire history of the Place. You begin

to read the history of the Place in its various previous forms, and to hear Stieglitz tell stories out of his life about the past. Every time you think, "Now I have the essence," and then you come back, and the sunset varies. You begin to feel hopeless about ever communicating any of it, because every time that you see something, hear something, it is something basic that you did not hear or see before.

The patch of sky is the same. The sun is the same. The landscape is the same. But the atmosphere changes constantly. According to the ability of those present to absorb, Stieglitz tells less or more of what is the whole of a feeling, of a story. He never tells a story save to illustrate some concrete point, and the points which any one story can illuminate themselves vary. Stieglitz is constantly growing, constantly seeing more deeply. You have grown, yourself.

Again the challenge: "There is no such thing as the impossible if you really want to do a thing badly enough. If you have to do a thing with all of your being, then you find a way, even if you have to die for it. Having to: that is the only wanting I recognize." Or, he will say, "If you have ten miles to walk, you must walk the first mile first. If you don't want to walk the first mile first, but the ten miles all at once, you will never even get started."

You are puzzled, because you are told how one must force nothing; how one must know in oneself what one must do. One must not do anything that does not satisfy oneself. "What takes form within oneself will be felt outside oneself. But, if one begins with the idea of satisfying someone else, one will satisfy neither that person nor oneself. That is the difference between esthetics and ethical formulæ; the creative and the being in bondage to the attempt to do good deeds. The subconscious pushing through the conscious, driven by an urge coming from beyond its own knowing, its own control; trying to live in the light, like the seed pushing up through the earth—will alone have roots, can alone be fertile. . . . All 'idealism' that does not have such roots must be sterile; must defeat itself. . . ."

Someone after a conversation with Stieglitz asks him in wonder who he is. Stieglitz replies, "I am the moment. I am the moment with all of me and anyone is free to be the moment with me. I want nothing from anyone. I have no theory about what the moment should bring. I am not attempting to be in more than one place at a time. I am merely the moment with all of me." And again: "When I am no longer thinking but merely am, then I may be said to be truly living; to be truly affirming life. Not to know, but to let exist what is, that alone, perhaps, is truly to know." How can this be reconciled with the challenges to do? He has challenged one to be true to the moment, but always with a sense of direction. "I am a Fatalist, but with one eye on Fate."

You begin to wonder why Stieglitz himself does not write his own biography; then there would not be this inadequacy of others doing something that they can never know the whole of. But Stieglitz has various things to say about that. He says he is too busy living his life to write it. He says that he does not want to write his autobiography until he can sum up the whole of his life in one page. He tells how if he could really put down the line of the mountain and sky as they touch, as he has seen it across Lake George from his house on the Hill, it would include all of life. He tells how he cannot write his autobiography because so much of the actual evidence of events has been destroyed, and he does not see how one can trust one's memory about things in the past and tell exactly what has happened. His diaries and so many of his letters have been destroyed that he feels it would be futile to attempt to reconstruct from memory, and, short of telling and showing everything, there would be bound to be or appear to be a falsification. He has this too to say about autobiography: "Everyone has his blind spot and until one knows what one's blind spot is, anything that one has to say about oneself must be meaningless." Then slowly you begin to realize that the Place and Stieglitz are so much one thing all the way through, that every story he tells, every photograph he takes, every incident at the Place, actually communicates the essence of the whole meaning of all of them, as well as that insight into that which we call the universal, without which added illumination nothing whatever would have been communicated to begin with. You realize that if you could tell but one incident, repeat one story or discovery, communicate the meaning of but one photograph, by interpreting its meaning in full, with all of the implications clearly included, you would communicate the essence of the whole thing.

And then the time arrives when, like the child that comes forth from the womb without one's having anything to say about it, the life beating within one must be born or wither for all time. One must face the consequences. One must accept the child for what it is, even if it is not precisely the child one might have wished to bear; even if it is not perfect as it rears its unpredicted head; even if it will be difficult to say that it is this or it is that, if it is indeed alive and has any living qualities whatsoever of its own. . . .

What else is Stieglitz saying about work that one does? You hear him tell about the man who complained because a certain picture was perfect except for one line, and how the painter replied that he knew that the line was imperfect but if he could make a perfect picture which also included that line painted perfectly, he would not have had to paint the picture. "There are two ways of looking at a thing. Either you feel that a thing must be perfect before you present it to the public, or you are willing to let it go out even knowing that it is not perfect, because you are striving for something even beyond what you have achieved, but in struggling too hard for perfection you know that you may lose the very glimmer of life, the very spirit of the thing that you also know exists at a

particular point in what you have done; and that to interfere with it would be to destroy that very living quality. I am myself always in favor of practising in public. There are, of course, those people who say, 'But the public is not interested in watching people practice. It wants the finished thing or nothing.' My answer is that if one does not practise in public in reality, then in nine cases out of ten the world will never see the finished product of one's work. Some people go on the assumption that if a thing is not a hundred per cent perfect it should not be given to the world, but I have seen too many things that were a hundred per cent perfect that were spiritually dead, and then things that have been seemingly incomplete that have life and vitality, which I prefer by far to the other so-called perfect thing. It is one thing to think about a piece of work as a scientific or objective entity that will stand up a hundred years hence, and another to think of the living quality of the person doing the thing and of his development. Is the thing felt—does it come out of an inner need—an inner must? Is one ready to die for it? . . . That is the only test. . . ."

Again, there is a sad chuckle: "Everywhere I find myself surrounded by perfect people. Question a single action, and you are told that you are utterly mistaken to question. I suppose I am the *Isle of Imperfection* in a *Sea of Perfection*." "It seems never to occur to anyone to go into himself; to question himself. Automatically the other person is wrong. To grow more tolerant towards others, stricter with oneself, seems unheard of. Freedom for all—tolerance towards none, seems to be the slogan."

Again. A man stands before some paintings at the Place. He points to one picture that has been recently painted and remarks that he likes it better than the others, painted at an earlier stage of the artist's development. Stieglitz turns to him: "I suppose you like the full-blown flower better than the bud? I suppose you like the Beethoven Ninth Symphony better than the Beethoven First Symphony? Such distinctions do not interest me. All of my life I have been told such things: that sculpture is greater than painting, because sculpture has a third dimension; that painting is greater than photography, because painting has color and photography is 'mechanical.' It is as if there were a great Noah's ark in which every species must be separated from every other species, so that finally, as they are all placed in their separate cells, they grow so self-conscious that finally, if one were to take them out and put them together they would all fall upon one another and kill each other."

While it eases a little the pain of one's imperfections to hear these words about concentrating upon the white light illuminating the darkness, rather than engulfing in darkness what light one finds, still there remains a stern discipline to be adhered to, wherein the spirit is as rigorous as the letter, save only with the difference that the spirit builds while the letter destroys. Instead of reaching out for something that you do not feel within yourself, something that is not born out of your own body, there is the necessity to know when to let your very child pursue its own inevitable course and to stop trying to mould it into something that will kill the very spirit you wish to let live. Just as knowing *about* a thing is not the thing to center upon, but rather the absorbing of its spirit, and the transforming one's knowledge into action, so imperfection and perfection, agreeing or disagreeing, right or wrong are not the things to center upon, but the spark of life wherever one finds it, and the letting live that spark of life in the creation of a man which it is as essential to protect from death as the life of him who has created it.

And as any single story must give the essence of the whole, so, unless what holds true of what you have derived from the message of the Place holds true of everything that you feel about life, and its spirit is communicated to everything you do in your own life, then what you say about anything else will be untrue to the spirit of the Place, and what you say about the Place will itself be untrue of the Place.

3

You FEEL YOU HAVE the essence of what you want to say clear within you and that you are writing down the man and the Place, and then you feel it is that elusive quality just beyond, that you haven't quite captured, that is the core of it all. . . .

It would not be difficult to reconstruct any number of convincing portraits of Stieglitz and the Place, but the moment you try to pin it all down and fit it into a theory or derive a theory from it, you betray it. You can take up the varying aspects of what Stieglitz says and of what the Place is, and you can be quite convincing, but it will all be but a starting point for something beyond that you want to say.

There is the title "An American Place." What does it mean, and how does it relate to the meaning of Stieglitz? You hear Stieglitz tell about his feeling for America, and while he speaks you begin to see what he has done in the light of what he tells.

He tells how when he was a child he could not listen to fairy tales but preferred instead to read over and over again of the American Revolution. Nathanael Greene was his favorite hero. It was the strategic retreats he made that fascinated Stieglitz, because, without ever winning what is called a victory, Greene always defeated the enemy. One quickly sees the significance of this early reaction and how later he himself was to do likewise. Greene was a corroboration, not an ideal. There have been Stieglitz's own retreats to victory. There was his necessity in photography at once

to withdraw from the orthodox methods in use at the time, and in doing what had not been done before to create what those who had no such inner need, no such vision guiding them, and who kept to the worn-out paths, did not create. He withdrew from business because he would not be forced into doing imperfect work in order to conform to the prevailing methods of business, for he could not see how in turning out great quantities of a thing at maximum speed, without any respect for quality, one could do a job that was "just as good as" the best one was capable of doing, which latter alone could have any significance in a living way for any workman. This feeling was no theory either, but was rather something he felt within himself and that he heard corroborated by others who had respect for their work and were not allowed to do the best work of which they were capable under the prevailing spirit that dominated business methods.

You will hear him tell how, if people would only stop talking about the brotherhood of man and talk more about the brotherhood of man and the machine, it would be a great deal better. He will say too how it is the workman and not the "worker" he cares about, and how if people would think more about their work and less about their "ideas" and themselves, it would all be better too. For at the same time that he began suffering himself from the tyranny of the shoddy and heard others suffering too about not being allowed to do their best work, he also began to hear employers complain because they could not find workmen who were properly trained or cared about their work. It was a vicious circle, which he did not allow to imprison him. He withdrew, his withdrawal a protest, but in reality an affirmation of something positive.

Next he led what was called the Photo-Secession, its very name a sign of retreat. Again a retreat into victory in a greater sphere from a lesser one. And then he withdrew from becoming part of an art game, when with all of modern art available to him for little money he could have turned the whole of his work into a material success rather than into a creative source. It is a retreat all along the way from the personal and the sterile, to make room for the larger than the personal and for the creative in the true sense. In his own qualified use of the term true he has said how all true things being equal to one another is the only democracy he recognizes, and it was a democracy he was fighting for even as had Nathanael Greene—but necessarily on his own terms.

And then there is a story you will hear him tell about how when he went to Europe to study when he was young, he had his glorious vision of America, inspired by his history books, and one imagines by the natural patriotism of the young, as well, which with him was a passion. He defended everything American against the skepticism of the Europeans to whom, on the whole, America was not to be taken too seriously. A professor who claimed to have studied very carefully the principles upon which the Brooklyn Bridge had been built, maintained that they were faulty, predicting the collapse of the bridge within five years. Stieglitz, who had never seen the bridge, completed while he was abroad, who knew nothing of the technical problems involved, who had never even given the subject a moment's thought before, defended the bridge because he felt intuitively that the professor must be wrong. It was his America he was defending, like a lover defending his beloved, and the America he envisioned was his own spirit at work in life, even though probably he could not have told you what that spirit was. When he returned to America some years later he found the Brooklyn Bridge standing, but the America of his dreams was nowhere to be found. He asked himself whether his, perhaps, had not been the greatest fairy tale of them all.

And then we hear a great deal about the America he did find, where a great deal of individualism and anarchy and exploitation and a great deal of idealistic talk about "everyman" created the same discrepancy between word and act that had always troubled him even as a child, and was to trouble him always. . . .

Here in the land of promise he found it impossible to participate in life on the terms offered, and still it was this first love that he has never lost. It is at the root of his challenge to America, like a parent filled with love for his child, relentlessly criticizing. It is his child not only because he has taken it to his heart, but too, because it has sought him as parent. He has said, "They had promised me something that I did not find, and all of my life has been spent in search of that thing, even to the point where I have had to create a world of my own, wherein the principles they preached to me, can actually be practised."

It was not mechanization or business as such that he protested against. It was the sacrificing of the living spark, of the element of deep caring, of love—for the dead and the non-caring, which robbed all living beings of the throbbing contact of the alive with the alive, on whatever terms—and upon which contact the human being depended for survival—that was a torture to him. One might say that Stieglitz fell in love with that which represented caring or love in their simplest terms, for whatever man found himself in contact with—to the existence of which love Stieglitz was innately sensitive. It was this love that moved him, and what moved him he must photograph, must liberate. This is a center, a secret core of his photography, of his life.

There is a portrait of a lone street sweeper on a rainy spring day, conscientiously plying his trade with all dignity and tenderness of movement, as tender as the young budding tree next to which he stands, encased though it is in what seems like a prison of wire fencing. Behind him rise the buildings of a new world. There is a constant song in his photographs of the ever present vestiges which

man somehow manages to preserve for himself, of the individual in contact with and caressing the simple, the breathing, and the enduring in life, in terms of its most fundamental being—in the very face of a new and brittle world encroaching upon it and to which it cannot bend. There is the challenge to persist, to touch, to transform the ever changing, ever new world with the light of love, of caring, of responsibility towards it—of man-ness in harmony with it, harmonizing it wherever possible to man himself at his best, through man's own loving touch upon it. And there is not only the championing of the old integrity, fighting for its life in the new world, but there is the recognition of, and faith in the flame persisting in that new world itself. There are the photographs of the frameworks of new steely skyscrapers, illumined as with a holy light, touched by the sky—rearing their heads over the world below, helpless and passing in darkness, unless illuminated in turn by these symbols of fresh incarnations of light, which must themselves be concrete manifestations of the very emerging power and integrity they symbolize. The qualitative values of the subject matter Stieglitz photographs are communicated without any comment other than the sensitive registering or recreation of the very values symbolized, in the prints themselves.

There was persistent a dream, too, that there could be a coming together of those individuals who in their hearts must be seeking, even if unconsciously, such a coming together, whereby their ability to function as integrated human beings rather than as maimed ones could be maintained. He felt that the same drive which had led men to unite once must lead them so to unite again—a true *e pluribus unum*. . . .

He had the intuition, and he found response to it in those who had aroused and so had corroborated the intuition, that despite the fundamental aloneness of spirits sensitive to the underlying core of living, denied in a growing sense by the very way of life of a country actually founded on a principle of democratic caring about "everyman," there was still militant in each individual deep down in his very being as man, a yearning for that same and only freedom, that only order, that he himself yearned for: the right to function as a creative, throbbing being, true to one's sense of responsibility towards whatever one undertakes. And as Stieglitz's photographs are a perfect recording, so his acts have been likewise indicative of his faith in and love for the emergence of that tenderest, most dependable, most lonely individuality that is the core of everyman, forging through the chaos and purgatory that is life, wherever—into light—the light of fulfillment through touching with his own center that point beyond self; that point which in bringing one into contact with all living; in revealing the universe, includes the center of all men. Through the touching of this point beyond self only, can one finally complete self and so free oneself to *be,* in the creative sense of the word, and thus only to be at one with all men; with all living.

There was a growing conviction, never rigidly formulated but ever more surely functioning, that was like a rekindling of that same fire that had led his heroes of the American Revolution, ill-equipped, outnumbered, poor as they were, to attempt to create a world wherein men might again function free of tyrannies, which, for no qualitative reason, would but once again sacrifice the many for the few. But the battle must necessarily be waged on new terms—the end must be even more clearly seen. . . .

To the ever recurring question, "Do you believe in Communism for America?" Stieglitz's invariable reply is, "It isn't Communism or any other 'ism' I'm thinking of. Show me a Communist or any other 'ist' who lives the spirit of what he believes he is preaching; who is prepared to bring to what he preaches the spirit of what he believes himself to be saying; who is ready to die for the thing he preaches and pledges his allegiance to, and I will follow him to the ends of the earth. Short of creating one's own world about one, wherever one is, in the spirit of what one preaches, one cannot protest against the world as it exists. Unless one creates in embryo what one wishes to see flower in full; unless whatever a man does is a symbol of the thing he claims to be fighting for— then what he says and what he is fighting for in the end can have no significance." To wish for something without being that thing; to want something for nothing; not to be ready to die for whatever one puts one's signature to; not to wish to be one's best self and to free others to be their best selves, to do their best work; not to earn the right to live; to wish to overthrow without having recreated in the image of what one wills to be; to predict without already having experienced—such allegiances are not for Stieglitz. Protest must be affirmation first. The ism is of secondary importance.

There is the desperate love of a parent now for those who in their corroboration of one's own touch upon life are one's especial children; of one's own blood. Every attack from without upon one's beloved who are life to one is like the potential death of a child. "It isn't starving I'm thinking of, but of seeing one's loved ones starving and being unable to feed them." One thinks of Chekhov's portrait of Posetski in *The Black Monk.* A horse tethered to one of Posetski's prize apple trees, "surely," as he remarks, "by some villain," rubs the bark of the tree in three places. Posetski cries in despair that "they have dirtied, spoiled, damaged, ruined my orchard. . . . It is lost, destroyed."

"What," he asks, "will become of the garden when I die? . . . In the condition you see it now, it will not exist for a single month without me. The whole secret of its success is not because the garden is large and there are many labourers, but because I love the work—you under-

stand? I love it, perhaps more than my own self. Look at me. I do everything myself. I work from morning to night. I do all the grafting myself. I do all the pruning myself—all the planting—everything. When I am assisted I am jealous and irritable to rudeness. The whole secret lies in love, that is, in the vigilant master's eye, in the master's hand too, in the feeling that when you go anywhere, to pay a visit of an hour, you sit there and your heart is not easy; you are not quite yourself, you are afraid something may happen in the garden. When I die, who will look after it all? Who will work? A gardener? Workmen? Yes? I tell you my friend, the chief enemy in our business is not the hare, not the cock-chafer, not the frost, but the stranger."

It is a perfect picture of Stieglitz. And what else is an American Place than an expression of a poet, who like a Chekhov or an Isaiah stands in his own land among his own people, seeing before other men a *fin de siècle,* sensing its meaning clearly, yet carrying within himself more than any other the seed of a rebirth? There is the cry, "They have ruined my orchard," and there is, too, that incommunicable point beyond and within: Better let the orchard be destroyed, if they have not the proper spirit with which to carry it on. The seed is sturdy. It will arise again.

4

But, LIKE A SCIENTIST TOO, who has at last perfected a technique, on which he has spent a lifetime of experiment, Stieglitz, with his faith, isolates a single living cell on which to continue to concentrate his research on the human body of America; isolates a small space, simply a place in America: An American Place, not only as a living cell out of the body entire, but as a laboratory in which to study the cell itself and by means of which to create the body entire anew. But just as for such study the cell must be a healthy, a representative, a fertile cell, with all of the potentialities within it of the body entire, so An American Place must be a healthy specimen of America; must also be as a laboratory for its study, and must have within it all potential apparatus for that proper study.

As, in the words of Stieglitz, everything within An American Place is tested by whether it functions as a necessary force for what is outside, so everything that is within must stand the test of the light of day; of the world beyond—falling upon it from without. There are the large windows.

As An American Place must represent and be a tool for everyman, so everyman must be free to come to An American Place, not only to be observed in the laboratory that must know him before it can help him, but so that he too may observe, not only himself, but the whole universe in concentrated form, in this same laboratory, which to help him must first show him to himself: as part of the whole to arise through him. There is the door open to all. . . . There are the photographs, not of celebrities, of special men in the worldly sense, but of the inner light of any man: of the elevator boy, the simple country folk of a passing era, the gentle city folk; of the essence of that which, in moving one, is worth fighting for. Such moving beauty, if one can but open one's eyes to see it, exists in everyman; and in proportion as he is given the opportunity to show it will it flower. There is no pandering to clichés of wealth or worker, but a losing of self to work and to the fertile spirit, wherever. There is true caring, which is *act*. There is the democracy of taking any space, whether a garret or a loft in an office building and through respect for one's materials and concentration upon the actual problem involved, without theory, transforming the materials of the market place into a veritable shrine, with the corroboration of Stieglitz's vision of America upon the very walls. Better to have a prophet create a *place* into a shrine than a shrine without a prophet become a mere place.

But again, as that which is within must stand in readiness for all who would enter, so those who enter must decide for themselves if what is within is necessary to them, and in accordance with that necessity, there is the challenge of the Place: how to protect that which stands in readiness for all, since the fate of its very existence rests in the hands of those who need it. When for years Stieglitz did not lock the doors of that precursor of An American Place, 291, it was not merely because the idea of locking things was one foreign to his nature, or because energy expended upon keys was energy taken from more vital activity, but because of something even more important that was again at stake. As the Place is ever on trial, so the people themselves who enter and need are on trial as to whether they are able to preserve for themselves that which they claim to care for and to need. But this they must recognize for themselves. It cannot be told. "Automatically, if anything is stolen, the people will have forfeited their right to that which exists for them if they but know how to guard it. . . . I cannot conceive of art as property, or as other than belonging to the people, but until the people protect what is theirs, they will deny themselves of the very thing they seem to hunger for, and this mess of art being turned into property will continue. . . . I do not feel that I can call a thing 'mine,' unless it is available for all."

That there are locks at An American Place is a symbol not only of the changing status of the so-called value put upon the work he guards, by the very world from which he must protect it, but of the misunderstanding that is bound to arise about Stieglitz's own attitude towards the whole question involved. For himself he refuses to regard as property the work over which he is guardian. Yet, in order to protect the makers of it, he has been forced to forego his own inner necessity to let the people guard what is theirs—the very essence of trust. This is a constant hurt to him, and we can understand Stieglitz only if we understand the nature of the paradox, that although the doors are open to all by day, at night they are locked, (even though Stieglitz stands ready to open the Place to any who seek it, at whatever the hour). Only thus can we understand the deep hurt engendered within him, born of the very love that he must betray in order best to serve it.

He has said how if you believe in a thing sufficiently, it exists in the world, one's belief, one's need creating it. This portrait may itself be a starting point. It is possible that part of it, through corroboration and belief about something that exists in the form of Stieglitz's life, rather than through any completeness of communicating it as a whole, may touch a point that is part of the story. But there are other phases of the prophet standing looking at a world crumbling about him. There are endless phases.

"It is like this," he has said, "I live in a house near a river. The house is of wood and not very solidly built. Each year the river overflows, even though to no very great extent. Somehow I feel that some day it will overflow more violently and our house will be submerged. I warn the others in the house that we must rebuild it with strong, deep, steel foundations, so that we shall be prepared. They say that the other houses are of wood; that the river has never come near us; that there is no reason to expect that it will; that they have their work to do. One day the river overflows as it has never overflowed before, and the house is flooded. Everyone is wildly excited and afraid and calls out to rush to the top of the house. I stand on the ground floor, and continue with what I am doing. They call desperately to me to come quickly to where it is safe. I refuse. I say that I shall remain where I am. There is no other choice for me as I see life."

To see and to see even beyond the point of seeing. It is the revelation of this point beyond that illuminates his photographs, as it is in the quality of the light that it takes so long to fathom at the Place. "Everywhere in life there is a common desire for something that seems to be brought to life when two forces potentially meet, achieving a Yes to a Yes, but even when that point is seemingly achieved, there is the straining for the point even beyond." The Place is the touching of the point beyond touch, what Stieglitz calls a relationship more intimate than between any two persons, for what is art does not change, and there is no earthly limitation, no third or personally disturbing element that can come between oneself and one's experience of this kind. The Place is the point of contact between those who are seeking and those who have found. "When I am permitted to give what is mine to give; when I see someone simply, openly communicate what he is getting at the Place, putting it into form in his own life and for the benefit of the one who has given him that something, then that is my pay for what I am doing."

As with a camera, light is used by which to see and as the active agent in the very process upon which photography depends. That which is beyond man: the question what is life, is left in darkness, while out of contact with life, out of essential living, comes light itself. Dark room, light room. Stieglitz is ever the photographer, going far below the outer surface of appearance, showing to each his essential self, writing his signature within his work and not possessively upon it. "When I was young, for a time I would sign my name to my photographs, but soon I felt that if my work did not carry its own signature within it, then the easiest thing to forge would be a signature."

There is the problem of how to show color to the color-blind, play music to the deaf. There are the two opposing forces driving one. There is the voice saying that it cannot be achieved. There is the other voice, stronger, active, ever sensitizing new surfaces upon which one's message may be written. In proportion to the intensity of one's vision and one's necessity to communicate that vision shall exist one's power to sensitize surfaces never before written upon by man, to probe beneath surfaces never before realized by man. It is the key to his preoccupation with pioneer work, with the fostering of pioneer work, as of the patient impatience of Stieglitz with those who have not yet "seen," not yet "heard." And in his own contact with the world, there is the passion and the discovery of an Einstein, a Freud, a Bergson, as he goes below the surface of appearance, seeking and finding the inner reality. Light is the symbol, the goal, the test of An American Place.

Stieglitz speaks of one who, despite his professed caring about the welfare of the Place—which is the welfare of all concerned—in a situation analogous to shipwreck, stands concentrating upon the petty deficiencies of those involved, deflecting attention, as he does so, from the important work at hand, which is the saving of the ship and of the lives of those aboard. In the end the professed friend will have caused all about him to drown. "And you will drown with the rest," the answer is made. Stieglitz replies, "But at least I will have seen what is happening."

To see. Ever to see more deeply. Stieglitz is seventy. He stands tending his garden all day, every day. To be away is to have a heavy heart. . . . What might he be neglecting. . . . Truly this is the curator of a museum of a new order, born of love. To keep together and to protect the work of his co-workers and those co-workers themselves is one of his main preoccupations. He has even said, "Everyone is part of the Place, as I see it, whether he knows it or not." "To see the work of any artist scattered here and there is to see the work of an author scattered leaf by leaf, over the face of the universe. When will the people learn to husband what

is theirs and keep it intact, thus only *having* it? . . ." "If I cannot go to the Louvre, the Louvre does not come to me . . ." Or again, he chides his America: "If the American had his way, he would put his Niagara Falls and his lakes and his trees and his rivers into Ford cars and show them the world. . . ."

There are certain things he particularly demands from himself: ever to have more strength; to leave no edges ragged; to follow through what he has begun. . . . "To have the physical strength of a scale that can weigh a thousand tons of coal, plus a psychic sensitivity equal to the sensitivity of the scale that can weigh a ray of light."

There is always that something ever beyond one.

Again the prophet stands at the window looking out upon the world. You will hear him say that it is not art he cares about saving, for if all of the art in the world were to disappear and something *out there* were to be born in a pure spirit, that would concentrate a little upon some "common decency" instead of so much upon what is called "common sense," then art would inevitably flower again. No, it isn't this that interests him. It isn't "art" and "literature" that preoccupy him, but that which moves one and *becomes* art and literature in time. It is not the spasmodic burst of activity based on "ideas," but the sustained growth and the devotion to a dominating force, upon which one's very life depends, that moves him. . . . The eyes reach far, gazing into the point where all points meet—photographic, anti-photographic, surface, below the surface, personal, impersonal. He looks out upon America. The door is open to all, as if for the door to be closed to some were to shut out light; as if to shut out light were to shut out vision, were to shut out life itself. . . .

As in a laboratory, to see is the end; no solution, no slogans are sought. But, as in a scientific laboratory, where no practical or material end is sought, what is found is ultimately applied to the physical welfare of man, so in a laboratory such as An American Place, what is found is in the end applied by man for his own spiritual well-being.

As the form of a Gothic cathedral is a symbol of its reaching towards the skies, and includes in the magic of its very being the point it aspires to touch, so the clean, sharply defined cubes that are the parts of An American Place, enclosed as they are, save for the windows opening upon the city beyond and the door leading out into the office building itself, are in simple and forthright manner a symbol of a holding the Kingdom of Heaven within.

Fully to be; to see; to let exist what is; to nurture: of such is the containment and life-giving force that is the calm and all-inclusiveness of the square, light-filled rooms that are An American Place. The reaching towards what is beyond anything one can see with the outer eye, if it cannot be achieved wherever one is, cannot be achieved anywhere. If one cannot take materials available to all and use them in such a manner as to transform them into something beyond themselves, then surely one's use of more precious materials must be meaningless—depending upon some external qualities not created out of one's own being. "I am here," says Stieglitz. "Whether they come or whether they do not come: I am here." It is that simple, as Stieglitz tells it. . . .

To ask Stieglitz how to attain "salvation" is to be told swiftly, surely, "You can do only what you are doing. You must do exactly as you are doing. The blade of grass does not ask what it is meant to do, but continues upon its way: a blade of grass." For those who would evade suffering, who would use some external means for solving their problem, Stieglitz has little encouragement to offer. Another law of the interplay of forces: "If you try to spare someone from some inevitability, you will create a situation worse than the one from which you are attempting to protect." He is no evangelist going forth, promising an otherworldliness not attainable on this earth. His is the relentlessness of the oracle never moving forth; of the Greek chorus timeless and all-seeing; of the speaker of parables—without compromise reading life to those with ears to hear. He tempts tragedy itself, it would seem, by affirming it so nobly, almost seeming to call it forth to test some truth, prove some truth, that he has found repeating itself, predictably—given certain conditions. . . . He has no illusions, "Fatalist with one eye on Fate." His faith transcends tragedy, else it were not faith. . . . When someone asks him what he understands by the word "justice," Stieglitz replies, "There are two families, equally fine. They go to a hillside, and there they build their farms. Their houses are equally well built; their situations on the hillside are equally advantageous; their work equally well done. One day there is a storm which destroys the farm of one of them, leaving the farm of the other standing intact. That is my understanding of the word justice." Another man comes with a tale, "A terrible thing has happened. A friend of mine has betrayed me, even knowing that I am financially ruined. He has ruined others as well. How can men do such horrible things to one another? I do not understand." Stieglitz, quietly withdrawn, replies, "God, too, does terrible things to men, you know."

He speaks his message: always a variation on his theme, which like Lohengrin departs once you ask its name; which cannot be told any more than one may say what life itself is. For he has faith that there are those who will hear, and that through the hearing there may be an opening up of closed worlds. His message is not a promise to create worlds where none have stood before, taking unto himself tasks beyond the scope of man; worlds which must crumble, but rather: ". . . to let one another flower, and through what each takes from the other, the soil shall reënforce itself." There is the challenge to communicate out of darkness into light, as a seed flowers under the warming touch of the sun. . . . But always there is the knowledge of the point beyond seeing, beyond action, beyond communication: the symbol of life, mysterious, absolute: the first and the last cause. Out of the infinite into the infinite. . . .

Stieglitz stands looking at the point where all points meet: "I will be sitting with the plate of a picture I have just taken in my hands. It will be the picture I have always known that some day I would be able to take. It will be the perfect photograph, embodying all that I have ever wished to say. I will just have developed it; just have looked at it; just have seen that it was exactly what I wanted. The room will be empty, quiet. The walls will be bare—clean. I will sit looking at the picture. It will slip from my hands, and break as it falls to the ground. I will be dead. They will come. No one will ever have seen the picture nor know what it was. That, for me, is my story of perfection."

PART TWO

Ralph Flint

Post-Impressionism

THE EMERGENCE OF MODERN ART from a distinguished but somber nineteenth-century parentage was as essentially spectacular and unpredictable as the appearing of electricity in a world long accustomed to a less incandescent illumination. As manifestations of the same spiritual impulsion, these kindred phenomena were definitely part and parcel of the new progression that has been ousting from the social scene these past threescore years one phase after another of established ritual and routine. This evocation of a new era, with its harnessing of strange powers and gathering of fresh impetus, with its steady but inevitable insistence on new alignments and its unforeseen adjustments, undoubtedly characterizes the boldest, most vital and intensive assault on the human probabilities yet recorded; and it is hardly surprising that art, perhaps the most sensitive of our seismographic agencies, has from the first felt and recorded each cosmic thrust of this long progression with clairvoyant accuracy. Such liberation of latent forces, bringing into experience a mounting manifestation of light and power in swiftly increasing intensities, has led us to penetrate beyond the accepted outlines of a hitherto static and cloistered world toward horizons so boundless that we can but watch and wait in growing wonder at the unfolding panorama. Even those pioneering souls instrumental in shaping the first luminous statements of the new creed could hardly have guessed what exciting chapters lay ready for the turning of the page. Edison, sufficiently sensitized to capture the first faint but revolutionary rays of the rising electrical effulgence, made the year 1879 outstanding by setting the first electric bulb glowing in his Menlo Park laboratory. In much the same way but less dramatically, Monet started a new cycle when, stimulated by the splendor of the Turners at the National Gallery back in 1870, he began to develop the possibilities of transposing the play of direct sunlight to canvas.

From the very beginning, this electrically conditioned epoch has been fraught with untold potentialities. In America a pronounced metaphysical awakening, following hard upon the country's stand against human slavery, was set in motion; at the same time, a like stirring was noticeable in caste-ridden India toward new social attitudes. But however one may interpret this concerted approach toward a more emancipated basis of thought and action, the increase has definitely been along the line of light, metaphysically as well as physically; and any record of modern art at all cognizant of cause and effect must give that English landscapist, J. M. W. Turner, special credit for having been the first pictorially to brave the sun and bear away a coherent record of its radiance. His habitual concern for the logical ordering of natural phenomena —be it tree or rock or cloud or wave—was an integral part of his raptly focused vision which brought to his work a vitalizing grasp of form that has much in common with the interpretation of nature that the great Chinese painters have given us. Without some sort of introduction to Turner's rare appreciation and grasp of the laws of natural growth, such as Ruskin offers in his voluminous *Modern Painters* to anyone sufficiently courageous to take the plunge, it is quite possible to overlook this most important aspect of his art, although many of his water colors and most of his splendidly conceived and executed "Liber Studiorum" plates would seem to offer an easy clue. It is little wonder, then, that the Turners which Monet encountered in the National Gallery for the first time were sufficiently revealing to start him off on a new tangent, to induct him into a special and all-absorbing study of light which was to resolve itself into a definite school of far-reaching consequence.

Once the nucleus of the new movement was well organized, it did not take Monet and his sun-worshiping accomplices long to lure the painting fraternity from the shady retreats of Fontainebleau into the sunlit fields and sparkling riverways of the provinces, where each slightest variation of atmospheric effect was promptly charted on canvas with a zeal and exactitude more characteristic of the laboratory than the studio. A fine period of sunny incubation set in for those artists attuned to this new order of painting, where form *per se* became submerged in the general illumination and iridescence of the whole scene. A healthy individualism arose, with each man free to wander where he would in this newly achieved outdoors. The romantic revolution in French art that reached its

does not seem so bright now because everything is bright

climax prior to the outbreak of the Franco-Prussian War had prepared the way for this sudden adoption of the plein-air latitudes of
Impressionism: with the traditional hold of Church, State, and the
academies in abeyance, it was every man for himself, and the sky
definitely the limit. The devotees of this new form of painting
basked luxuriously in their new-found freedom, and it was a richly
preparatory period for the strange and unconventional findings that
were so soon to crowd upon the scene. Technically, this loosening
of traditional procedure lent a greater pliability to painting than
had been known before and paved the way for the startling innovations that were to be released with the rending of the Impressionistic veils. Representation for its own sake having reached a
stage of superlative refinement at the hands of the classic and
romantic masters of the nineteenth century, the soft and languorous
envelope that Monet and his associates drew across the face of
nature lulled to a great extent the long ingrained and decidedly
overworked instinct for close depiction of natural objects. Furthermore, a new agent had appeared in the shape of the camera to take
over the responsibility of supplying a facsimile record of the human
scene, leaving art freer than ever before for plumbing the more
intangible problems of painting.

With the thickening of the Impressionistic mists and vapors, new
dynamics, soon to drop like sharply revealing lightnings, were
steadily generating. A breaking-up of old-time considerations of
technique, a brand-new layout in prismatics, a complex weaving of
brush strokes that merely approximated form—these innovations in
painting had wrought sufficient consternation in the camp of the
conservatives; but the general reaction to Impressionistic dicta was
as nothing compared to the storm that broke loose in Paris with
the first realization of what the new pictorial formulæ bearing
Cézanne's authentication implied. The transitional steps leading
from the light-hearted, gently ruminative modulation of tone and
manipulation of accent of the plein-air painters to the highly
charged and incisive handling of the Master of Aix are not easy to
detect, for Cézanne himself had little or nothing in common with
the practices and preferences of Monet and his friends, although he
was to inherit something of the general lightness of brushwork that
came in with Impressionism. Excessive concentration on volume and
flow of form was apparent from the first in Cézanne's painting, as
is clearly set forth in his Man in a Blue Cap in the Bliss Collection,
a study made prior to Monet's historic visit to the National Gallery.
This advance from the tonal pleasantries and sunny platitudes of
Monet to the searching, searing inventions of Cézanne would
seem to parallel the course of events in the field of electrical phenomena where the early manifestations of light and power were
slowly but surely superseded by an increasingly significant and
determined control of this all-transforming element. And so the

luminous complacencies of the Impressionists merged inevitably
into the dynamic postulates of the Post-Impressionists.

In Cézanne we reach a peak of pictorial fervor and effulgence
that definitely separates the long progression of European art from
the newly conditioned epoch that has come to be known as Mod-
ernism, and we may well look upon him as the Great Divide of
painting. No one man has ever exerted such a potent spell on art
as this simple-minded but marvelously informed and informing
artist. Even today it is unlikely that we have fully gauged the
significance of his epochal career, but at least it can be safely
assumed that there can be no going back to a pre-Cézanne basis in
painting any more than there can be a return to a society uncon-
ditioned by electricity. It was a master stroke of fortune—for us, at
least—that he was circumstantially shut away from the Paris of his
own time and its doubtful advantages. Denied a place among the
leaders of the day, thrown utterly upon his own resources, he was
obliged to fight out his pictorial problems alone with nature and
his own driving sense of beauty. His beloved Aix came to have for
him the seclusion and security of the laboratory. There was nothing from without to disturb him in his self-appointed vigil; there
were no contrary voices or vainglorious promptings to impinge
upon the inherent integrity of his life purpose. He was reserved by
fate to discover during the long and often lonely watches of his
painting career just how far it was possible basically to revalue
form and color, just how far the singing quality of a pictorial statement could be advanced. The art world of our own time, responsive to the throb and beat of Cézanne's inspired orchestration of
effect as to no other single influence, has readily profited by this
realignment of pictorial forces, the essential idea of which Clive
Bell has so happily summarized in his phrase "significant form."

There has appeared recently a critical analysis of modern art that
is likely to stand for a long while to come as the most illuminating
commentary on the complexities of this much discussed and, in
many quarters, little understood phenomenon. I refer to Herbert
Read's *Art Now: An Introduction to the Theory of Modern Painting and Sculpture,* a volume worthy of study by all students of
twentieth-century art. While the author deliberately excludes from
his survey of the astounding diversities of contemporary art any
attempt to establish "a causal chain in this uniform aspect of confusion," he has nevertheless set down with remarkable lucidity and
sympathy the general nature and the essential factors underlying
the seemingly "catastrophic character" of this revolutionary period.
He graphically sketches the emergence of the "Symbolist" attitude
of the Post-Impressionist, so aptly summed up in Cézanne's dictum:
"I have not tried to reproduce nature: I have represented it," an
attitude wholly at variance with either the "scientific" or the
"empirical" methods of the European schools of the previous five

82

centuries. In *Art Now,* this all-important Symbolist credo is given a thorough and exhaustive airing. This radical departure from facsimile painting, so signally embodied in the work of Cézanne and to a lesser degree in the painting of Gauguin and Van Gogh, not only opened the way for every sort of pictorial inventiveness and experimentation, but brought European art for the first time into direct alignment with the principles of ancient Chinese painting and its insistence on metaphysical content. Such a sudden shift from the time-honored objective standpoint in art to a subjective state of reasoning, where ultimate satisfaction inevitably rests in symbols, is perhaps responsible for the meretricious aspect of much modern work. Confounding liberty with license has resulted in a flood of ill-considered and soon-to-be-forgotten productions. But in the main the beginning of a genuine rapprochement between the art processes of the East and the West can be discerned, however dimly.

In his desire to "get away from the exact mechanical reproduction of that imaginary mirror-like level onto which, in the act of vision, we conventionally project things," Read points out how Cézanne was continually projecting "a metaphysical conception of painting; a notion that there existed in the sense-data of the painter a 'real' vision independent of the intellect and beyond, at the back of, the emotions." To quote further:

But Cézanne was a simple man, though a passionate one: and he had no Sérusier to formulate a system on the basis of his passionate practice, his dogged insight. His method was, in a sense, still empirical. He kept to his ideal of the "real" vision, but he sought to arrive at the representation of this vision by tentative means. He explored the structure and the colours of an object, tirelessly, endlessly, with maddening persistence, until he felt satisfied that the form and colours on his canvas did in fact represent his "real" vision. It was a method that required the patience of a saint, and because saints are very rare (even among artists) it was not a method likely to become popular.

Because of the intensity of his feeling for form and color, Cézanne was able to subjectify the most objective material, so that his most prosaic still-life composition emerged monumental, individual. He sublimated each incidental part of the pictorial whole, giving to the finished painting an enduring vitality that enables one to return to it again and again for fresh delight. Such conceptions embody more than the painter sees at a given moment, for they acquire in the process of subjectification an absolute identity of their own, a living force, a presence that greatly endures. This sort of painting is far removed from the mirror-like processes of the so-called "scientific" painter who uses any means to make his "study" as like nature as possible, setting up thereby a comfortable assurance for himself that "God's in His heaven, all's well with the world." In this mirror-like semblance of the visible universe, the man who runs may gain a comforting glimpse of his own identity as part of a well-ordered cosmos, but he is not likely to have much relish for the work of the artist who sets out to establish a sequence of pictorial findings possessing an individuality of their own apart from what are commonly known as personal likes or dislikes— beauty, as Whistler pointed out, being ever present to the trained eye, whether in the rose or the dunghill. The true modernist thus begins to draw upon the inexhaustible funds of truth and beauty that lie outside a purely personal sense of form and color and line.

Such art is born of a kind of divine impulsion, whereby the ordinary rules and regulations do not apply. At such times technical inventions and necessities are suddenly established, to the confusion of the uninitiated. In painting of this order—and the myriad pale imitations of Cézanne's style only prove how universally he was endowed—a new manifestation of pictorial power is brought to light, conjuring up some fresh phase of absolute beauty from out that illimitable storehouse of abstract form and color that Plato indicates so lucidly in his *Philebus* when he says:

I do not now intend by beauty of shapes what most people would expect, such as that of living creatures or pictures, but, for the purpose of my argument, I mean straight lines and curves and squares, if you understand me. For I mean that these things are not beautiful relatively, like other things, but always and naturally and absolutely; and they have their proper pleasures, no way depending on the itch of desire. And I mean colours of the same beauty and pleasures.

Surely, this is as cogent and conclusive a statement concerning Cézanne's break with the traditional handling of form and color as could be framed. Here is form established for its own sake, not dependent on any other consideration or relationship, application or purpose—form that is beautiful "always and naturally and absolutely." Cézanne, in his avowed attempt "to make out of Impressionism something solid and enduring as the art of the museums," was actuated by no clear-cut Platonic theory, but, as Read points out, he staked everything on the "inherent form" in contradistinction to the impression of natural vivacity that had actuated the schools of painting "from Constable to Manet." This accounts for his abiding passion for "planes, volumes, and outlines, which tended to give his paintings a geometrical organization." But, as if this was not enough, he added to his concern with "the cylinder, the sphere, and the cone" the further attribute of color, a condition that in his eyes gave to form its ultimate force and distinction. "When colour has its richness, form has its plenitude." Here, in Cézanne's own words, is set forth the whole story of his art.

In order to achieve this dazzling display of imponderable form and rich color without depending on the involved processes of the older masters in underpainting and glazing, Cézanne was obliged to arrive at a technical mastery that necessitated a surpassingly flexible touch and rhythmic flow of form that is perhaps only to be matched in the work of the great Chinese painters. He undoubtedly possessed the most sensitive touch in all Occidental art, a touch that is, *mirabile dictu,* equally alive and varied in the ponderable oils as in the lighter medium of water color. Of course, his earlier paintings are more loaded than his later work, but the same marvelous sense of swelling, salient form is there throughout. It is this instant, directly contrived rendering of form that gives his least effort an inescapable thrust of pattern and plane. No one ever produced such solidity in paint with as little technical manipulation. The Venetian wizards and certain other masters, notably Rembrandt and Velasquez, accomplished astounding feats of pigmentation by means of intricate and long sustained processes of underpainting and glazing. They built up their lights scientifically, often repeating the preliminary stages of modeling as many as twenty times, contrasting heavily loaded passages with transparent glazes to such a degree that enlarged photographic studies of certain sections of their work appear more like sculpture than painting. They achieved the effect of powerful form in this indirect way without actually having fully to master the problems involved. What Cézanne perceived and recorded almost at a glance, they arrived at circuitously, creating remarkably deceptive semblances of swelling form but minus its dynamic content. They reasoned out their effects through the well-tested processes of the schools; he attained his goal through sudden realization and sharp necessity. Cézanne knew instinctively the true balance of forces in nature—the intimate and exciting relation between the angle and the arc, the power of softly focused strokes massed against razor-like slash of final accent, the sudden compression of pictorial interest like crossroads meeting on a map, the sly and subtle use of elision, the necessity for points of rest, the dynamic insistence of clustering lines drawn into some centrifugally managed whirl, the dramatic value of sudden pauses or blanks cutting in on the general drift of the pattern. His calligraphic touch remained the same in all his work, and he could shift from oil to water color without loss of tempo or delicacy. Not only does his marvelous brushwork keep his painting alive, but the supremely important faculty of constantly transcending the visual facts of the case was also his. Examined from a purely anatomical point of view, his large Male Figure, which is undoubtedly the *clou* of the Bliss Cézannes, discloses enough peculiarities of form to send the academically-minded to the madhouse; and yet I doubt if there is a more significant example of Post-Impressionist painting to be found. From the purely realistic angle, the whole work appears most unnatural, even suggestive of the novice in art; arbitrarily managed outlines cut in

upon the fleshly parts of the figure in a most alarming way, and in certain cases accents have been introduced into the anatomical structure that might seem more appropriate to a textile pattern. And yet it is one of his most exciting, most satisfying pieces of representation, sustained throughout by the intensity of his vision, bringing into focus all the bright and glowing facets of his pictorial sensibilities through that "maddening persistence" which enabled him to arrive at his "real" vision.

Here, then, is the central genius of the Post-Impressionist group, whose shift of balance from the objective to the subjective set in motion a reversal of form in all departments of twentieth-century art. There were of course those two other luminaries, Gauguin and Van Gogh, who, in their individual ways, manifested much the same sort of pictorial intensity as Cézanne. With Gauguin it was mainly ·mood and color that caught the new intensities, particularly in the final Polynesian period, when his natural feeling for rich hues and cabalistic design burst into sultry flame, adding a new and provocative note to the symbolic attitude toward nature that was being so rapidly formulated by these later painters. Van Gogh, too, broke into violent reaction against the prevailing serenity of the Impressionists, reconditioning their timid strokings and tenderly planted color vibrations to such a degree that he practically burned himself out in the process. He went about as far as the law allows in the direction of fiery manipulation of pigment and boldness of accent, setting a pace that no other painter could follow. Although less turbulent by nature than Gauguin and Van Gogh, Seurat brought to this Post-Impressionist group a similar sensibility for heightened power of effect that characterizes the best work of this special period. He also took the Impressionistic technique to further conclusion, giving it a more complex and formalized treatment that in due time resulted in Pointillism. He, like Van Gogh, came to a point where he could advance his technique no farther, his ultimate rendering of the Impressionist formulæ resulting in lovely sensitive patterns never to be surpassed in this special field of painting. Like Gauguin with his flaming evocations of the South Seas, like the tempestuous Van Gogh in his dizzy, impassioned assault on nature, Seurat, too, produced painting that was distinctly climactic. Something of Cézanne's ultimatum is to be felt in the work of these three so dissimilar artists, whose combined influence was to lead on into even more diversified modes of painting. But while the work of Gauguin, Van Gogh, and Seurat served primarily to heighten the general feeling for greater individualism in art, (as soon came to pass with the *Fauves,*) Cézanne's particular conception of form and color founded a royal dynasty that was to spread out and embrace all nations. The work of the other three left little room for further elaboration or even emulation, so strangely individual was each in his own estate; but what Cézanne had broached in his tireless experimentation along the lines of pictorial organization and abstract beauty directly prepared the way for the geometrical innovations of Cubism.

The time was ripe, by the turn of the century, for the first direct steps toward a wholly abstract art. A growing sense of the machine with its increasingly complex scheme of living was leading to some sort of climax that would terminate the outmoded methods of the nineteenth century. Each mechanical advance was a direct call for a further supply of electrical power. On the esthetic side, Cézanne's feeling for "formal structure" found a true affiliation with this mechanistic trend of thought, and the modernistic mélange was further augmented by a sudden interest in primitive and savage arts. El Greco, after a comfortable repose of several centuries, was sympathetically resurrected as the foster parent of the whole movement. The *Fauves,* with Matisse at their head, were frantically experimenting in all manner of new pictorial schemes. Dérain, Braque, Rouault, Dufy, Vlaminck, and the rest outdid each other in self-determined distortion of form and in willfully "unnatural" color harmonies, and Paris rang with their passionate protests at the conventions. But more significant yet was the appearance of Cubism in 1908. Here was the Cézanne credo of form for its own sake taken to a logical conclusion. Picasso, together with Braque, became the leading protagonist in this new phase of the modern spirit. While the *Fauves* were instrumental in carrying on the emotional and symbolistic tradition of Gauguin and Van Gogh, it was mainly the efforts of Picasso, owing to his special aptitude for abstract form, that evolved this wholly subjective, mechanistic ordering of area and line. The zero hour had indeed struck, as far as facsimile painting was concerned. From that point on, the story of art was to be built up out of new elements, was to flow in many and diverse streams, toward undreamed-of objectives. The existing order of things pictorial was being plumbed with a vengeance.

In those transitional days Matisse was a lively, dominating figure, trying out each new scheme on his palette in true opportunist fashion, cleverly combining the best of each and ultimately arriving at a highly calligraphic and personal style that has become one of the dominant characteristics of modern painting and that assures him an important place in the historical progression stemming from Cézanne. Brightness of color, breeziness of style, an all-over checkerboard patterning that hails in part from Persian art, a fine simplification of chiaroscuro, a charming naïveté and instantaneousness of vision, a vision that Read defines as "primarily integral," as "prelogical" and the "delight of the innocent eye"—all these essentially "modern" qualities became in time part of the Matisse equipment and helped to round out a talent that has produced perhaps the most exhilarating still-life painting that has ever been seen. So completely is Matisse the perfect embodiment of the still-life painter in

the broadest sense of the word that his figures seldom emerge outside the general diapering of his canvases. Matisse is wholly within the limits of his period, intellectually straightforward, an outstanding example of the modern artist who has made a success of his art and an art of his success. His few excursions into the unseen or the semi-abstract have not been altogether happy, and his best work has been done as the *Fauve* fever has given way to a more mature, prosaic interpretation of the natural scene. Braque, like Matisse, has remained quite within the French tradition, and although he worked side by side with Picasso in establishing the Cubist cult, he has hardly ever exceeded that initial proclamation of pictorial freedom, save to elaborate constantly his original formulæ. His latest compositions, such as Paul Rosenberg brought this past season to New York, are the acme of a most distinguished talent, but they are still securely linked to his first Cubist utterances by a sublime contentment with the creed that he and Picasso so signally set forth in 1908. His pictorial inventions have grown constantly richer with the years; innately French, they curiously recapture the Louis Quinze feeling for squat and formal elegance.

With the bursting open of the power plants of the world in 1914, when with frightful suddenness the sense of power as power could no longer be humanly sustained, a new directional influence was found actuating the general scheme of affairs. A period of power-put-to-use sets in, a period of penetration, with earth and sea and sky and time and space as new and more enticing targets to aim at. Penetration goes forward in the perfection of the radio; in improved forms of communication; in the rapid conquest of the air; in stratospheric and bathyspheric experiments; in the evolution of more resilient metals; in new conditioning of light and in ever more dire explosives; in increasingly powerful telescopic ranges; in television; in the new photography that pierces solid matter and fog; in the creation of the cinema, an art form for the many and not the few, and the first attempt to link together three such dissimilar elements as science, art, and commerce, without any one of which the cinema as we know it in its broadest sense today would cease to function,—to mention some of the outstanding marvels of the electrical pageant that our century has seen come to pass, a picture certainly that for sheer audacity and swift seizure of fresh opportunity through skill and daring has had no counterpart in history.

And what is the counter record of this period of penetration in the course of contemporary art? One has only to glance through the pages of *Art Now* with its dizzy assortment of modernly minded pictures to see just how far the penetrative spirit of the day has been reflected in our thinking, to realize what strange and weird and wonderful inventions in art have come to pass since the Great War shattered the complacency of this particular planet. And of the generous company of artists who have found this post Cubist period to their taste, Picasso has come to be the one name to conjure with. Standing head and shoulders above his fellow workers, this spirited, shock-trooping Basque has kept Paris the focal center of artistic thought and development ever since he got into his stride in 1908. He has taken the so-called School of Paris out of its traditionally French envelope and stamped it with an authority that is responsible alone to some extra-territorial impulsion difficult at the moment to determine. The prophetic note that Eugenio d'Ors sounds in his illuminating monograph on Picasso is probably as near to the facts as we can come just now:

The nineteenth century was dying when Picasso was in his adolescence. . . . But even at his very beginnings, in those inevitable moments of pristine babblings, when the spirit is bursting to speak; even before he left Barcelona . . . he produced precocious works so out of keeping with the Impressionist atmosphere which then dominated artistic circles, so precociously foreshadowing artistic tendencies toward construction and the neo-classicism, that they may almost be said to seem later than the Picasso of 1912 or even the Picasso of 1928. He who looks at them marvels, and would be moved to speak of miracles—or of fraud— if he were not persuaded as I am that in the vocation of men there is a force more intelligent and unifying than the consciousness of men itself: a force which, far from presenting the cosmic dispersion of the unconscious offers a superconscious coherence which we can only call angelic —witness the guardian angel of Tobias or the familiar daemon of Socrates.

Just as Cézanne epitomized the Post-Impressionist period, so Picasso is the special embodiment of the next great division of the pictorial progression that we call, for want of a better term, modern art. What seemed in the early days of Picasso's painting to be merely a peculiar restlessness, a vagrant and unsettled will, an unequaled precocity, we can accept today as a direct response to the underlying tidal flow of human aspiration toward a more emancipated, more buoyant state of being. Darting here and there, boldly appropriating a hint from this painter or that, seldom stopping more than to define the nature of each fresh invention, despising in his highly sensitized and overcrowded mind the delights of surface painting, digging feverishly into each fresh vein of thought, sometimes achieving a comic gesture of salutation to the gaping throng, sometimes mocking directly a special style or fashion in art, but making each new premise a logical step in his own evolution, Picasso has delivered the *coup de grâce* to pedestrian art. Despite the various group tendencies of the Ecole de Paris, he greatly dominates the situation today and doubtless will until he signs his last canvas. Only this past year has he taken stock of the surréalists

in a series of amazingly brilliant and daring water colors, matching them stroke for stroke on their own grounds.

Without wishing to alarm unduly, I feel certain that the art of the next few decades stands in grave danger of being further than ever removed from the realm of the predictable. Paris, highly feminized, centralized, will doubtless continue to be the main locale for the operations of the modern school, will doubtless continue to exert her prior claims as focal point for Occidental art until, in the course of slow time, some other center sends up a more potent call to pictorial arms. Where else than in Paris could the Impressionists have found a more fitting cradling for their newly conceived adventure? Who other than a Parisian would have had the instinct to discover what lay concealed in the work of Cézanne? Or what other metropolitan kaleidoscope could have supplied the requisite elements for the shaping of a talent like that of Matisse? In what other capital than Paris could Picasso have found a public sufficiently alert and ministering to sustain him and his art and to keep them both in proper circulation? For unlike Cézanne, he has needed the applause of the crowd, the gentle flattery of a de luxe press, and an emotionally constituted critical fraternity to broadcast his least utterance. The stamp of Paris is still supreme, no matter whether the outside world relishes it or not. By constantly radiating her supercharged reactions to the various other art centers of the civilized world, she has served the cause of modern art as no other community could have possibly done. What will come to pass after this rich period of recapitulation has rounded out its term is not for us to say. There is small chance of going back to outmoded positions, however. The world today is progressing rapidly toward new states of mind, toward new attitudes and receptivities, and in that direction the story of modern art is bound to proceed.

Advancing along the line of light from power to penetration, we should ultimately arrive at a period of revelation. Already the surréalists have coined a new vocabulary, and no matter how valid their communications may be, they have at least been ready and willing to try the impossible. The sudden demand for further streamlining of our equipment today is quite likely to carry over into our esthetic problems; slipping along our terrestrial courses with increasing ease, we should find some equivalent in our mental processes. Picasso has already taken flight at seemingly dangerous angles: he has touched upon the psychic to a degree unrivaled by his contemporaries. Surely, in the course of modern art, there has not been vouchsafed us a more haunting piece of mental conjuring than his Seated Woman, which dominated Chicago's Century of Progress exhibition of art last summer by virtue of its fierce intensity of mood and its macabre enchantments. While others play about the studios making unusual and often fascinating patterns, Picasso seemingly gets his supply of ideas from more authentic chambers of imagery. Securely established in the midst of a most phenomenally successful and spectacular career, he might well cry out: *"Après moi, le déluge!"*

As far as Post-Impressionism in America is concerned, the story runs a more checkered course—at least, until within the last few years. Today, thanks to the enterprise of certain enlightened art lovers in New York, a museum has finally been established which permanently houses one of the finest collections of modern art in this country as well as assuring for the cause the official sanction of society. From now on, judging from the popular success of the loan exhibitions at the Century of Progress in Chicago in the summers of 1933 and 1934, the task of converting America to modern art should be comparatively easy, not to say painless. The older museums, such as the Metropolitan Museum and the Museum of Fine Arts in Boston, are still strangely unaware that anything of consequence has occurred in art since the time of the Impressionists; but such younger depots as the new Hartford museum, the Fogg Art Museum at Harvard, and the handsome new Worcester Museum, as well as several of the more inland art centers, make it their business to keep abreast of the times. So far, however, only Hartford can boast a museum of the fine arts devised entirely in the modern mode. To the credit of all concerned, Hartford also rose to the occasion by inaugurating its new museum with a loan exhibition of works by Picasso that ranked with anything yet achieved in Europe. The rank and file of good Americans, however, are yet a long way from sensing any issue at all. We are still rather too inclined to suspect this new art, hailing for the most part from Paris, as the outcropping of a decadent and worn-out European society. Characteristically, foolishly, pardonably, perhaps, we cling to a nationalistic idea of art, priding ourselves on our immunity from such alien and disrupting influences. After getting off to a flying start in the field of mechanics, after grasping to such a widespread extent the metaphysical aspect of this electrically conditioned era, it is strange indeed how laggard we remain when it comes to esthetics.

Until the famous Armory Show in 1913 put Post-Impressionism on the map, art in America suffered from provincial anemia. There was little or nothing in our artistic make-up to keep us abreast of the times. Only at the close of the 'eighties did such names as Van Dyck, Hals, Rembrandt, and Turner appear in the catalogue of paintings at the Metropolitan Museum, thanks to the Marquand Bequest. The average buyer at that time was busy acquiring Bouguereaus and Meissoniers, favorites who gave place to the Barbizon masters, who in their turn were superseded by Mauve and Israels with their pearly sentimentalizings. Inness was the principal

American challenge to these importations: and he must have enjoyed a considerable local patronage, for the Metropolitan Museum lists the acquisition of two important canvases from his hand as early as 1887. The big money, however, went for such works as Rosa Bonheur's famous Horse Fair which fetched something like fifty thousand dollars at public auction, while for Meissonier's equally spellbinding 1815, depicting Napoleon surrounded by his faithful troops, a price of upwards of one hundred thousand was cheerfully paid. Henner's alabastrine nudes were popular items in *fin de siècle* collections, and Detaille's martial numbers were also much the vogue. Realistic "panoramas" with elaborate plastic foregrounds likewise intrigued the art-loving public of that parlous period: art "with a message" was the thing, and Millet's Angelus toured the country with overwhelming success. The Metropolitan Museum could stage a provocative and instructive exhibition of these popular "buys" of the 'eighties and 'nineties, listing the original prices against the probable figures these relics would bring today at open market.

However, there was one individual in the New York art world whose sense of values was sufficiently developed to catch the first oncoming vibrations of the new movement. Alfred Stieglitz, with a considerable European background to his credit, had returned to America in 1890, full of enthusiasm for Rubens, the newly discovered wonders of Egyptian antiquity, and the possibilities of the then underestimated camera. It did not take long, however, for this youthful enthusiast to size up the American situation, to sense the course of the prevailing winds, and to discern which way lay salvation. From the beginning, because of his ability to perceive the immediate significance of each phase of our esthetic evolution, he has kept several laps ahead of the procession; and this sense of the contemporaneous has kept him from ever losing sight of art as essentially related to life. Instead of regarding photographs as such, or of thinking of pictures as items to be marketed like securities on exchange, he has insisted on their significance as vital documents of human thought and aspiration, to be kept fresh and alive and functioning, lest one choke to death on them in the end. Documentary tags and the dusty deadweight of officialdom have never been allowed to accumulate on any work bearing the Stieglitz cachet of approval. From the very beginning of his long labors as champion of certain clearly defined issues, Stieglitz's forwardness of vision has automatically kept him in the limelight as the leading exponent of living art in the New World. Instead of waiting for a convenient season in which to acknowledge some special talent, instead of waiting to see how well early promises were kept, he has continually matched each phase of art the moment of its emergence with an equally immediate acceptance.

For this reason Stieglitz was the one inevitable focal point where the first intimations of Post-Impressionism in America were to register with any outstanding effect. The Impressionist attitude had found echo in much of his early photographic work, but it was not until the more dynamic phases of the modern movement began to ripple their way across the Atlantic that his sympathies were genuinely aroused. He took to the new art from the start. Although his principal concern had been with the issues of the rapidly unfolding art of photography—he had already taken many revolutionary steps both artistically and technically—the academic complications of the photographic coteries began to cramp his free spirit. Had there been the slightest touch of commercialism in Stieglitz's approach toward art, either in photography or in painting, he could easily have retired years ago a multimillionaire; for it was his privilege and prerogative to introduce to America the outstanding men of the new movement. Long before the average New York collector was aware of the implications and importance of the Post-Impressionists, Stieglitz had hung their work on the walls of 291. But his only excuse for handling art at all lay in his keen appreciation of the lasting significance of each esthetic experience as relating, first of all, to the individual artist, and then to life in general. And so his returns for handling art on his own terms have been deposited where no collector of internal revenue would think of looking. There they are, nevertheless, and Stieglitz stands the richer in the end.

Now that we in America have become less laggard in the matter of the fine arts, having caught up with our artistic heritage even to its earliest colonial beginnings, it may not seem such a colossal feat to have been the first to represent the work of Cézanne, Matisse, Picasso, Braque, and the rest before an indifferent public. But to one who has any knowledge of the intensity with which Stieglitz wages his campaigns for esthetic liberty and freedom of expression, those early days at 291 have about them a decidedly Lincolnian ring. Whatever the issue at stake, all through the various chapters of his extraordinarily active and extended life, there has been no concession to the second-rate, no deviation from his self-appointed course to follow the line of least resistance. He has continually courted fate by shaking out a challenge to measure up to his standards. From the beginning of 291 up to the present time he has withstood the solicitations of the crowd, has remained insulated but not isolated from "the common life" and its deadening values. Through long years of acknowledging only the best in art and life, Stieglitz has come to acquire that "toughness of mind" which Van Wyck Brooks refers to in his study of William James (*Sketches in Criticism*) as belonging to "men who have values." This very ruggedness has long been characteristic of Stieglitz, for he has steadfastly looked conventional life in the face and rejected it, "not

through any neurotic need to escape, but at the command of a profound personal vision." To many this "toughness of mind" is tiring, troubling, hardly to be endured. While it acts for them as a barrage through which they may not pass, it serves him protectively by keeping out those not worth the trouble of admittance. His reputation for being blunt and even bellicose has prevented many discerning folk from seeing the real man beneath the protective coloration, and many are the recorded incidents where inquisitive and often unprepared visitors have had their foundations shot from under them by Stieglitz's sharp inquisitiveness and booming oratorical periods. His clairvoyant thrusts have caused others to forego their pleasure in whatever art he may have been showing at the time.

Having stripped himself for a battle to the death with the shams and stupidities of the ordinary round of living, Stieglitz's insistence on the eternal verities is hardly comforting to the average citizen content with taking things as he finds them. Brooks complains that "American society is like a cogwheel that has lost its cogs," that we in this curiously compounded country invariably lack conviction because we lack values. "How much," he adds, "we should enjoy the spectacle of a sour-faced American Schopenhauer, an indigestible American Tolstoy, an insufferable American Ibsen, an incredible American Nietzsche—just one true-blue solitary rhinoceros." Well, I think we have just such an one in Alfred Stieglitz, and it is little wonder that from the beginning there has clustered around him a considerable though shifting body of men and women —artists, writers, thinkers, workers in many fields—who have found in his stern and rockbound attitude a place of refuge from the indecisions of a cogless, overcrowded society, who have relished a point of contact with one whose life purpose has been so indomitably maintained, so unflagging in its demands not only on himself but on those who have come to vision something of his purpose. A keen sense of sportsmanship for its own sake has helped him to run the good race, enabling him to keep on going long after most men would have been glad to call it a day. This unremitting concentration of purpose, this incessant hewing to the line, this same sporting sense that led him as a lad to run a twenty-five-mile race around the cramped circuit of his New York cellar, has undoubtedly toughened him to the task of seeing the whole thing through, of supporting the issue of modern art from the early showing of Rodin's drawings in 1908 up to the 1933 exhibitions of Marin and O'Keeffe and Dove. By every sign, Stieglitz was the one man qualified to express in American terminology the essential qualities of Post-Impressionism.

His own direct contribution to American art has been, of course, through the camera, a highly objectified and mechanically circumscribed medium, but for once carried far beyond its ordinary limits by the sheer mastery of the artist. From the start Stieglitz has matched the mounting issues of modern art in this country with clear, well-timed photographic statements, a record that begins with the early impressionistic plates of picturesque New York byways; that merges into the more personal, biting, and boldly conditioned studies of the people and places during the Post-Impressionist days at 291; that includes those lovely lyric interludes at Lake George which have marked each summer season; that rises to those rarefied and transcendent Equivalents which would have sent Ruskin skyrocketing at such profound interpretation of the heavenly hosts in all their intricate counterpointing; and concludes with the thrilling skyscraper studies of modern Manhattan that climax his photographic career. These latest New York prints mark the acme of photographic interpretation, where so-called mechanics give place to a persuasive animus that is indeed the artist's very self—an open demonstration of mind over the machine, if you like, but, at any rate, photography taken to higher pitch of perfection than has come to pass at the hands of any of the myriad practitioners at work today throughout the land. Stieglitz brings to his camera work much the same sense of sheer veracity and pictorial penetration that Cézanne brought to painting. A born cameraman, a master technician, a poet, a seer, a practical student of the humanities, a fighter, a sportsman (without a sport), a rare friend, an acknowledged philosopher and guide, he has forced the seemingly conditioned camera to rise to unsuspected heights in a way that defies analysis. The camera has served him well throughout the years, served as a "cave of his own soul" where he might retreat to find "new frames of mind, new attitudes, new standards of measurement." It has offered him a handy dark-room retreat where he might enjoy the solitude necessary to every artist.

While Stieglitz was primarily responsible for the rapid development of photography in America, as well as being a vital factor in getting Post-Impressionism off to a flying start, he has stood back of the best of art, no matter of what nature or of what provenance, with a strict impartiality. It would have made little or no difference to him if Marin had been a Canadian or O'Keeffe of Mexican stock so long as the work they produced was definitely alive and related to the moment. It has been from the beginning art as a whole rather than any special group or aspect that has commanded his interest and support. Looking on art purely as a manifestation of social values in the highest degree, he has naturally attracted to himself work of special significance. This, especially in his earlier days, resulted in his becoming a veritable storm center for all the radically minded in the town, but his long-established policy of nonresistance and watchful waiting have afforded him valuable protection and enabled him to weather whatever crises may have arisen along the way. At heart, he has always been remarkably cool and

contained, and there must have been many occasions during the early days of 291 when it was necessary to keep calm in the midst of the fiery discussions and contretemps of his sometimes too zealous followers. Even at the Intimate Gallery, there was still much of the *sanctum sanctorum* atmosphere hovering over the scene; and it was only when the Intimate Gallery in its turn gave way to An American Place that the real Stieglitz emerged in all his elemental vigor and essential simplicity. Perhaps the nature of An American Place, with its clear-cut, business-like atmosphere and unpretentious setting (although no gallery in the town was ever so scrupulously polished and painted), made him realize more completely than ever before the main idea back of his gallery work. Here was Stieglitz functioning true to form, a "minor prophet" (as a somewhat bewildered news reporter had it on the occasion of his seventieth birthday) in "a makeshift gallery." Here was art set forth like some rare table in a wilderness of bartering and social jockeying; here the final resolution of the Stieglitz idea as embodied in the work of Marin, O'Keeffe, and Dove, the three Americans who round out a full picture of his artistic credo. The first two particularly—Marin with his intensely masculine outlook and inspirational approach to art, and O'Keeffe with an equally intensified pictorial viewpoint springing from the more emotional nature of the woman—would seem to have arisen as if by magic to complement each other, to provide him with a perfectly balanced instrument through which to realize to the fullest extent the emotional gamut of his vision. Such patronage, where one artist voluntarily sponsors, inspires, and sustains his fellow artists, protecting them from the worldly cares that ordinarily beset the creative thought, and building up for them a following of distinction, is indeed a labor of love that has no exact counterpart in the history of the arts. In the case of Marin, Stieglitz has watched him unfold during the course of some twenty-five years—his stand for the water color as a medium of equal importance to the more showy oil is a story in itself; and I am certain that the delight in watching the pictorial thought of this extraordinary artist expand and ripen into fullest maturity has more than repaid him for the labor involved in bringing and keeping him before the public.

Particularly at this moment, when art in America seems to be heading toward a more proletarian basis, does the Stieglitz contribution to art and criticism seem more than ever providential, more than ever an essentially vital step in our unfoldment. Without a certain remnant and a qualified leader, as Brooks points out in his study of William James, no real development can ever take place in society. "Values have to be recreated—or at least restated—in every social group and in every generation; and when this re-statement fails to take place, one has the stagnant epochs and the stagnant peoples." With Stieglitz as standard bearer to continue reframing our esthetic credo, there can be little doubt that art in America is safe for posterity. I am equally certain that with the passing of the years his influence will increase and multiply, will serve as a mark for future generations to aim at. We shall be increasingly glad of our "one true-blue rhinoceros," our "minor prophet" and his far from "makeshift" gallery. It is this enduring, even prophetic note in the Stieglitz make-up that will probably carry farthest down the course of time, if my premises are correct. The initial idea of light, now grown in power to penetration and performance, will undoubtedly propel our art along this line of development toward an increasingly inspirational standpoint. As a nation we have gone farther in giving woman her place in the sun than any of our neighbors, and since woman, "clothed with the sun, and the moon under her feet, and upon her head a crown of twelve stars," stands for revelation, it should follow that in the course of, say, the next hundred years, American art reflect states of mind that we today may but dimly discern.

The history of our art is doubtless as fine and honest as it should be. The first great trio of true-blue Americans—Homer, Eakins, and Ryder—affords a firm base for any superstructure we care to raise (even if we have but comparatively recently seen our way to the full acknowledgment of their various virtues). Sargent and Whistler, contented expatriates, have their place as historical ornaments rather than as solid blocks in the building of our Pantheon of the arts (although Whistler in his etchings must rate among the elect). From then on, as the various influences of the Impressionists and the Post-Impressionists have affected American art, the building blocks have become smaller and smaller, although of such increasing numbers as to make up in quantity what they might lack in importance. We have today in our midst a greater array of what may be called second-, third-, and fourth-string artists than any other country. Our big annuals are marvelous outpourings of intelligence and skill; they have all the diversity and animation of a five-ring circus. But out of the first ten, or the first "Nineteen" as the Museum of Modern Art once had it, there are precious few who possess the magic touch that will lift their work into an assured place among the very great. Marin and O'Keeffe are of this group: they both have something of the revelatory touch—Marin as no other painter living today, O'Keeffe particularly in her early inspirational work, when strange fires flared up as never before in the painting of any woman. And since these two artists in particular have been brought up with such consideration for their peculiar talents, since their art has enjoyed a unique presentation and environment through Stieglitz's devoted ministrations, something of this special atmosphere and enfoldment should be devised to carry over into the future. I should like to see some small art center created to house the work of Marin and O'Keeffe, to present a carefully selected group of their paintings in a setting that would let one enjoy them at their full value. Marin's work, the best of it, being couched in that little comprehended medium, water color, will otherwise only be seen in obscure corners of our public institutions where water colors are usually consigned. The O'Keeffes should be carefully selected, with special reference to her early work (including the little-known water colors), in order to bring out the whole range of her pictorial thought. I should also like to see, placed on the same level of importance with the Marins and O'Keeffes, a generous showing of Stieglitz's own work, all the outstanding plates that he has created during his distinguished career. Then, too, for good measure, and because they have both figured to a large extent in Stieglitz's residual group of protégés, there should be a representation of the work of Dove and Demuth. Here would be a metropolitan meeting place for those who choose to think of art as necessarily contacting the ideal at all times, a rendezvous for those who cherish the implications of art more highly than the works themselves, a clinic for such as like art of a medicinal nature, a rarely suitable monument to the genius of a great American who managed, through unswerving devotion to truth, to complete "the arch of his thought."

Harold Rugg

The Artist and the Great Transition

ALFRED STIEGLITZ'S PRODUCTIVE LIFE has spanned precisely the period that I call for emphasis the Great Transition. I mean the forty years of drastic social change that have passed since the premonitory events of the eighteen-nineties. It was in these forty years that the First Industrial Revolution catapulted into the Second; that the wasteful Machine Age passed quickly over into the efficient Power Age. It was in these forty years that Stieglitz achieved the distinction of being the first artist to use successfully the camera, a mechanical instrument, to reveal the organic character of the nature-thing. And it was in these same four decades that he stood out as the Teacher—fighting his cultural warfare, denouncing and deriding the marts of esthetics, creating the first unique American Place, and furthering the concept of honest, indigenous American life. Thus he is both artist and teacher, and it is as such that he has provided us with indispensable concepts and an equally indispensable example for the educational reconstruction of the years ahead.

2

THE BREAKDOWN OF OUR ECONOMIC INSTITUTIONS in the past few years has rudely awakened us to the truly interim nature of our generation. We have been suddenly compelled to recognize that our Western civilization is not merely enduring one of its periodic business depressions. On the contrary, it is passing from one cultural epoch to another, from the first stage of industrialization into the second.

It is of the greatest importance that all workers who are concerned with social and educational reconstruction recognize the initial character of the industrial stage out of which we are now passing. The two centuries and more of engine and machine invention, of construction of power plants and factories, transport and communication systems, and in general of large-scale business enterprises, have produced for the first time in all history a highly productive economic system. In many unique respects it was the *first;* for example:

(1) The *first* invention of efficient power-driven machines.
(2) The *first* central electric stations transmitting power over long distances.
(3) The *first* vertical corporations with their giant concentrations of capital, their mechanism of automatic, integrated, and interchangeable fabrication, standardization of parts and processes and specialization of labor.
(4) The *first* unhampered application of the concept of laissez-faire in economic life. Given efficient prime movers and machines, men, for the first time, were really free to exploit—people as well as things.
(5) The *first* attempt to organize the collective economic affairs of nations on a world-wide interdependent basis. As a result six hundred million people are now dependent on the uninterrupted operation of a fragile world mechanism of specialized production and exchange, with fluctuating units of money, wages, and prices, and an intercontinental market based on widely varying national standards of living.
(6) The *first* experimentation with the concepts of political democracy—notably those of government by the consent of the governed, freedom of movement, of assemblage, and of speech, trial by jury, and the like.
(7) The *first* experimentation with the concept of education for all the children of all the people.

We need not multiply cases. Our list documents sufficiently the initial character of the period of exploitation at the close of which we now stand. In these and in other ways the stream of events of the past two centuries constituted the dawn of a new culture. It was a First Day.

As a First Day it advanced by utterly unique economic and social trends. Not only was a new physical civilization suddenly produced: deeper-lying psychological problems emerged as well. These are the devastating social and personal problems with which we are confronted today. But to understand them and to devise solutions for them we must know the characteristics of the social trends and the human traits which propelled them. Succinctly, what are the special traits of this first industrial and social revolution of modern times?

3

FIRST, *rapidity of growth.*

For more than two centuries, during the fumbling experimentation of Porta, the Marquis of Worcester, Papin, Savery, Newcomen, Watt, Arkwright and company, the industrializing process gathered momentum very slowly. By the middle of the nineteenth century, however, it began to pick up speed, and the next five decades—from the American Civil War to the World War—were a period of swift expansion. Every phase of it grew at positively accelerating rates—the production of goods, the aggregation of populations and their concentration in urban communities, the radius of the market, horizons of communication and exchange, the interconnections of cultures, the time-beat and rhythm of urban life. All was positive acceleration.

The engineers have recently reduced the past century of growth to mathematical order, plotting curves and fitting equations to the trends of production of the basic commodities. They are all parabolas, and many have equations of high exponents. Whereas population increased as the square of the time, the curves of production mounted as the third, fourth, even tenth power of the time. Witness steel . . . rubber . . . automobiles . . . electric power! The men in the street as well as the owners in their chambers of commerce, guided the expansion by a simpler quantitative slogan—"Bigger"—and added their naïve concept of quality, "Better." But the basic idea was the same—More! More people to buy more shoes, more houses, more food. More power stations, more factories, more cars. More goods to export to "backward" populations. No concepts are more adequately descriptive of this era of expansion than this one of positive acceleration.

Not only was acceleration of growth true of the volume of production; similar mathematical laws governed the swift increase in the productivity of the worker himself. The equations which fit the parabolas of "man-hours per unit of production" also have high but negative exponents. After 1910 the increase in output per man-hour became so vast that in the early 1930's the engineers could generalize a century of growth in this way: *no longer does a relation exist between what a man can produce and what society can pay for it.* Thus have physical power and purchasing power gotten out of relation to each other. And all this within less than fifty years after the filling in of the last American frontier.

Second, absorption in physical construction.

Naturally, the first stage of industrialization was an orgy of building. In America, especially, it could not have turned out differently. Given: isolation from the quarreling courts of Europe, the world's most favored virgin continent, a population descended from the Nordic adventurers of trade and migration, and the guiding theme of life in the nineteenth century was bound to be physical conquest. Dynamic catchwords energized the struggle with geography and with native owners. Conquer and settle. . . . Build. . . . Construct. . . . Make it big, make it stunning.

Moreover, these concepts of construction were given a patriotic rationalization. "America" must be built. There is not much time, so hurry. The good of the individual will be guaranteed by augmenting the wealth and power of the group. Hence build, for the sake of the country. But do not spend too much. Acquire and keep. Save for tomorrow. Accumulate. Pile up a surplus in order that you may invest—in more land and more factories—and export your surplus capital to undeveloped lands. Thus also we shall build America.

Third, undesigned and uncontrolled exploitation.

The virgin continent, the cyclonic climate, the drives of human nature, and the pressure of hordes of immigrant newcomers, all contributed to a restless haste to get immediate profits. So everything in the earth was mined—the top soil, the forests, the coal and the oil, the iron, the copper and other metals. Everything in the earth was taken in a mad, unrestricted, and unplanned race for gain.

It was an uproarious period of hectic trial and error—mostly error—and waste! The concepts of private ownership and free competition made "design" in the first era of industrialism utterly impossible. Although, even at the beginning of the debauch, thinking men counseled the imperative need for plan and social control, most of the energetic, shrewd, and ambitious men threw themselves into the race for money and power and rationalized their conduct by the French economic philosophers' doctrine of laissez-faire. The Western man translated the physiocrats' dictum to suit his personal desires: "Freedom to exploit." . . . "Every man for himself—and the devil take the hindmost." And he did; that is, he took the rank and file of the people of the industrial countries.

Fourth, the nervous tension of life.

Changes in the tempo of living in the new régime paralleled those of the new mechanical occupations, transport and communication. Faster and faster beat the basic rhythms of physical life. "Cutting down elapsed time" became an obsession of the man in the street as well as of the pony-express riders and the drivers of locomotives, automobiles, or airplanes.

For well-nigh three hundred years tension has marked the nervous life of the American. Physical danger on the frontier and economic insecurity in the jungle of the market served the Western man alike—to produce a continuum of alertness, of restless, hectic movement. Inevitably the attention span and interest span remained short.

The compulsion of hurry ever confronted the American—whether set by the climatic exigencies of the growing season or by the competitive race with one's economic rivals. Hurry! Get it done! Beat the season, or your neighbor. . . . A higher jump. . . . A swifter crossing. . . . A new record—for speed, size, or endurance.

Neither thoughtful design nor contemplation was easy in such an intellectual climate. Mental life consisted of a succession of fairly obvious problems, each to be solved by impulsive generalization. Naturally, thinking was for most men mere perceptual reaction. The inhibiting of impulse for moments of thoughtful choice between alternatives became a rare occurrence. Percept ruled over men's minds, and but few achieved the attitude of problem-solving and conceptual generalization.

Fifth, the guiding concepts of language.

The grip of the physical and mental climate on men's minds showed itself in their language. The vocabulary of the Westward movement—either of the frontier or the towns that rose behind it—abounded in action words. Utterance was primarily specification for construction. Build. . . . Make. . . . Do. . . . Tear the old one down, put the new one up. So widely pervasive did these ideas become that even a child in a city school responded to the question: "What is the first thing you do when you put up a new building?" with the confident reply, "You tear one down."

Although on Wednesday evenings and Sundays men monotonously hymned the words—Spirit . . . Soul . . . God . . . Heaven . . . Rest—it was lip service only to the words of meditation and contemplation.

The nouns as well as the verbs of the Machine Age vocabulary help to set for us subtle psychological problems. Although surrounded by a superabundance of natural resources and of skilled labor, machine technology was still undeveloped throughout the nineteenth century. So even in the midst of the enormous production of the World War and of the "prosperity" of the twenties men continued to speak the language of an economy of scarcity. Guiding their behavior were such concepts as: Increased production. . . . Free play for private initiative. . . . High profits. . . . Save and cumulate a surplus. . . . Invest in capital goods.

The compulsion of hurry ever confronted the American—whether set by the climatic exigencies of the growing season or by the competitive race with one's economic rivals. Hurry! Get it done! Beat the season, or your neighbor. . . . A higher jump. . . . A swifter crossing. . . . A new record—for speed, size, or endurance.

Neither thoughtful design nor contemplation was easy in such an intellectual climate. Mental life consisted of a succession of fairly obvious problems, each to be solved by impulsive generalization.

Thus the language was appropriate to the initial period of physical exploitation. It was the language of *defining,* not of *seeing;* and this was also inevitable in a First Day, in the dawn of the new technological culture.

4

SIXTH, *philosophy became merely a method of solving problems.*

One other mental trend seems to me as inevitable as the physical and social ones; namely, the evocation of American philosophers and of their pragmatic experimental philosophy. Between the Civil War and the World War both were produced by the evolving culture of industrialism. Two thinking men—Charles Peirce and John Dewey—blazed the new intellectual paths.[1]

Again we see how the culture produced the men and the theory of life. Peirce and Dewey were surrounded by the driving exploitation of the period of American expansion. Both were devotees of the scientific method. Peirce was practised in the processes of technology. He was, indeed, world acclaimed for his technical researches. He knew the physical basis of the new industrial culture "internally, in its own terms." Moreover, both Peirce and Dewey were professed students of logic. How predetermined it was, therefore, that the life work of each should have been given to formulating the scientific method of thought, rather than a theory of life. Pragmatism (or "pragmaticism," as he called it after his quarrel with James) was to Peirce, and Experimentalism was to Dewey, just that. It was a way—no, *the* way—of thinking. To neither one was it a way of living. Today, in chaotic transition years, it serves us as a perfect phrasing of one important kind of mental procedure, but not as a statement of objects of allegiance for a bewildered world.

It was, of course, a tremendous intellectual achievement, one that guarantees the two men an enduring place in the world's

---

[1] I exclude William James because he seems to me to have been much more the artist than the intellectual philosopher. James's whole creative life, from his youthful painting to his warping of Peirce's "pragmaticism" from a method of thought to a way of life reveals that. The point can be made best by comparing the productive work of James and Dewey.

annals of human thought. Standing aloof from the immediate action of the society, and seeing from a height its need for design, for plan, they saw what most men missed: namely, the prior need for a clarification of the processes of thinking. A technological civilization was in the making. The mental processes of invention and research and their application in the building of America must be subjected to scientific study. Psychology must be made scientific in order that a new generation of clearer minds could be produced. Hence "how we make our ideas clear" became with Peirce, and "how we think" with Dewey, the orienting objective of a life of study.

Living in a dynamic changing society they built their psychology on novel concepts. The first was that of *active* response. The new dictum of learning and growth became: We *react with* meaning; we do not absorb meaning by some passive process. A generation later schools began to rebuild their programs of study and their methods of teaching on the new idea.

Living in the midst of the research physiologists, neurologists, endocrinologists, Dewey perceived the significance of the integration principle in human behavior. We respond as living wholes— not as aggregates of separate traits. The nervous system, the anatomy of the body, the viscera, the glandular system—all constitute a unified whole. Moreover, the environment and the individual are fused parts of the same situation. Experience is correspondingly a unity. Ends are not separated from means. Mind is not independent of body. All are fused into one dynamic organic whole. Body and mind are Organism, not Mechanism. Thus the philosopher avoided the pitfalls of the mechanistic theories which trapped many of the psychologists of his day.

The foundational importance of these two concepts illustrates the manner in which the experimentalists sensed the scientific need of the closing years of the First Industrial Revolution. The Western world was rushing faster and faster toward the end of an epoch, and with it overwhelmingly complicated problems of social control. Whether the pragmatists generalized with respect to the problems of the economic-social system I am not sure. I doubt if even they saw that far beneath the surface of the social trend. But whether they did or not, they succeeded in building the chief psychological tool needed in our day for the social control of the environment. They gave us a clear idea of the method of problem-solving, an indispensable instrument to the industrial or to the social engineer.

But that they have generalized too far I am equally confident. Enamored with the charm of their experimentalism as a scientific method of thought, they conceived it to be *the only way* of re-sponse. "Thinking" to them constitutes all of mental activity. The experimental attitude of inquiry is the only psychological orientation to life. Life is visualized as a succession of problems. And the steps of problem-solving—viz. Dewey's *How We Think*—have been accepted by them as the only way of decent human response.

Thus they subsumed the two problems of design of our generation—social control and self-cultivation—under one category. The deliberate adoption of the problem-solving attitude was accepted as the appropriate means of orientation to either kind of situation. All "problems" were regarded as socially set; the end as well as the content and the method was found in the objective conditions of the external world, not in inner temperament. From their language was excluded the vocabulary of mood. The concept of "spirit" was anathema to their psychology. Appreciative awareness was explained in terms of measurement and analysis.

Correspondingly, the purpose of art became communication, message-giving, not self-cultivation. Artistic expression came to be regarded as language, not self-portraiture. The measure of excellence in the product was its rank order of comparison with the products of others, not with one's inner self.

These, then, are typical examples of the propulsive concepts and attitudes, and the guiding outlook of this First Day of industrial culture. It is not doubted that they produced remarkable physical achievements—a better standard of living, the general lengthening of life, the reduction of human fatigue, the increase of leisure activities, the creation of world-wide communication between peoples, the building of literacy among 600,000,000 people—to name only a few conspicuous changes which the new temper and ideas brought about. But that they also produced baffling social and personal problems for us who live just at the dawn of the second industrial stage is equally clear. Let us note next the manner in which our transition years were born out of the close of the first one.

5

CAREFUL ANALYSIS of social change, aided by the engineers' curves of technological advance, show us with some precision the approximate time at which one epoch definitely took the shape which marked its merging into another. The most pronounced point of change was the short period of the World War, 1914–1918. In these years population curves reveal points of inflexion, production curves rise more sharply, man-hour measures change more swiftly. Premonitions of the coming economic and social changes had, of course, been heralded a quarter century before, at the very moment of Stieglitz's return from Europe. Witness: such new inventions as the automobile, wireless communication, the motion-picture mechanism, the electric generator, and the central power station; the sharp changes in immigration from Nordic to Slavic and Latin Europe; the filling in of the last frontier; the marked drift from farm and rural village to manufacturing town and city; and the swift alteration of family, neighborhood, and community life and of long-established loyalties and allegiances.

From our vantage point of perspective today we can see that even if the First World War had been put off for another generation, the advance of social trend would have guaranteed that Western industrial peoples would shortly awake to find themselves in a new epoch. The probability is very great that the points of inflexion in the curves of social change would have emerged by the nineteen-forties. But the war was precipitated in 1914, and did speed up invention and technological advance enormously before 1919. Moreover, it altered every aspect of industrial culture, piling up national and international debts, upsetting the relations between interdependent peoples, and dislocating markets, currencies, popular faiths, and the march of political experiment.

Very few people perceived the accelerating influence of these on the changing economic-social system for more than a decade after the close of the war. For seven years dazed America danced on into another trade cycle of seeming prosperity. This short-lived period was marked by feverish expansion of production, construction, instalment buying, and the erection of a top-heavy structure of credit. The curves of debt claims mounted more rapidly even than those of production. The whole economic system became tenuous and fragile. Even the people of "education," anesthetized by the prosperity (a prosperity that even professed economists as well as two American Presidents declared was "here to stay"!), threw themselves into an orgy of speculation. Men appeared really to believe that an economic system could continue to expand on the principle that many of the people could live by getting something for nothing.

Meanwhile, in the research institutes of the great corporations, invention was subjected to the methods of mass production, and technological efficiency advanced by great strides. Every phase of the economic system was speeded up—the energy-converting power of engines, the integration of power, machines and processes in the automatic factory production; the productiveness of human labor, and hence the permanent displacement of workers. Even during the prosperous nineteen-twenties there were never fewer than two million unemployed workers in America. Competition for jobs became fiercer, and standards of living turned downward once more.

Increasingly the bargaining power of the owner and the employer was enhanced, but the worker lost control over his job, his wages, his standard of living, and his craftsmanship.

6

THEN CAME the well-known events of October, 1929, the crash of the financial house of cards and the shock to the economic mind of the nation. I have no space, and there is no need, to rehearse the manifold physical and psychological effects which followed upon these shaking happenings.

But one result is of far-reaching importance: namely, the dazed awakening of a thoughtful minority, at least, from the fantasies of the previous decades, and the vigorous launching of new scientific studies of industrial culture. The signs of the depression had scarcely revealed themselves before a brigade of students of the economic-social system began producing new analyses of it. In 1930–1931 a whole library of criticism and protest prepared the way for many careful studies and "plans" for a controlled economic system. The latter came from the pens of publicists, economists, historians, chambers of commerce, captains of industry, labor leaders, bishops of the churches, presidents and faculties of colleges.

A new body of creative students also entered the sociological laboratory. Engineers, ousted from their professional work, and free of the academic blinders of classical thought, graphed economic history and fitted equations to the curves of the trend. World-renowned scientists applied their concepts of energy and life and their scientific methods to the study of the economic system. Thus the current years have launched what promises to become the most creative period in the history of modern thought and social organization.

As a consequence, it has been made clear to us that we today are caught between two stages of economic and social change. These stages are, at bottom, very different. A few contrasting characteristics will illustrate the difference and set the chief cultural problem which our generation must solve.

First: Whereas the first epoch was one of *expansion,* of positively accelerating growth, the second is to be one of *consolidation.* As a single example, consider the change in population growth. Although the American population doubled every twenty years from 1790 to 1920, it has now reached a plateau; births and other accretions only barely equal deaths and withdrawals. No longer can the concept of "more people" motivate the operation of the American economic system. Our language must now discard that concept and use that of a "static population."

Second: The orgy of sheer physical building is over. The major part of the economic system is erected. We have passed out of the wasteful Machine Age of crude steam engines, slipping belts, and creaking pulleys and gears into the Power Age of efficient giant generators, long-distance power transmission, and automatic continuous straight-line process factory production. The implications of this for thinking men are clear; they cannot deal with the problems of the new day with the concepts of the old one. For example, *we no longer live in a régime of scarcity; we have already passed into the day of potential plenty. For the first time in the world's history man in America can now produce a civilization of abundance for all.* And our language and thought must from now on show that we know it.

Third: The initial exploitation for immediate private profit and personal aggrandizement of the first epoch must give way in the second to designed and controlled production for the total group. Our new era of plenty is only a potential, not an actual one. To bring it into existence will require the building of a distribution system which is coördinate in effectiveness with the production system which has already been erected. But to do that in a democratic society, many minds must be made aware of the necessity of deep-running changes in the ownership and operation of basic utilities and industries.

That is, new problems of social control now confront us, and to deal with them we must build a new language of discourse. In a régime of initial exploitation of virgin continents, the concepts of laissez-faire, of success via competition, were useful, perhaps indispensable. But in a régime like our own, (1) in which an efficient production system has already been erected; (2) in which there is no longer any relation between what a worker can produce and the share of the social income which society can pay him as purchasing power; (3) in which it is increasingly evident that profits and fixed charges take an undue proportion of the social income; (4) in which competition interrupts the operation of the system and withholds much of it from use; in such a régime, I say, the concepts of *scarcity, laissez-faire, private ownership and control of basic industries and utilities constitute the vocabulary of a foreign and useless language.*

Fourth: As a final illustration, we must note that intellectually and spiritually the second industrial age is also new. We have moved from an epoch which demanded action and percept above all things, into one in which design and realization are possible. Indeed, two crucial problems of design confront us in the Great Transition. There is first the problem of designing a social structure that will produce the economy of abundance which is guaranteed by our resources and our technology. There is second the problem of designing a creative and appreciative personal way of life within that structure. The nub of the former is social control; that of the latter is self-cultivation. The guide to the former is the technologist and experimentalist; the guide to the latter is the artist. The truly great culture on the verge of which we now stand cannot be ushered in if either of these problems of design is ignored.

The documentation of the preceding pages provides abundant evidence that the problem of designing a controlled social structure is being vigorously attacked. The creative activity of the students of the "new social order" guarantee that these problems will not be neglected. Day by day the high potential productivity of the economic system is being better documented, and more and more minds are being convinced that the system cannot be run on a niggardly purchasing power for the rank and file of the people who must buy back the goods they produce. The brigade of creative students of social reconstruction is steadily being augmented. Space need not be taken in this essay to enlist more recruits for that enterprise.

7

To SKETCH briefly these sharp contrasts between the two epochs is to set the chief creative task of our transition years. The passing of an epoch inevitably produces chaos and bewilderment. So it is with our current years; they are essentially years of drift, of lack of direction, of confusion of problems, of ends, of next steps. Hence the dire need is for clarification—clarification of trends and factors, of problems and ends; clarification of alternative courses of action, of probable consequences, of loyalties and allegiances.

But for the clarification of meaning a new language is needed. We have seen that the problems of the second stage of industrialism simply cannot be thought about by means of the ideas and methods of thinking which dominated the mind of the first stage. New concepts must be found to fit the new situations. A new orientation, born of the current trends, is demanded. We are now confronted with problems of articulation in a period in which the language of our childhood must be discarded and a new one devised. And that will prove to be the major creative task of our Great Transition.

But the solution of these problems of social and personal design can be achieved only by means of a drastic revolutionary educational procedure. The Americans, at least a considerable minority of them, must learn how to combine efficient technological operation with democratic control, to establish government by the consent of the governed through education in tolerant and critical understanding; to develop interest and ability in creative labor; in short, to apply the scientific method to the Man-Man relationships and to live creatively as Artist as well as Technologist.

But, I repeat, to consummate these things under a democratic form of society (and any other form is totally repugnant to most of us) our recourse must be to education. Standing at the end of the first industrial epoch and at the beginning of the second, our problems, both social and personal, are educational ones. New minds are to be created. New personalities are to be brought forth. A new orientation to life is to be developed. A new language must be evolved. But these are all products of education. They can be brought forth only by many of the people taking thought about their society and their personal lives. So it is great teachers that we need in these chaotic years; teachers who see clearly through the tangled maze of current trends. Some of these must be rigorous students of social reconstruction; others will be masters of personal self-cultivation.

Can we expect to find these in large numbers in the present teaching body of the nation? We cannot, indeed. Teachers, whether of college or primary school, are adrift. Like the general population, they are the inevitable product of the mechanical system which day by day they perpetuate.

It was no doubt to be expected that the rank and file of teachers in the years of transition would be bewildered, uncertain, lacking either a social program or a design for personal living. We must not forget that the nineteenth century was the first in human history in which the experiment of universal elementary education was tried. Hence it would be asking too much of the first century of public education to demand that it achieve more than the administrative thing. That much, at least, was done, not only in America but also in Britain, France, Japan—in all industrializing nations. Ninety-odd per cent of the children of "educational age" were herded into "school" and classified into regiments and companies. School buildings—in America very efficient ones—were erected to house them. Teachers were brought together in "normal schools" and taught what "the book said." Courses of study of intellectual subject matter and sets of textbooks were prepared and graded to fit the year-groupings of the young people.

Thus in a century of hustling physical construction, a graded school system, national in scope and fitted to the chronological development of childhood and youth, emerged in every manufacturing country. Within it education was conceived to be: (1) something that went on in a "school," five hours a day, one hundred and eighty days a year, apart from the home and community life which created it; (2) something one did before entering life—a preparation for life; (3) something one did with books, with words, not with the body, the spirit, all the sensibilities, the entire organism.

This, then, was the outcome of the first century of universal education. In every industrial nation the result was much the same—a standardized mechanism, a national replica of the technological culture that sponsored it, perfectly appropriate to the mechanistic psychology that guided education within it. Most of the administrators and teachers were conformists and routinists following a disciplinary psychology of ancient history. And of those in the mass school who were "forward looking," the vast preponderance went with Thorndike and the behaviorist company rather than with Dewey and the organic group. Some tens of thousands were exposed more recently to the concept of active, integrated response, but of these only a very small number really understood the theory and its implications for curriculum and learning.

Teachers, then, have come out of colleges and normal schools utterly lacking either in personal philosophy or sense of social direction. Confronted by this crisis they lack understanding either of the pressing economic and political problems or of the historical trends and factors which produced them. Faced with the task of total reconstruction of the school program they flounder helplessly. Hence their need, like that of their people, is not only for a social program; it is equally the need to build a personal philosophy of living. And for these there are two types of teacher and guide—the technologist of social reconstruction and the artist.

8

THANKS to four centuries of scientific inquiry, and to the experimentalists' heroic efforts to phrase the scientific method of thought, the sources for a new language and a new theory of social control are fairly well developed. Certainly it should not be a superhuman task for the creative energies of Western men to construct in the next generation working hypotheses for a collective society. It will of course be infinitely more difficult to put them into practicable operation, with the log of intelligent understanding and the social control of education and the other agencies of communication among the chief obstacles.

But the real danger of the Great Transition is that its creative minds shall take their cues solely from the students of social control, either the practical technologists or the theoretical experimentalists. For the problem of designing a personal way of life appropriate to the new Second Day of industrialism not only parallels in importance and difficulty that of designing the new social structure itself, *it is in addition a different problem*. Men must live with themselves as well as with their fellows. This presents the unique problem of appreciative awareness and self-cultivation. The danger is that men of creative potential, absorbed in the insistent social problems of the day, will ignore the equally imperative task of self-cultivation.

That brings us to the artist, for he is the master of self-cultivation. Whereas the scientific student of society supplies us with concepts and methods with which to build a new social order, the artist supplies us the key to the design of personal living. The concepts and methods of both are necessary. No matter how efficient its technology or how humane its government, no culture will be truly great if it does not instil a high order of appreciative awareness in the people. It is clear, therefore, that the adventure of beauty calls us as well as the effort of reason.

Herein, I think, lies the true importance of Alfred Stieglitz to our troubled times, and the reason why we should celebrate his life by striving to see the rôle of the artist in the difficult years ahead. He is important because he integrates the twofold rôle of the artist and the teacher in one personality. In an economic period in which it was practically impossible for the true artist to secure an audience and earn a competence, Stieglitz has, in spite of obstacle piled upon obstacle, maintained his integrity as a creative artist and a teacher of Man-as-Artist.

As for the former he imposed upon himself the task of employing the most difficult medium of all the means of personal expression—the camera—to portray organic life. That is, he employed Mechanism to reveal Organism. Most of his contemporaries in the arts—painters, sculptors, dancers, and others—used the more natural means of expression, the human organism, to portray organism; most of these succeeded only in achieving superficial photography. Their art products were little more than representation of the superfices of life. Thus Stieglitz has served his baffled era first by a life of creative expression, by giving an example of the true artist; in his case by using a mechanical instrument to lay bare the moving life below the surface of organic nature things. For this achievement alone his record will persist long.

But in addition to the example which he has set he has served his times more directly as a great teacher. I refer to his quarter century of heroic effort, first to establish and maintain a purely American Place, and second, to help the artist to become articulate and to clarify his meaning of life and its portraiture.

In the former effort Stieglitz is the continuator in our time of the tradition launched by Emerson and Whitman and Louis Sullivan in their respective generations of American development. These men also strove to create the tradition of the American thing. They tried to visualize the unique indigenous American person, and through multitudes of him, the honest creative America. This, as I see it, is Stieglitz's great contribution to our day, for in 291, in the Intimate Gallery, and in An American Place he sheltered and prodded, disciplined and encouraged, a fine company of struggling and harassed creative Americans.

In the fullest sense of the word every community in America should have its American Place. This would be the true culture center in which people would come together both for personal self-cultivation through creative production and for social participation in the coöperative community. In such a place Persons—honest, efficient, and integral Persons—would be produced. Each person would respect and admire the integrity and efficiency of each other person. In such a cultural milieu the life of honest integral acts would be lived. The great society would be guaranteed because great individuals would be the product. To such an American Place the current widespread mode of hypocrisy would be an incredible way of life. The very basis of life in it would be the integrity of each human act—the spoken sentence, the answer to another's question, the production of any craft goods, of a book, a verse, a house, a dramatic scene. Each human act would be accepted as an honest objectification of the self. Each Person would be accepted as Man-as-Artist, striving constantly to speak, to write, to make, to live, *what he is*. Because of his personal philosophy of life that he had evolved himself, each would utter only what he is.

It is such a cultural milieu that I visualize for the ideal school; hence my admiration for Stieglitz's exemplification of the traits needed most in the American teacher. His American Place is a nurturing place; each school in America should become a true American Place. In a great society, "the school," in the broadest sense, would be the culture nurturing place, the true center of the community.

But Stieglitz has nurtured the artist in ways other than by practising his own art creatively and by sheltering the artist and exhibiting his products. He has furthered also the artists' struggle with the problems of articulation and clarification of meaning. And the need at this point is a dire one, for while the vocabulary of social control is being steadily augmented and a clearer theory evolved, that of personal culture is being sadly neglected. Most artists are, indeed, inarticulate about self-expression. Few of them write, and fewer turn their insight into verbal studies which will promote general understanding. But Stieglitz, through his publication of photographs and of essays, verse, letters, and other personal documents, and through his talk, has contributed to this crucial problem of clarification of meaning.

Many of the writers in this volume have commented on the fact that Alfred Stieglitz is always talking. I have long felt that as one of the most desirable qualities of the Place. I have, in fact, always sent my students to him with the direction, "Go, and look at Marin and O'Keeffe and the others on those clear walls, and if Stieglitz believes you are sincerely trying to find something there for your life he will talk to you. His talk may appear to be unorganized, if judged by academic standards. It may seem disjointed and even superficial to the casual listener or the pragmatic problem solver. But don't be a problem solver in his presence. Strive to be receptive and aware in listening to his talk as you will in becoming alive to the pictures on his walls. Remember that this man is struggling with novel problems of articulation and meaning. He is honestly striving to find out. And that alone justifies both speech and audience. Without systematic psychological design he is contributing his bits to the structure of a new language of appreciative awareness. Don't look for the everyday vocabulary of thinking, and don't pass over what may seem to be superficial comments. Look at the pictures of life on the walls and listen to the talk about life from the Man. Moreover, go back again and again and continue to look and to listen."

These, then, are the traits and the function of the American Place and of the Artist and Teacher who lives in it. These are what I crave for ten thousand centers in America. At last they can be produced if we will become sufficiently aware of the problem, and—if we commit ourselves to its solution.

Evelyn Howard

The Significance of Stieglitz
for the Philosophy of Science

WHAT IS THIS MAN Stieglitz? He himself has said that he is a workman who has been all his life on a strike.

Stieglitz has lived to do many things which are nevertheless always the same thing. He has lived to protect life: he has lived to shelter beauty—the all enveloping subtle beauty which interprets life, orders life, and gives it meaning. Stieglitz has seen very clearly into the significance of art—he seems almost to have seen the human spirit itself. The intense life of this spirit is its expression in art, and this life that flowers into beauty is so fragile, so tender, so beset with dangers outside and within itself. These perils are many, and the most insidious of them is the domination of the will-to-know.

From out of these enveloping dangers Stieglitz gives an incarnation and a home to beauty. This he does in many ways to some extent in every contact, however slight: it is a part of his being alive. His epitomized expression of himself is his photography, which is one of the most direct expressions the human spirit has ever achieved; direct and at the same time rich in its contacts with subtle complexities which prolong themselves into arborizations extending infinitely into mystery. He says many things in his photographs, but he also says many of the same things in words and inevitably in deeds. In various places he has hung on the walls the work of various artists, and he has worked to protect the pure life of true intensity, whether that life is in the artist who is trying to speak or only in the person who is trying to hear and to see. For Stieglitz is not concerned with individuals but with forces at work—forces which exist in various persons in many degrees of purity—forces which are attaining their maximum effectiveness in our time in such artists as Marin and O'Keeffe. Stieglitz has worked to protect even the physical life of these artists who are such important sources of significant life for all people. But while protecting the source he is always ready to give ear to the frailest voice of new-born truth in any of those who come to see the pictures that he has hung.

These people who come: they are the casual public in which everything exists—thrust and counter thrust—God and Devil. In them the world comes to Stieglitz, and he listens to them and says to them the things that his life is always saying in a thousand ways. He hears their voices and reënforces what is in them that is of the good. For there is always to be heard the voice of the living beauty, and often it is struggling against the lust for knowledge. There is the girl who says, "I love this picture," and there is the man who says, "What does this picture represent—what is the meaning of it—why do you consider it beautiful?" Stieglitz's answer to the man is, "Why is a woman beautiful?," and then Stieglitz goes on to say many things which mean that some things cannot be told —essentially we cannot learn from words because words are no greater than are we ourselves. Words are always less than we are —sometimes very much less.

Wagner's King Mark thought, when he had been told about the *Liebestrank,* that he understood life and could control living. But could he alter the course of conflicting loves by his desire for renunciation? Tristan and Isolde could not live: together they achieved the all-excluding death which together they had chosen at the first. The knowledge of the *Liebestrank* acted to protect King Mark from the realities of death and love—that knowledge gave him less contact with life instead of more.

And so the reality of the meaning of a picture cannot be explained, it must be seen: the living life of the picture must fuse with the living life of the man who sees it—he must drink it—he must eat this body-of-Christ—he must let it enter into him until he knows it in the same way that he knows that he himself is himself. And no man can help him in this knowledge—beyond showing him the picture, and shielding him from false sophistications. As for the artist who creates beauty—he must know surely that he does not know what he is doing—he knows that he dare not even look to find out—or looking, Orpheus he will become, with his beloved lost.

Must no one look? Is all knowledge delusion and a snare of sophistications? What is our science—has it any real life or is it just a set of rules in a mechanical game—rules which hold sometimes and then sometimes do not hold? In the daytime this game of science is very absorbing. In the daytime we are safely enclosed under the blue dome of the sky, everything can be seen clearly, and all is rational and safe. But at night—at night we see that the blue dome was an illusion, all about us is infinite space—infinite mystery outside and within. Science, what *is* the night?

In our far-off beginnings, when the desire to know first opened its eyes, science and religion were indistinguishable. They were the expression of man's first awe and love and wonder of the world of mystery which surrounded him. And so also art arose to express these feelings. Albert Einstein has said:

> The most beautiful thing we can experience is the mysterious. It is the source of all true art and science. He to whom this emotion is a stranger, who can no longer pause to wonder and stand rapt in awe, is as good as dead, his eyes are closed.

However, in the mêlée of our exuberantly verbal and triumphantly systematic civilization, art and love and religion and science have all become separated and have all become intellectualized. All alike suffer in the same way, although the devitalization of art and religion is more apparent to the man in the street than it is in the case of science. Science seems, judged by its practical results, to be exhibiting exuberant vitality. Could anything now be wrong in science?

It is the fortune and the misfortune of science that it can go a long way without breathing. Each time science really draws a breath, so much can be done with it that it is not necessary to breathe very often; in fact, it may be actually inconvenient.

Science advances in two very different ways. To take the more obvious way first, science is developed by taking as a basis known properties of things and measuring them more accurately, or more thoroughly, or under experimentally varied conditions, whereby certain already established patterns of concept relations may be strengthened, clarified, limited, extended, or negated. In this way, by proceeding step by step in logical sequence and in honorable toil, vast technical advance is made, and also theoretically valuable data are accumulated whereby important generalizations of our knowledge become possible. This aspect of science is easy to justify economically and consequently affords an occupation to large numbers of people. But this logically developed scientific activity is always based on sensually apprehended properties of things—and how is our awareness of these properties achieved? How else but by a direct perceptual apprehension which fuses to the sensual perceptions of the artist without absolute demarcation. It is from a kind of direct communion of the spirit of man with external reality that there arises in the minds of men a fundamentally new conception

of a property of nature. It is when this thing happens that science draws a breath.

The fact that the newly apprehended property of nature is natural does not imply that it is simple—it may or may not require elaborate experimental technique or elaborate ratiocination for its detection. Whether or not the newly apprehended property is classified as important fundamentally would seem to depend on the extent to which the new property is general in nature, but the degree to which this can be determined at any one time depends on the degree of advancement of science in general, as well as upon the intellectual skill of the observer.

The scientist, then, always is privileged to yearn and wonder and muse over strange little things that do not seem to fit in the established system of conceptual relations, and this yearning over tender, delicate little strange things, this sense of wonder in the face of nature's mystery, seems at present to be qualitatively as close as man can get to an understanding of nature. Quantitatively the communion can be enormously increased as our scientific awareness of phenomena and their interrelationships is increased—actually who can tell the possibilities of the future in this awareness of communion? We do not sit down and think out in the abstract what our future scientific progress is to be.

D. H. Lawrence says:

> *The mystery of creation is the divine urge of creation,*
> *but it is a great strange urge, it is not a Mind.*
> *Even an artist knows that his work was never in his mind,*
> *he could never have* thought *it before it happened.*
> *A strange ache possessed him, and he entered the struggle,*
> *and out of the struggle with his material, in the spell of the urge*
> *his work took place, it came to pass, it stood up and saluted his mind.*

And in that way science takes another breath.

Science demands of its greatest followers that they be capable of great living direct perceptual insight, roving hearts and eyes which forever refuse to be bound by their intellectual conceptions—and in the same breath they must be capable of intensive intellectual use of concepts. This duality of the greatest scientific natures we are inclined to forget. Far more of our so-called scientists achieve intellectuality than retain a sense of wonder. Men become expert technicians and can no longer look on nature face to face. All too often men judge science by certain dry-rotten academicians who are credited to be scientists—and forget that the real science is a far deeper, more mysterious communion with reality than the majority of professional scientists could remember they had ever dreamed of.

Our minds, in the grip of the will-to-know, demand that science explain phenomena. A student wants to know what electricity is, and why it is as it is. He takes a course in physics and learns certain things about electricity, certain laws which govern its action. It then may happen that he feels baffled because he cannot understand *why* these things are so. He may even feel that he cannot understand science, that it is all beyond him. But he is asking for too much, and the truth is that science does not explain electricity, it merely describes its properties. So the artist does not explain his picture, he merely creates it. Will science ever be able to explain the properties of matter? Who can answer? Meanwhile it lures us on.

Our scientific pattern of the universe at present is composed of certain descriptions of comparatively separate categories of phenomena. The thing as a whole defies description—although we are inclined to forget our ignorance in our self-satisfaction at what we have achieved. The comparative insignificance of the scientific laws which have been formulated up to now may well be epitomized by these remarks of L. J. Henderson:

> . . . the process of the evolution of the earth appears . . . as a continuous production of many systems related together in an orderly manner from few original systems, and . . . these systems are not only very numerous but also very diverse and often very stable. Further, we have seen that there is ground for the belief that the more important conditions which make possible this evolutionary process are the specific *characteristics* of matter and energy as they coöperate in the process, rather than the most general *laws* of physical science.

So our vast systems of knowledge can only conclude that the world is as it is because it has certain properties. Nevertheless, the interrelationships of these properties reveal most wonderfully ordered activities in nature.

The spirit of Stieglitz expresses that which is at the tip of the arrow of the direction in which our nature is working to move. That tip of the spirit strives to put man's psyche in relation to all the enveloping mystery in which man is swallowed up—the mystery that makes of man's own soul an inward unknown surrounded by a little shell of mind, floating in a vast sea of unfathomable universe. Art in its pure self is an expression of the intuition of the human unconscious regarding its own unknown life of sensation and emotion. Science is an approach toward the whole mystery using a different technique—a technique whereby the sensuality of color and sound is replaced by the sensuality of thought.

Science yearns over nature, as does art, trying always to touch with the sensualities of its truths, creating as it moves on always new perceptions of beauty in new truths or new enticing, luring mysteries. So as it goes it accidentally throws back over its shoulder telephones, X-ray machines, vaccines: conveniences for the body and perhaps inconveniences for the mind.

Living art leaves in its wake organizations of line and color and sound which speak much more directly to the longing and wonder in our minds—to the intuitively alive person art speaks directly—only needing as connection the impress life has made on us or on our ancestors. Through the crevasses which ecstatic joy or suffering have broken through the insulation of the soul—through these crevasses art can enter and communicate with the soul directly—pour through man's being its strong current. One of the chief differences between art and science is that, although science requires no greater discipline of its active followers than does art, it cannot give nearly so much at second hand. A scientist can "enjoy" art—but does an artist ever "enjoy" science? An artist can speak to all who are alive—by contrast a scientist is held almost incommunicado.

Yet art and science is each in its essence adoration of the one mystery—through different types of sensual touch. And Alfred Stieglitz, in serving the essence of art so valiantly, in so uncompromisingly taking his stand to keep alive the fragile and easily thwarted instinct in man to achieve a valid and direct nonintellectualized communion with nature—in doing these things Stieglitz has served not only art but also and no less science. Hermann von Helmholtz once wrote, when thermodynamics had just been born, "Our generation has continued to suffer from the thraldom of spiritualist metaphysics. The younger generation will doubtless have to protect itself against the thraldom of materialist metaphysics." We are now that younger generation, and Alfred Stieglitz has long been to us an unerring protector.

To return to Stieglitz's championship of the right of the picture to speak for itself: he can do this because he knows that in the scientific sense the picture is a real force which can actually cause a given effect in its beholder. Stieglitz has not only loved art, he has loved people also, and so, loving both people and art, he has studied their interactions. He has seen that certain abstract pictures cause certain effects in people—that these effects are reproducible from one person to another: they are not arbitrarily variable but they fulfill the condition of regular manifestation by which science is accustomed to establish the existence of material phenomena. So that extra-verbal perception is far from being reduced to an arbitrary stimulation with an unpredictable result. Naturally, the manifestation of the result may vary, since people differ greatly in the degree to which they react and in the degree to which they are able to express, or even be conscious of, their own emotional reactions; nevertheless, the emotional reactions occur as regular results of truly existing forces.

The reality of the action of a picture on people becomes most starkly evident in the case of an abstract picture: abstract in the sense that it does not represent any physical object. Such a picture is born of subconscious emotional symbols in the artist. These symbols can speak directly to the emotions of the beholder—if he has been somehow sensitized by life—or else not blinded by life. An abstract picture is one which is completely free of extraneous associational appeal—hence one in which the reality of art is present in its greatest purity. If an abstract picture is less powerful than a realistic one, it is because its art is less powerful, the power of the realist is not a result of his realism. I am enabled to say this because of Stieglitz's photographs, many of which are abstractions in the sense that they do not present images of physical objects. To say that a photograph does not present an image means that the image of the thing has only the significance that paint has as paint. Such abstraction existing so clearly particularly in photography is a challenging commentary on all art. It is Stieglitz speaking.

There is furthermore something of tremendous general import implied in Stieglitz's philosophy which is also implied by the generalizations of the scientist Lawrence Henderson. These two men, with completely different materials, are both pointing in the same direction, as would two different parts in the design of a picture. This picture is none other than the essence of our very lives; it contains ecstasy, and also it contains the crucifixion against which one writhes in impotent rebellion, and perhaps it also contains peace.

The current philosophical conceptions with which science has replaced the religion of former generations emphasize the unimportance of the individual. The explanation of physical phenomena as resulting from statistically random variations in molecular and sub-molecular entities is not edifying to contemplate: it reduces life to a game of chance. The conception of evolution as a resultant of random mutations and survival of the fittest: this neo-Darwinian statisticism, if it was ever actually accepted, would annihilate Nature's precious race by annihilating the individuals of which it is composed. For the necessary thing about life is that it seem important to the one who is living it—that the game be worth the candle.

When religion satisfied men it gave them the continual conviction that God was ever present and ever powerful in their daily lives. Man could accept in living peace the sorrows of Job if he continually believed that God sent them—a God just and good and powerful—and purposeful beyond his understanding. But if one believes that sorrow comes to one from chance, because a certain proportion of people always suffer owing to a chance unfortunate combination of hereditary and environmental influences—in the bitterness of such sorrow one cries why, why to unanswering heaven: why must life exist when it results in such purposeless

suffering—what possible reason can there be for the miserable concatenation of electrons that is oneself to struggle any longer to endure this futile torture? To such sorrow of the individual the spectacle of the evolution of the race as a result of fortuitous variation and natural selection offers very little consolation. For the individual can make himself important to himself up to a certain point, and beyond that personal point he is a small speck in a seething hostile chaos, unless he can envisage order in the universe, and, more than that, order in significant important relationship to his personal self.

Science has recently envisioned a new category of order, which almost seems as if it might grow to satisfy this terrible need in man.

It is a philosophical truism that an event may have a purposive cause and a mechanical cause at one and the same time. Thus, if a man starts the motor of his automobile, he starts it with the purpose of going somewhere, that is the purposive cause, whereas his act of putting his foot on the starter is the mechanical cause of the chain of mechanical events which results in the starting of the motor. In this example it is important to realize that the purposive cause operates via the mechanical cause and that the two are co-existent: the existence of one does not exclude the other. Medieval science was greatly hampered by its tendency to emphasize the purposive cause in an arbitrary manner rather than to attempt the study of the mechanical cause. Modern science studies only the mechanical cause: a true and valid approach to the purposive cause is our most fundamental contemporary problem.

This problem is nowhere more acute than in the attempts to understand the process of organic evolution. The hypothesis is current that evolution has resulted from random self-perpetuating mutations in the genetic units, and survival of those variations which proved favorable. Although this might account for certain characteristics, it seems difficult to account mathematically for the coördination of adaptations on such a basis. Furthermore, it is doubtful if anyone has ever actually witnessed the occurrence of a favorable mutation: certainly most mutations have less survival value rather than more, whereas adaptation to an unaccustomed and initially unfavorable environment seems to occur frequently. In short, the problem of teleology, or apparent directedness, in organic evolution remains quite unsolved. Lawrence Henderson has pointed out that there is superimposed upon the problem of teleology in organic evolution a similar teleology in the physical world. Henderson arrives at this conclusion from purely physical considerations of the properties of matter. He states:

The unique ensemble of properties of water, carbonic acid, and the three elements hydrogen, carbon, and oxygen constitutes the fittest ensemble of characteristics for durable mechanism . . . the fittest for mechanism in general, not for any special form of mechanism, such as life as we know it. . . . Nearly each of the properties of these elements is almost or quite unique, either because it has a maximum or a minimum value, or nearly so, among all known substances, or because it involves a unique relationship or an anomaly.

Thus the properties of the three most abundant chemical elements make possible the production of stable and diversified systems in place of the original condition of unstable homogeneity; in other words, favor organic evolution.

Nor can we look upon these peculiarities of the matter which make up the universe as in any sense the work of chance, or as mere contingency. There is, in truth, not one chance in countless millions that the many unique properties of carbon, hydrogen, and oxygen, and especially of their stable compounds water and carbonic acid, which chiefly make up the atmosphere of a new planet, should simultaneously occur in the three elements otherwise than through the operation of a natural law which somehow connects them together. There is no greater probability that these unique properties should be without due (i.e. relevant) cause uniquely favorable to the organic mechanism. We are obliged to regard this collocation of properties as in some intelligible sense a preparation for the processes of biological evolution.

Thus science is faced with the question, not only of the origin of teleology, or adaptation to a purpose, in the qualities of living organisms, but with the teleological adaptation of the inorganic universe itself. We see that what occurs in the organism occurs in inorganic nature—an adaptation to the purposes of life. The two categories, animate and inanimate, are working together. The activity of the universe is an organic whole. There is no line of demarcation between living and not living: all matter is organized for the end of organic evolution—whatever that may be.

So science has come around a great circle, and from demolishing the old conceptions according to which the sun moved around man's earth, science finds itself faced with an appearance of teleology omnipresent perhaps in every quality of the universe. Henderson points out that the significance of the properties of matter are only revealed by the passage of geological time. Compared to the implications of Henderson's conclusions, the older religious conceptions appear as child's play.

Teleology, then, is omnipresent, and it is so unattackable from the point of view of mechanistic science that we seem to be led to the conclusion that throughout all nature there is a purposive cause which coexists with the mechanistic cause. Hence it seems quite possible that any event has a dual aspect, it is a result of a physical "chance" juxtaposition of forces, and of a metaphysical purpose. Hence an event may occur as a result of general laws, and yet at the same time have a completely individual purpose.

The particular personal significance of an event is the meaning that is revealed in a Cézanne pattern of apples, or in a Stieglitz vision of a "chance" juxtaposition of clouds—or hands. It is that which gives human meaning to the greatest art. Nowhere is this purposive interrelationship of all things more consistently presented than in the work of Stieglitz.

This duality of causation which seems to occur in nature seems to extend also to one's personal life in a very definite way. In the realm of psychological mechanics, one may discern an absolute and necessary causal relationship of each circumstance in one's life to the past and to the future. At the same time one may discern a pattern which seems to be teleologically controlled. For example, one seems to fail at something in one's life—one often fails over and over again. If one can see clearly and honestly one sees that it is not life that is at fault, but one's self, because always the same things happen to one, different in circumstances but the same in inward personal significance. So one may discern Nature working on one—trying to mold something in one by a long laborious process. Changes are wrought one molecule at a time. Nature tests each new call before letting it enter into her established framework. This molding, this erosion of life—what is it but teleology in the personal sphere? Nature works on our personalities with a definite directedness. Nature is not always easy to understand, and especially when she sends us unhappiness we are inclined to conclude she is talking nonsense. But honesty and humility and courage, which together are the basis of art, are capable of coördinating what happens to us in a way which reveals its significant meaning. Tragedy becomes a great thing when its protagonist understands that he is receiving something vital and tremendous from life at the moment when he is most completely failing in what he wanted to do.

Very often we do not succeed in achieving greatness in tragedy or in discerning any purpose in the apparently blind misfortune that is always somewhere in the world. Better to leave tragedy unexplained than to force a false explanation. Our minds cannot grasp more than an infinitesimal part of the past and future implications of any happening. Our immediate world is always changing: the justice of yesterday becomes the injustice of today, and our source of glowing happiness becomes our most poignant sorrow. One may have his life arranged in tranquil joy, and then there comes a seemingly arbitrary devastation. Sometimes it only seems to serve to make one ask why—"Why should my happiness be thus destroyed?" Even to ask that question has its value. One may answer: "Possibly because all things are so utterly interrelated that no man may be secure in personal happiness while there remains one of his brothers who is unfulfilled." An ideal being would suffer as much from the sorrow of another as from his own, merely knowing of its existence. For those of us who are limited in our sympathy, the interrelations of circumstance perhaps arrange that we suffer eventually because of the results of the sorrows of others. Thereby life gives to man, belatedly, ironically, but actually, an aspect of the divinity which suffers from any sorrow. Each selfish man is somewhere vulnerable, has some point on which the chain of causation can work. No one can be sure of security for his children in a world in which insecurity exists. Sensitive natures who have achieved what most men consider as the conditions of personal happiness, become then explorers in the realms of sorrow: they must push on, detecting always new imperfections, their share of the blows that are welding the world.

The function of the greatest art is to discern and to avow the teleology in our personal lives, as science discerns the teleology in the external world. The utter purposive arrangement of all things which the scientist Henderson discerns in physical matter the artist Stieglitz sees almost every minute in the personal eventual world. So seeing, one can have nothing but complete faith. Every single thing that happens to one is literally and absolutely the speaking of God. Would God speak always in words of one syllable?

So science has destroyed a god which had died in our minds and become a graven image, and science and art together seem to be revealing something infinitely more perfect.

This faith in the complete presence of teleology cannot become dogma. Science has not proved anything. Science has suggested that something seems to be shaping itself to unknown ends but implicitly controlled in every detail. Art proves nothing. It simply exists and can be read. This faith is not based on ideas but directly on scientific concepts and on artistic feelings. It may fade away if too strong a light is turned on it, just as a delicate structure in a microscopic field becomes invisible if the illumination is too diffuse.

There is in all this no promise of anything. But there is a ubiquitous pattern of directedness in nature. There is the possibility of faith—a faith which not only frees but requires one's entire intelligence—a faith which, like life itself, is forever just ahead, forever waiting to be realized.

Waldo Frank

The New World in Stieglitz

THE CROWNING FUNCTION of a world is to create the energy that will destroy it, the idea and form that will replace it. This activity takes the form of a variant from the world's current values, and it is often personified in the lives of historic men.

Thus Socrates. He lived at a time when the ethos voiced by the Ionian school was breaking. Consciousness in these early Europeans had been a simple awareness of the Whole. The person was not objective; as a man came to know himself he knew at once the cosmos. And nature, to man, was not objective: it was composed of psychic forces—gods, or of one substance—as in Thales, Heraclitus, and not of elements each real in its own right. This world in our terms lacked both psychology and science. In its decadence, the pre-Socratic Greeks needed to become aware of parts—of self and of things. By analysis, they broke up the undifferentiate oneness of the archaic Mediterranean world; for if the components of existence were considered independently real, they might be examined and mastered. The dualism of the Eleatics marked the birth of this new ethos, whose first step was to separate the subject from the object. Now, vividly in his life, Socrates enacted the division of "soul" from body and from the things of nature. Like a chemical reagent, his *behavior* precipitated the monism of a childlike world into elements which Plato, Aristotle—Europe, would study and control: the "ideal" of reason and the "material" of nature.

Thus Paul of Tarsus. He lived at the time of the agony of national Judaism. Early Judaism had not been troubled by the contradictions of a culture that claimed to be both special and universal. But the Law had become too rigid to breathe. The arms of Rome and the thinkers of Alexandria precipitated the crisis: universal Judaism, in order to survive, needed to leave its parent, the national Judaism of the Law, taking along into another body the passion and the vision. In the life of Paul, who turned the Jewish Law into a symbol of the captivity of the Jewish nation and made of Christian Grace the symbol of release, this painful rebirth was personified and prospered.

Thus (to leap to our day) Karl Marx. The bourgeois-Protestant culture to which Marx belonged, the culture of eighteenth-century rationalism and nineteenth-century romanticism and capitalism, had nurtured the value of individual freedom and its postulate, social progress, which derived from the notion of individual growth. This became the liberty of private enterprise, which was capitalism's method. But now the accumulated enterprise of private persons, rationalized and organized in business and State, threatened human liberty. To preserve it, or more precisely to make liberty at last real, the bourgeois-Protestant-capitalist system, which the ideal of liberty had fostered, must go. Marx embodied the need of the bourgeois world to supersede itself in order that its own dearest values might live.

Thus Alfred Stieglitz. . . . I do not say that Stieglitz, like these others, is a historic figure. A man's historic importance depends not merely on his intrinsic traits but on the use that is made of him by following generations. Socrates, Confucius, Paul . . . these are men who have been deeply employed, and hence historic: it would be absurd to place any man, whose progeny is yet unborn, among them. And it must be that there were other men, at crises of transition between worlds, of like quality yet who were not used save perhaps by family and townsfolk, and hence men of no historical importance. Possibly Stieglitz is to be one of these. What is certain is that he embodies and projects for the experience of the coming generation *a variant value* within the old world, significant and perhaps crucial to the new world which all minds feel now stirring in the anguish of our epoch. Whether the individual articulation of this value which is Stieglitz is to be fecund, whether this value indeed comes to birth, therefore finally whether Stieglitz will be a historic man, depends on ourselves more than on him. Such questions may not here concern me. I confine myself to a brief description of the variant value in the man Stieglitz, and to a swift naming of the New World which the value in the man discloses.

2

I HAVE SAID that the nineteenth century was involved in a titanic contradiction. It had inherited and passionately fostered the ideal of individual value, of personal human value; yet it lived by means and institutions, themselves sprung from the ideal of that value, which progressively threatened to undermine it. Thus technics: a product of the human will in free pursuit of happiness and enlargement, which in the hands of an exploiting class became an enemy of human life. Thus Democracy, which exalted the sum of persons to be the nation, in lieu of a qualitative symbol incarnate in a king, yet served (since the citizens were not liberated of their ignorance and lusts) to strengthen a new class of leader who personified and exploited, not the potential strength of the people but their weakness. Thus finally industrial capitalism, child of Democracy and of technics, which actually rationalized the hold of a few congregated thieves over the mass of the exploited.

Why did these instruments and institutions for human liberty become liberty's destroyers? If we analyze them, we have the answer. At the heart of each element of nineteenth-century civilization we find *the cult of the person*. Protestantism, rationalism, rational idealism (hostile sisters), established the mind and conscience of the person as the seat of Truth; Democracy made the person the theoretic integer of State and nation; the machine aimed to extend the power of the person; capitalism ennobled—in place of the old caste—the privilege and enterprise of the person. Yet none of these examined what a person *is*, none demanded a norm, a discipline, a method, for establishing true persons. Therefore Man agonized; Man was in danger of dying. Because the prevalent concepts about the person were false, all means to invigorate or to uphold the person were doomed to failure.

We must remember that the idea that "true persons" had to be formed—technologically created *out of* the state of nature—is as old as the Hindus, the Chinese, and the Egyptians, from whom possibly Pythagoras and the Hebrews took their first lessons. But although precise methods for this purpose have always prevailed in the East, the West could not accept them, since they worked from and toward an unacceptable notion of what the person is. The Mosaic Law with its more than six hundred commandments is also such a method. When Paul rejected the Judaic norm of the person, he rejected not only the Law but all human methods, and relied on the ecstatic energy of Grace to make what he deemed true persons—waiters, in passive perfection, for Christ's immediate return. Paul's ecstatic energy of Grace has almost vanished, and the belief in the Second Coming with its concomitant contempt for human works. Yet Paul's rejection of a human norm of the person and of a human method to produce real persons has prevailed throughout the history of Europe.

The creative spirits of the nineteenth century were alive to the crying need: Save the person, save belovèd Man! Yet even in the lurid light of Catholic Europe's failure, and of the modern technological obsession in all realms of nature, amazingly few envisaged the primary problem: Learn what Man is and how to produce him. Much preparatory work was done: in lyrical exhortation (Blake, Rimbaud, Stirner, Nietzsche, Whitman); in analysis of the mind and of the social body (the psychologists culminating in Freud and Dewey, the great novelists, the social historians). Yet by and large, the individualists, children of Rousseau, took the person for granted and thought to "save" the person, by withdrawing him from the social system; and confused the individual's barbaric will with the essence of the true person. The collectivists, realizing that the person is rooted in the social body, prescribed merely methods for changing that body. Implicit in both groups, the anarchist and socialist, is the *personal* value: the need of creating a culture-bed for persons. But the romantics merely transposed the source of Paul's ecstatic energy from Christ to "Nature"; and the collectivists were content with a political-economic method of revolution. Marx, the greatest of the latter group, was in this sense, like the anarchists, a disciple of Rousseau: he made no study of the intrinsic nature of the person, of a methodology of man; he took his basic human value romantically for granted.

This brings me to Alfred Stieglitz. Born in the North of the United States during the Civil War, which corresponds to the earlier revolutionary struggles of Europe that nurtured the young Marx, he also was born into the great bourgeois-Protestant world. He also derives his values from that world, and his work from its need. *That value is the person*. In this, he is one with Marx and a thousand others. But his work has been a searching of the person's true content, a revelation by his own life of the true person's nature, and thereby a discipline for his emergence. In this Stieglitz has been almost alone.

3

SINCE THE Stieglitzian exposition of the person is simply and wholly his life, there is no direct way to learn it save to experience his life by watching him live and living with him; and there is no direct way to describe it except by describing his life. This description, manifold yet single, is the body of our book. Gradually the surfaces, depths, forms, exterior relations of this man's behavior—which is his work, which is his methodology—are revealed in these pages. And the reader who has followed will apprehend the organic portrait. Now the main forms are there, I draw certain lines along them, as it were with an identifying pencil, in order to make more visible the difficult because unexampled portrait of *a person*.

The reader will have noted two conspicuous traits in Stieglitz. There appears to be not the slightest demarcation between the man's values and his humble daily behavior, between his life and his work, between his being and his doing. Stieglitz, for example, is never "busy," since any interruption becomes spontaneously his business; is never "working," since everything that occurs, any word that is spoken and his reply to it, is part of his work; is never more intimately involved, less intensely concerned than in any other event, since all of him is always open and ready to be engaged according to the demand and capacity of the event before him. The second conspicuous fact is that the man's incentive is totally wanting in the will toward self-aggrandizement, whether in terms of money or of reputation.

These two characteristics are revealing. A class society, such as that which gave birth to Stieglitz, is a dualistic system splitting reality into parts which mutually thwart one another and yet rationalize their destructive separations. The terms soul as against body, play as against work, art as against amusement, duty as against pleasure, etc.; the divisions of men into stranger, enemy, ally, friend, partner, rival, casual acquaintance, etc., are pointers not to the reality of man and of life, but to the rationalized conflicts of our social structure. Each individual, to survive in this world, must split himself also into a series of responses—not to life, but to the conflicts between the thwarted and thwarting separatisms of the system. His survival in the discordant whole depends on the success with which he conforms not to the whole which is life, but to the *discord* which is death. His success, paradoxically, will derive from his acquisition of some sort of *separate* and divisive reward which, if analyzed, is seen to be an abstraction from the whole—a taking-away from what other rival individuals are also seeking. If we may assume that a cancer is a cell which seeks aggrandisement beyond its integral function in the human body, we might say (without forgetting that we deal with metaphor) that our society is a body in which the individual, in order to succeed, must become a cancer: that our social system consists of cancerous cells organized into a ruling class, and of subject cells made morbid and progressively destroyed by the cancer which, in order to "progress," must end by destroying the entire body. And the reason why this metaphor appears incongruous is that our very language expresses the values not of the whole body but of the cancer.

The two traits of Stieglitz which we have named might be summarized as the man's refusal to "split his responses" in accord with a discordant world: the refusal to accept the language of a cancerous system. But these are mere clues to the design. The life of Stieglitz might be more simply plotted as an ethical triad, consisting of a thesis, an antithesis, and a synthesis.

The *thesis* is the acceptance by the man of all life. I mean "acceptance" in the mystic sense of knowledge of the self as belonging to the whole, and of knowledge of the whole as belonging to the self. This acceptance does not preclude criticism of parts or even deliberate and mortal hostility of parts; it merely precedes and subsumes them. It is the recognition of a connection with life strictly analogous to anyone's connection with and acceptance of his body. Indeed, the simple mystic is one who "knows" the cosmos immediately (before analysis or control) as the babe knows its body. The mystic may not have the word "mystic" nor the word "cosmos": neither, in fact, is in the language of Stieglitz, whose words are not vocables but actions.

This thesis of acceptance is variously uttered by the man, as our book reveals. For example, it is uttered by his relations with friends —a multi-faceted form that is recorded in the *Variations,* and particularly in the section "The Man and the Place." His acceptance of a friend may be a mere nurturing. If the friend's life-will is weak, the influence of Stieglitz may even seem to accentuate the weakness, since it establishes a kind of protectorate over the friend forever. If the individual is strong, Stieglitz's acceptance acts as a challenge, a bringing-forth into the open of the other's essential problem, a constant call to battle in which the friend may emerge a victor . . . to go on to deeper battle. The thesis of acceptance is uttered no less in the man's relations with casual acquaintance. The stranger dropping in to the American Place may be a dividing, hence death-dealing individual. Stieglitz will touch that theme of his life, and in all probability the stranger will hate himself—find this unbearable—and save himself by turning his hate against Stieglitz. Acceptance in the sense in which I use the word is not collusion: it is dynamic recognition.

The thesis is in the photographs, of course; and here most directly accessible to the world. It has been said often enough that the remarkable value of these prints is that Stieglitz has used a machine as a means for making beauty. This is a half truth. (More or less directly machines have been used by creative men ever since the Pyramids were builded, and the machine in the raw is merely an extended tool—a tool within which man's intellectualized will is integrated, instead of being merely imposed upon it.) The significant feature in the photographs of Stieglitz is *that a man has accepted the factual world, which a recording machine gives him, to make beauty*.

Every artist, of course, accepts his world as the material for his art; and the bounds of his world are the bounds of his capacity to experience and to absorb. One may say that every artist accepts, for the material of his art, as entire a world as possible. And since his art is a unification of his vision and the objective world, his vision in the last analysis determines the world he can accept; determines the excisions and distortions to which he must subject it before he can employ it. The so-called "realist" who abounds today is the shallowest of artists, since what he takes to be the world is a mere surface record of his dogmatically rationalized senses—the record, indeed, not of direct experience but of an *inherited language* which, in turn, is a series of symbols for discordant parts and not for the whole of life. The "tendentious" artist, moralistic or political, is also shallow since (if he lives down to his creed) the world he accepts is within the confines of a temporal program, which means that it is a "world" delimited by the language of a specific human function which, being within the world, is *not* the world. Few artists, in the past bitter centuries, have had the serenity of vision sufficient to accept, as the material for their art, an unrationalized and "unprogramatized" world so entirely as Stieglitz. The camera in this man's hand is his enacted assurance that the material of his vision shall be as humbly, as minutely, as wholly, the objective world, as it can be; and his acceptance of this objective world, to be transfigured *by* his acceptance, is the man's certainty that his subjective vision is true: *i.e.,* that his vision and reality are one. I have said that few artists in recent times have had such strength and such faith. Those few are the mystic artists, the masters who can employ the whole of life as their material, because of their acceptance of the whole of life. And the true analogue to Stieglitz with his camera before a patch of sky, a city street, a face, a tree, a hand, is no "artist" in the modern sense at all: it is Blake recording his poem to the Tyger; it is, more precisely, Saint Francis preaching his adorable sermon to the sparrows.

Magic, the Hindus wisely said, is "a change of attitude," and acceptance of life, in the mystic sense, is alchemy: it transfigures the objective world into terms that can be humanly experienced, and it transfigures personal experience into terms that are sensed as the mystery, and the *good,* of all life. By the alchemy of acceptance, Stieglitz reveals within the common fact, recorded by his lens, his subjective vision. This alchemy of acceptance is nothing but the dynamics of the recognition of the truth. For truth recognized *is* action. If a man knows life in anything, it is humanly significant, it is beauty, it is truth. That is the message of these prints. The function of the camera is merely to state the nature and degree of the man's acceptance. The prints are merely one utterance of the man's thesis.

As his camera works, his life works. The casual encounter, the crisis of a soul, the dollar problem of an artist, the love of a woman, the bickering of an antagonist . . . all that occurs to the man and with the man is focused (*photographed,* one might say) by the lens of his acceptance of life: is made true, that means, by recognition. And this, I repeat, is as precise of his behavior with a casual

visitor at the Place as it is of his photographic statement of a belovèd woman's breast. The relatedness to the whole is everywhere, and is *the thing*. The camera merely proves it, by establishing the essential equivalence of what it records with what surrounds it. (This explains why a Stieglitz print of a woman's torso or a tree's branch is never episodic.) But the man's word, gesture, attitude, also prove it to those who understand his language. The thesis is acceptance, always, of life: and this means creation, for it means the suffusion of unity into the chaos of events, of wholeness into the false and painful fragments of individual existence.

I have spoken of language; I have said that the value of Stieglitz's prints lies in the fact that they are builded, not from the rationale of an accepted language about "facts," but from a direct unitary experience of the objective world and from the need to know—which means to "control"—this world. But this need is at the source of language. The prints are, hence, a kind of primary language—or, more exactly, of neo-primitive language. I have said also that the words of Stieglitz are not "vocables but actions." This must have brought an incredulous smile to many who know him slightly and have been bombarded by his stintless stream of talk. But the reason for their impression is precisely that Stieglitz is trying to employ words as he employs the objects that he photographs. He is refusing to take words as things-in-themselves; refusing to abide, as does the rationalist, by the assumption that each word is precisely and exclusively what it "means." Stieglitz feels that words, like separate things and facts, are pointers—pointing to what, in ever widening concentric circles, lies beyond them; pointing to life which no separate words can convey. Hence the ever widening circles of his talk. He is trying to use words plastically in order to build up an organic statement that shall be different from the sum of the words, as a live body is different from the sum of its constituents. If one lacks the key to this intention, the man's vast circuitous monologues are verbose; but if one understands his language, the talk of Stieglitz often takes on the organic dimensions of a page from Dostoievski. Yet it must be insisted that, although Stieglitz's intuition about words is profound, his craft in words is faulty. He is not a Dostoievski. He is a better craftsman in the control of photogenic objects than in the control of language.

To return, then: the man's *thesis* is the acceptance always of life. The *antithesis* is the refusal of everything that refuses, implicitly or actively, his thesis. That "everything" is our contemporary culture and civilization. It is our business, our politics, our laws, our morals, our popular arts. It is the system based on dualistic principles of individual and class aggression. The antithesis in Stieglitz is therefore his refusal of the bourgeois-capitalist world. Deepembedded for fifty years in American life, this refusal that is the man has lived and acted. But deep in the American world, older than the Republic, lives what I have called elsewhere the Great Tradition, which is the enacted love of man for God. The antithesis in Stieglitz, refusal of the present American world, is but the function of what is positive and enduring in the American world.

Thesis and antithesis, together, make the person. What kind of person, our book endeavors to portray. If we generalize, we find this to be an "integral" person: one in whom by the dynamics of acceptance, the elements of everyone, the values of everyone, the harmonic needs, in consequence, of a hale social body, have come actually—in individual form—together: one in whom the value of life (what we call vaguely beauty and truth) has a realized, functioning, individual existence. But everybody, whether he knows it or not, partakes of the whole social body which formed him, feeds him, and which—toward health or disease—he continues. And everybody above the brute lives by the axiom on which all religion, all art, all law, all constructive revolution, indeed, all behaviors of decency, are premised: the axiom that life has value. Therefore, an integral person such as we have constructed from the behavior of Stieglitz is one in whom the implicit content and value of all humans has become explicit and active. The integral person, by strict logic, is the true person. The sole real or realized person. And the *reality* of a person must be measured by the degree to which the health of the race and the value of human life has a focus and an utterance in his behavior.

Such an utterance is the *synthesis* of the life of Stieglitz.

either by crucifying them or by turning them into gods—displacing them into some transcendental realm where their example would not impede the wolfish laws of the day. The life of Stieglitz, also, has been a crucifixion, in that he has been constantly assailed by the world which (in order to survive) had to refuse his unitary implications; and it has been a constant resurrection, by virtue of the energy of his own unquenchable life acceptance.

The integral society in which a true person can live will be one in which the whole, by its normal function, gives health to its individual components, even as its individuals, by their normal function, give health to the whole. Such a society implies, no less, the existence of integral persons. In it, the universal sub-person of today—the power man, the schemer, the prowler, the exhibitionist and megalomaniac—will be as dangerously out of place as a Stieglitz in Hitlerian Berlin. If by some miracle such a society were to be established somewhere in the present world with the present types of sub-persons yet prevalent, they would destroy it and replace it with a society like our own, a world in which their greed, blindness, separatism, servility, and egolatry could again safely prosper.[1]

In its barest outlines this integral society may be defined as one without *economic* classes; one based on collaboration and not on exploitation; one in which the values of life and the disciplines of leadership will be totally dissevered from the possession of goods. In a word, a communist society which (as Marx said) will be the beginning of a human culture, because (as Marx neglected to explain) *in such a society alone, true persons can live.*

4

THE IMPACT OF THIS LIFE upon other lives must be revolutionary. Stieglitz's behavior, by its contrasting key, brings out the latent discordant motive (from the standpoint of the whole) in every man and situation he encounters. It reveals at all moments the dominant trait of our social system, which is the denial of life, and of which the tendency toward war and the prevalence of unemployment are but symbols pointing to inward war, inward poverty and unemployment. An integral person like Stieglitz cannot truly *live* except in an integral society: hence his positive acts are a rebuke of the world, call forth a constant negative from the world, and are, above all, an implicit cry for a different world—a new world—in which the integral man may live.

This has always been, since all history is a series of class worlds premised on human exploitation and destruction. And whenever integral persons have appeared in them, it has been to struggle and at last to die. For the will of the world must "put them away,"

5

WE AGONIZE in the death of a world: the emergence everywhere of the hideous leaders of the hour, in statecraft, finance, art, journalism, and what calls itself "religion," is a sign of our world's agony. The day's command is to mother, from the life of the past worlds that breathe within us, the new world: not one in which we may live as we and our fathers have lived, but one in which Man at

[1] Of course, such a "miracle" is nonsense. Social evolution is organic, which means that political-economic change does not come independently of change in the individuals who make up the social body, who effect social change, and are affected by it. As the true person slowly and tragically rises in the social texture, its nature also changes (even as any organic substance changes when the chemistry of its ingredients alters); and the social structure, as slowly and tragically, conforms to be the matrix for the birth of true persons. The double process can be divided only arbitrarily, for the sake of language. In the comparatively simple, formed organism of a man it is impossible to separate mental, physical and "spiritual" change. In an organism so vastly complex and inchoate as mankind, to endeavour to dissociate the growth of the true persons from the growth of a true society, would be to surrender to folly.

last—the Man potentially in us all—may be born. Myriad creative men and women, teachers, workers, artists, scientists, toil together, although unknown to one another, in passionate obedience to this command; toil in ways as variedly profound as must be the world in which the new-born Man—the true person—with his exquisite sensibilities and his enormous powers, may prosper. The work of these myriad good men and women is a symphony; and although they know it not, the major theme of all their complex music is the creating of true persons.

This fact makes manifest the share in their labors of Alfred Stieglitz, whose life is an art form of the true person, whose work is a method for the creating of true persons.

1 ALFRED STIEGLITZ *Winter, Fifth Avenue*, 1893

2 ALFRED STIEGLITZ, *The Terminal*, 1893

3 FRANK EUGENE, *The Horse*, 1895

4 ALFRED STIEGLITZ, *In the New York Central Yards,* 1903

5 ALFRED STIEGLITZ, *Five Points, New York,* 1892

6 ALFRED STIEGLITZ, *Night, New York,* 1897

7 JOHN MARIN, *Fifth Avenue – 40th Street, New York*, oil, 1933

8 ALFRED STIEGLITZ, *Wet Day on the Boulevard, Paris*, 1894

9 ALFRED STIEGLITZ, *The Steerage*, 1907

10 CAPTAIN PUYO, *Montmartre*, 1904

11 ALFRED STIEGLITZ, *My Parents' Home, Lake George*, 1907

12 CLARENCE H. WHITE, *Illustration*, 1904

13 ROBERT DEMACHY, *Ballet Girls*, 1904

14 ALFRED STIEGLITZ, *Sunlight and Shadows*, 1889

15 D.O. HILL, *Mrs. Rigby*, 1843 – 1846   16 D.O. HILL, *Handyside Ritchie and William Henning*, 1843 – 1846

17 D.O. HILL, *The Bird Cage*, 1843 – 1846

18 EDUARD J. STEICHEN, *Rodin, Le Penseur,* 1902

19 PAMELA COLMAN SMITH, *Death in the House*, drawing, 1907

20 EDUARD J. STEICHEN, *Gordon Craig*, 1905

21 EDUARD J. STEICHEN, *Yvette Guilbert*, 1905

22 BARON DE MEYER, *Marchesa Casati*, 1910

23 GORDON CRAIG, *Ninth Movement*, etching, 1909

24 ALVIN LANGDON COBURN, *Reflections*, 1908

26 JOHN MARIN, *Outgoing Schooner – Maine*, watercolor, 1923

25 HUGO HENNEBERG, *Villa Falconieri*, 1900

27 GERTRUDE KÄSEBIER, *The Manger*, 1899

28 THEODORE AND OSCAR HOFMEISTER, *The Churchgoers*, 1903

29 HEINRICH KÜHN, *On the Dunes*, 1900

30 PROFESSOR HANS WATZEK, *Sheep*, 1900

31 J. CRAIG ANNAN, *Mountain Tops*, 1898

32 ALFRED STIEGLITZ, *Goats Outside of Paris*, 1894

33 MARSDEN HARTLEY, *Deserted Farm, Maine*, oil, 1909

34 ALFRED MAURER, *Landscape*, gouache, 1909

35 *MSS* Cover, designed by
Georgia O'Keeffe, 1922

36 *Camera Work* Cover, designed by
Eduard J. Steichen, 1902

38 An American Place Announcement,
handwriting of Alfred Stieglitz, 1932

37 *291* Page, designed by Paul Haviland
and Marius de Zayas, 1915

39 ALFRED STIEGLITZ, *Brancusi Exhibition at "291"*, 1914

40 ALFRED STIEGLITZ, *Primitive Negro Sculpture Exhibition at "291"*, 1914

41 JULIA MARGARET CAMERON, *Thomas Carlyle*, 1862   42 FRANK EUGENE, *Sir Henry Irving*, 1896

43 ALFRED STIEGLITZ, *Marsden Hartley*, 1915

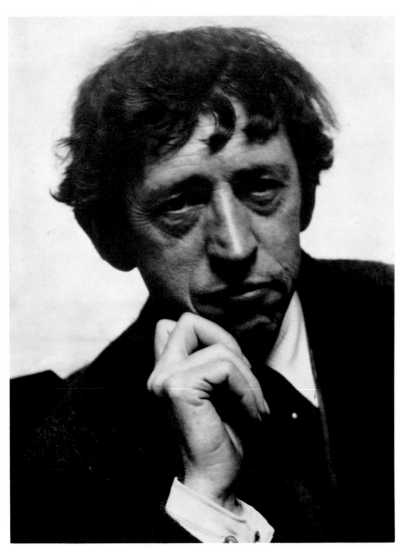

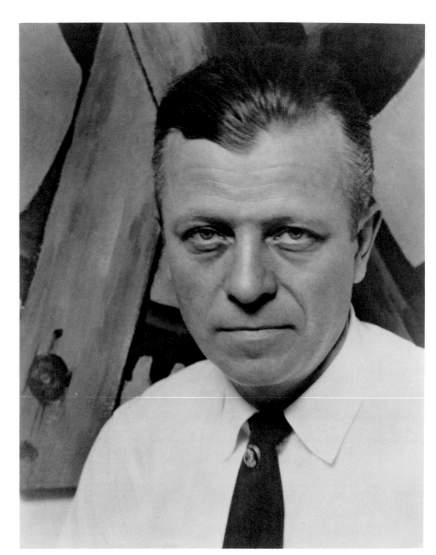

44 ALFRED STIEGLITZ, *John Marin*, 1922   45 ALFRED STIEGLITZ, *Arthur G. Dove*, 1915

46 PABLO PICASSO, *Sculpture*, 1909

47 MARIUS de ZAYAS, *Charles Darnton*,
charcoal drawing, 1913

48 ABRAHAM WALKOWITZ, *Portrait*,
pencil drawing, 1910

49 HENRI de TOULOUSE-LAUTREC, *Une Spectatrice*,
lithograph, 1893

50 PABLO PICASSO, drawing, 1910

51 MARIUS de ZAYAS, *Alfred Stieglitz*,
charcoal drawing, 1913

52 CHARLES DEMUTH, *For "Distinguished Air"*
by Robert McAlmon, watercolor, 1930

53 CHARLES DEMUTH, *Pears and Plate*, watercolor, 1929

54 HENRI MATISSE, *Nude*, watercolor, 1907

55 HENRI MATISSE, sculpture, 1910

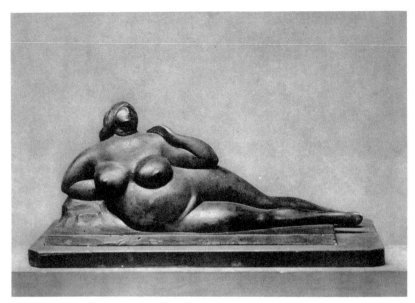

56 GASTON LACHAISE, *La Montagne*, sculpture, 1919

57 RENÉE LE BÈGUE, *Nude*, 1904

58 ALFRED STIEGLITZ, *Elie Nadelman Exhibition at "291"*, 1916

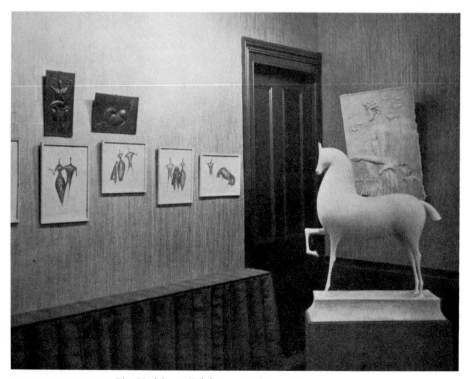

59 ALFRED STIEGLITZ, *Elie Nadelman Exhibition at "291"*, 1916

60 AUGUSTE RODIN, drawing, 1909

61 MAX WEBER, *Landscape with Nude Figure*, gouache, 1910

62 PAUL CÉZANNE, *The Bathers*, lithograph, 1898

63 GEORGIA O'KEEFFE, *Cross by the Sea – Canada*, oil, 1932

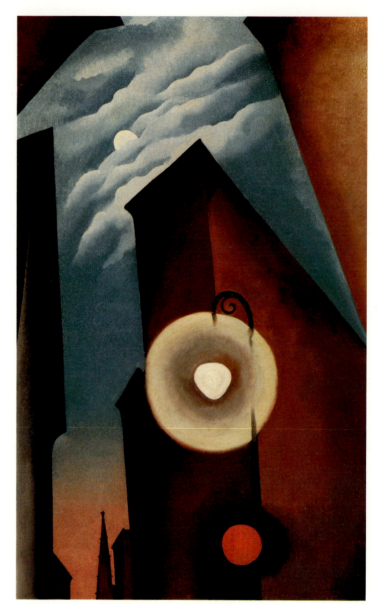

64 GEORGIA O'KEEFFE, *New York with Moon*, oil, 1925

65 GEORGIA O'KEEFFE, *Petunia and Coleus*, oil, 1924–25

66 GEORGIA O'KEEFFE, *Jack in the Pulpit No. V*, oil, 1930

67 ARTHUR G. DOVE, *Portrait of Ralph Dusenberry*, 1926

68 CHARLES DEMUTH, *Sunflowers*, watercolor, 1920

69 STANTON MACDONALD WRIGHT, *Abstraction on Spectrum (Organization 5)*, oil, 1914

70 MARSDEN HARTLEY, *Carnival of Autumn*, oil, 1909

71 ARTHUR G. DOVE, *Clouds and water*, oil, 1931

72 MARSDEN HARTLEY, *Cemetery, New Mexico*, oil, 1920

73 ARTHUR G. DOVE, *Sea Gull Motif (Sea thunder)*, oil, 1926

74 JOHN MARIN, *Mountain Forms, New Mexico*, watercolor, 1930

75 JOHN MARIN, *Sea Movement Green and Blue*, watercolor, 1923

76 JOHN MARIN, *Sunspots*, watercolor, 1920

77 JOHN MARIN, *Movement, Fifth Avenue*, watercolor, 1912

78 JOHN MARIN, *Brooklyn Bridge*, watercolor, 1910

79 JOHN MARIN, *The Red Sun, Brooklyn Bridge*, watercolor, 1922

80 ALFRED STIEGLITZ, *New York, North From An American Place*, 1931

81 ALFRED STIEGLITZ, *From My Window at the Shelton, New York*, 1930

82 JOHN MARIN, *From the Window of "291" Looking Down Fifth Avenue*, watercolor, 1911

83 ALFRED STIEGLITZ, *Night, New York*, 1931

84 ALFRED STIEGLITZ, *From the Shelton Westward*, 1931

85 ALFRED STIEGLITZ, *From the Shelton Looking North*, c. 1931

86 ALFRED STIEGLITZ, *Georgia O'Keeffe*, 1918

87 ALFRED STIEGLITZ, *Georgia O'Keeffe Hands – No. 27*, 1919

88 ALFRED STIEGLITZ, *Georgia O'Keeffe*, 1918

89 ALFRED STIEGLITZ, *Dying and Living Poplars, Lake George,* 1932

90 ALFRED STIEGLITZ, *Equivalent*, 1922

91 ALFRED STIEGLITZ, *Equivalent*, 1929

92 ALFRED STIEGLITZ, *Mountains and Sky*, 1924

93 ALFRED STIEGLITZ, *Equivalent*, 1931

94 ALFRED STIEGLITZ, *Lake George From the Hill,* 1931

95 ALFRED STIEGLITZ, *Hedge and Grasses, Lake George,* 1933

96 ALFRED STIEGLITZ, *Grasses,* 1933

97 ALFRED STIEGLITZ, *Dirigible*, 1910

98 ALFRED STIEGLITZ, *Airplane*, 1910

99 ALFRED STIEGLITZ, *Hand of Man,* 1902

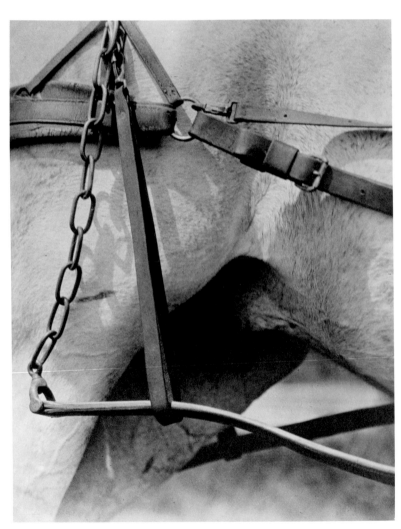

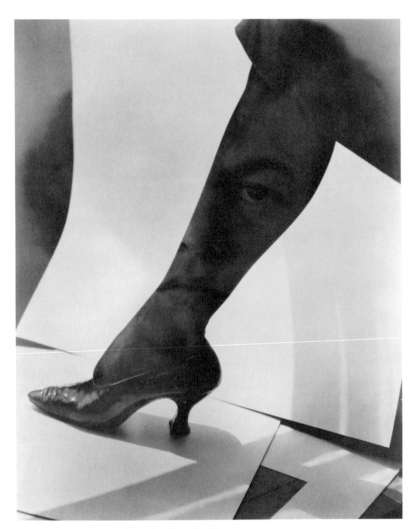

100 ALFRED STIEGLITZ, *Spiritual America*, 1923

101 ALFRED STIEGLITZ, *Portrait, Dorothy True*, 1919

103 PAUL STRAND, *New York*, 1915

102 PAUL STRAND, *Kitchen Bowls*, 1916

104 ALFRED STIEGLITZ, *The Last Days of "291"*, 1917

105 DOROTHY NORMAN, *An American Place*, 1946

VARIATIONS ON THE THEME

Elizabeth McCausland

Stieglitz and the American Tradition

A s NEW ENGLAND CANNOT be rightly seen save by the light of a cold Northern sun striking obliquely across stark hillsides, so Stieglitz cannot be understood except by reference to the distinctive sun which beats on America. Viewed in that symbolical light, all the volumes and masses of his significance are illuminated. Yet to be sure that the precise quality of this American sunlight has been defined, one must explore the American tradition, the American character, before considering Stieglitz himself.

Is there in fact an American tradition, by which "American" can be taken to mean more than a geographical or political affiliation? Is there an American character, forged on the frontier and welded into spiritual unity by latter-day Americans? Is there an attribute of the American soul by which it is set apart from other national psyches? Surveying our past and our present, one answers yes. That character, that tradition, is perhaps the last outburst of romanticism in the Western world, the last crudely spontaneous outgoing of the pioneer spirit, the last outbreak of childish self-confidence in a society already turning to sterner disciplines. But for the centuries behind us romanticism has dominated the American scene and the American mind, given our creative workers the energy for centrifugal and extravagant labors, breathed nostalgic faith into the artist, set the nation on fire with poetic zeal for the westward movement, that naïve yet passionate race against the setting sun.

Romanticism in this sense must be, one imagines, the inevitable state of a country where the sod is yet to be broken, the forests hewn down, the wilderness conquered. Energy in such a world must always be outward-moving, dramatic, tense with effort and struggle. A corresponding life of the soul is evolved, a life focused on feeling, that is, on emotional movement, whereas in an older world thought rules, fixed at dead center, unmoving, the source of serene and classical styles. In the realm of American political life, also, this spirit early found expression. And in spite of the inescapable facts of modern industrial organization, it is not too much to say that libertarianism (the equivalent in this field of the centrifugal outward movement of the soul in the esthetic) is still the mood of American popular life, still the ideal of American thought. Liberty, freedom, happiness, free speech, no interference from the next man, these are common American rights, however debased in practice.

To preserve these rights from corruption has been Stieglitz's endeavor. Listen to what he has to say, and "free" is the overtone of almost every word. Free to work, free to be himself, free to live without selling his soul, these are rough translations of the eloquent speech which Stieglitz has wielded for years as other men wield weapons. A worker must be free to do his work; that is said as one says it is an inalienable right of man. There is no hesitation here, no conciliation; freedom is the right of men, but especially of Americans, because their whole history has been based on this premise. That modern industrialism completely nullifies freedom, that the fathers of the republic were motivated not only by idealism but also by economic determinism (plus splendid rhetoric), does not alter Stieglitz's position. If an idea is true, that is all that matters. In another society the concepts which control this fidelity would be other concepts, the direction of his lifelong struggle would therefore be another direction. But the fundamental philosophic purity of his endeavor would remain the same; for after this exegesis of his ideas has been made, a more important conclusion emerges. To be sure, Stieglitz derives from the American tradition, he exemplifies the American character. These facts are true enough; but they are unimportant except in relation to a more basic and universal truth. In life it is evident that there are forces for evil and forces for good, that life can only be completely understood in terms of affirmative and negative values, of creative and destructive energies. When this is understood, one has no choice except to take his stand on the side of good: certainly this is true of Stieglitz. Purity, integrity, complete faithfulness to the thing done, these are the standards by which life is to be judged after this choice.

With Stieglitz the choice must have been made in the cradle. The uncompromisingness of his external life, the arrowlike sureness of his flight, the unerring taste of his perceptions, his uncanny foreknowledge of events, these are the best indemnification for good faith. Such integrity of the spirit one finds in earlier Americans: Emerson, Whitman, Emily Dickinson. One finds it too in Marin, O'Keeffe, Dove. These painters, one believes, are as American as Stieglitz, as truly one with the romantic ebb and flow of American energies. Yet in viewing their work, that work which Stieglitz so passionately asserts must be permitted to live without domination from the external world (the world of art dealers, collectors, museum directors, critics, and an indifferent public), one understands again how the American tradition operates, pulsing through the nation with a stifled sigh of regret for the past, boundless belief in the future, naïve friendliness, exuberant zest for beauty, how in the last analysis freedom is the right word for the American heritage.

For the work of these artists (and we write of them and leave out many others, solely because they most aptly symbolize this American sunlight, this American energy) freedom as a way of life is justified. Here freedom does not produce anarchy or lawless self-indulgence; it does not lump three diverse lives under one subhead: *homo americanus;* it does not sacrifice universal or human truth for an easy nationalistic imprint. It does, however, permit these splendid workers to live under the American sun, sucking up strength from the American soil, rooted in the American earth, beating in time with the American tempo, each achieving that special and individual happiness for which in the American mind liberty is the antecedent condition. Liberty, freedom, these words could not fascinate the mind if they did not correspond to a vital hunger of the soul. The sun falls seductively on these American acres precisely because they are rich soil for dreams. Stieglitz could exercise no sway over the imagination, nor could the human exemplars of his idea command a compelling loyalty if they did not speak to a truth deeper seated than the reason can reach.

If one says, then, that romanticism turns outward, its energy moving from the center of emotion and thought to the circumference of expression in art, one means that the individual has transmuted himself and his experience of life into a symbol, a work of art, not because he seeks to exhibit himself or to exploit himself, but because he profoundly believes in the sanctity of life, because he knows (by the light of this naïve and nostalgic American sun) that the Holy Ghost is every man, and that to deny himself is to deny Pentecost. Thus one may define romanticism as a tremendous concentration on feeling, on humane and humanistic values; a tremendous concern for the individual (not necessarily in the sense of nineteenth- and twentieth-century humanitarianism) but in the sense that to the romantic the fate of the individual seems moving and important; a tremendous hunger for self-realization; nostalgia; passion; a naïve idealism; energy; inventiveness. But when one says this, one implies also that these values are chiefly important because

they transcend the individual while at the same time depending on the individual for that incarnation which will give them tangible life.

It is this being more than human yet always human that makes Stieglitz profoundly significant for America, this distillation of American romanticism till by concentration even nostalgia becomes a major emotion. With Marin and O'Keeffe and Dove the same raising of emotion to the *n*th degree takes place. One can love nature and still be fighting beside the fallen Lucifer; but one cannot love nature as Marin loves it and be anywhere except on the side of the Everlasting Yea. One can create perfect symbols for one's perception of life and still be only a minor poet or a little master; but one cannot burn with the incandescence of the burning bush, as O'Keeffe burns, and not push this highly personal and romantic art over into that region where all great art resides, whether romantic or classical. One may play with theories or juggle the external aspects of the world as some people toy with phrases, and the result is scarcely important art; but one cannot so tenderly and so humorously yet withal so mystically experience the informing spirit of the world, as Dove does, without bestowing on his creation new and profound meaning.

Affirmation is a favorite word of Stieglitz's. There is a very good reason for this: to make an act of faith is a spiritual necessity of the American character. This compulsion drove John Brown to bleeding Kansas, to the gallows. Faith is the motive power for these painters' lives; the resultant acts are to be understood as acts of faith in the ultimate sense of

> *Faith is a fine invention*
> *For gentlemen who see;*
> *But microscopes are prudent*
> *In an emergency!*

Prudence, caution, calculation of personal advantage, do not enter into this equation, nor do they indeed enter into the romantic American character generally. Certainly Emily Dickinson did not live with her eye glued to a microscope; rather her sight was always fixed on an inner revelation, as is the vision of these present-day inheritors of the American tradition.

This revelation comes back to spiritual terms. Honest work, honest craftsmanship, these are ideals Stieglitz has exemplified in his own work, as pure creations as the twentieth century has produced; they are ideals, too, which he has sought to cherish wherever he has found them in the world: witness those early exhibitions of Cézanne and Picasso and Matisse at 291, the Marin retrospective exhibition of 1933, the O'Keeffe retrospective exhibition of 1934. Of these ideals we must say that they represent in art that condition of purity and immaculateness for which the human soul desperately longs and that to speak of honest work, honest craftsmanship, is to imply this spiritual passion for perfection. And indeed Stieglitz would not create the impression of a prophet bewildered because his revelation is not wanted by the world did he not combine in his own nature these two strains of the American character, this fanatical and rhetorical conviction that freedom *is* the right of man and this desperate need for perfectness. American history's long and weary list of self-betrayals springs from this naïve faith, so integral in the national character. And that Stieglitz's life presents, in so many respects, the parable of the prophet without honor in his own country must be ascribed to the fact that this belief (almost like Rousseau's) in the perfectibility of mankind is deeply if unconsciously ingrained in him as the heir of the American tradition.

There are those who will say that romanticism as a philosophy of art has run its course, that the last waning energy of the Renaissance has spent itself, and that if, indeed, romanticism is the banner under which America has marched in the past, it can do so no longer and live. To be sure, in great societies of the past, the emphasis of art has been on the group rather than on the isolated individual. To this Stieglitz will assent; he too conceives of the artist (and this word accurately should be "worker") as an organic part of society. The tragedy of Stieglitz—and the opportunity of Stieglitz—has been that he has lived in an age when the artist cannot be an organic part of society because society itself is not organic. Thus Stieglitz and his "group" may be thought of (from a somewhat artificially Olympian and detached point of view) as survivors of a shipwreck, clinging to battered spars, struggling to resist the waves, yet somehow rescuing that precious spark of life which we call art. That art has been colored and conditioned by the disintegrating world which gave it birth; that art, however, is by no means itself disintegrating. As romanticism can rise superior to its own intellectual flaws, if endowed with sufficient earnestness of purpose and intensity of emotion, so art can achieve an existence independent of the crippling circumstances and the handicaps which surround it. Of that independent and free existence, as the symbol of the American tradition, more than any creative worker or critic of our times, Stieglitz has been the champion.

americans:
1) freedom is right of man
2) need for perfection

society fragmented, industrialized

117

The Man and the Place

John Marin
The Man and the Place

QUITE A FEW YEARS AGO—*say twenty-five*—
there got to be—a place.

*This place was made by the locating there of a man
and a small group of kindred spirits who gathered about him.*

*The place grew—the place shifted—for
when the door was closed the place was where this man was.
This statement will have to be altered—juggled—or built upon—
for the man is quite apt to say
"You don't get it."*

*Let's see—This place shifted.
Shift is quite a word—a here—there—everywhere sort of word.
—Shift—is something that cannot be tied—cannot be pigeonholed.
It jumps—it bounds—it glides
—it SHIFTS—
it must have freedom.*

*In defense
upon coming upon the unclean—the corrupt—the petty it shifts.
In offense
upon coming upon these things—it efforts to shift them aside—
that is if the right party gets ahold of the shift.*

So you have here an intangible word—a spirit word.

*This spirit place took form—cared for and nourished by this man.
This spirit had to be fought for offensively and defensively
for this spirit had its reason for existence
from there being surrounding opposing spirits.*

*Ever since life started—a battle ground existed—
the battle ground of the spirits of light and those of darkness.*

*To which band does one belong—no one knows—one only feels.
This much common horse sense tells us—
both sides claim us in part.*

What's one to do? How's one to tell?

*Well if you glance along the top fence rail
you won't see the powers of evil astraddle the rail
—they're too positive.*

*What's one to do how's one to tell—
No—You do—
And the* doers *haven't time to straddle fence rails.*

*It seems those who do that worth the doing
are possessed of good eyes—alive eyes—warm eyes—
it seems they radiate a fire within outward.*

*The places they inhabit have a light burning—
a light seen from near and far by those who need this light—
and this light sometimes dim—sometimes brilliant—never out—*

*A place that is never locked for those who can produce a key.
A place that is never locked to anyone—
anyone can enter and walk about—
but if one got nothing then the* Inner *remained closed—
they hadn't the key.*

*To realize such a place—
a very tangible intangible place was and is this man's dream.*

*How much realized.—Well—this man being human—
working and being associated with working humans—
Those round about and many there are—
have sensed that things had happened—that things were happening—*

118

that work had been done and was being done—
that the way had been lighted up—
that cheer had been given to many to carry on—
that the place has carried on with the conviction that
the place does exist.

And as to whether or not everything there done
was the best possible doing—
whether or not mistakes were made—
whether or not those who were identified with the place were the
*   better—*
whether or not the better work was shown or the showers the better
or as to whether more or less could have been done—

All this answers nothing.
It's this—
did one get—had many gotten of their desires
a portion of these desires in this place
where there was a lacking elsewhere.

Even without their knowing it.
If so
the man of the place—Alfred Stieglitz—hasn't just dreamed a place.

That such a place exists to the extent that a certain human
or certain humans can realize an existence. . . .
artists create a conciousness

Marsden Hartley
291·and the Brass Bowl

THE ENTRANCE of Seumas O'Sheel, the then young Irish poet, into my friendship's circle, O'Sheel full of fire for the Irish revolution of the time, all for going to Ireland and becoming as he said a real Irishman and not a Christopher Street one, gave shape to the course of my whole life.

O'Sheel said, do you know Alfred Stieglitz—he has a little gallery at 291 Fifth Avenue—he might be interested—let's go up and see him, and we went up the next morning.

291 Fifth Avenue was an old brownstone house of the "elegant" period, and had been left like so many of its kind to fate and circumstance, and had been taken over by various kinds of business enterprises.

At the foot of the iron staircase leading to the upper floors of 291 was a small showcase with a photograph in it, the name "PHOTO-

SECESSION" and a gold disk between the words. The photograph was of a great celebrity, I don't remember now whether it was of Maeterlinck, of Duse, of Rodin; one of them it certainly was, but it was a photograph made to look like and to have the quality of a painting, and that was the fashion of that epoch, as we have since too well learned, the trend being now of course toward "pure" photography and nothing but, the presiding genius of which is still Alfred Stieglitz, who even at his advanced age holds the field to himself, and who certainly has not been excelled by anyone.

O'Sheel ushered me eventually into a small room on the top floor of that building that opened out from the elevator, it too a tiny affair, allowing never more than three or four to ascend at one time.

A shelf followed round the walls of this room, and below were curtains of dark green burlap, behind which many mysteries were hidden, things having to do with the progress of photography in those days.

In the center of this small room was a square platform, also hung with burlap, and in the center of this was a huge brass bowl.

I didn't know the meaning of brass bowls any more than I do now, but I suspect it was a late reflex from the recently departed eighteen-nineties, and the spirit of James McNeill Whistler seemed to come up out of this bowl like a singular wraith. The bowl, as I say, meant nothing much to me, as the paintings of Whistler never meant much of anything, though I learned later to enjoy the realistic etchings of the Thames series, these meaning more than the whispery effects of the Venice ones.

I was eventually presented to the presiding spirit of this unusual place, namely Alfred Stieglitz with his appearance of much cultivated experience in many things of the world, and of some of them in particular.

Since a photographer never had to fulfill the idea of conventional appearances as the artist and poet are supposed to have done, the photographer could always look like a human being, and therefore Alfred Stieglitz looked like a very human being, and it was through this and this alone that he made his indelible impression upon me.

Under the nimbus of voluminous gray hair there was a warm light and a fair understanding of all things, and anyone who entered this special place, entered it to be understood, if that was in any way allowed, and the special condition for this was the sincerity of the visitor himself.

I am certain that I never confused the presiding spirit of this place, for I had no talents for such things, so I was taken literally on my face value, and I had some sort of an impressing face, for all that was in me was on its surface trying to find a basis of unification with the outside and what was and still is earnestly under.

I was taken in therefore to the meaning of this place, and O'Sheel said to Stieglitz that I had come down from Maine with a set of paintings seen by no one outside of the brothers Prendergast, Glackens, and Davies, upon which these men had set some sort of artistic approval.

Stieglitz, about whom there was a deal of glamour without trace of esthetic fakery, of which there was a great deal at that time, remarked that if I wanted to send the pictures there, he would look at them.

A morning in this room with the brass bowl was revealing, for a smart array of stylish personages appeared and stood about, for there was no place to sit except on the edges of the brass bowl and few there were who felt courage enough to disturb this very awesome symbol, so they mostly stood, and the more nervous stood first on one foot and then the other.

I was, of course, impressed by the people, for I had never seen quite so many stylish ones. I soon learned also that many of them could be seen on Fifth Avenue of a morning, for it was the fashion to walk and be seen walking then, and if you wished to learn who was who, and to see the casual international face, you walked too, and the walking seemed to lead, curiously enough, to this small and, of itself, not too interesting room. Certainly it was not the room, but what went on in it that mattered, just as a stage feels so empty when the play is absent. The room was, however, full when the little shows were centered in it. So much seemed to be happening.

Stieglitz said to me, the pictures having arrived, if you will leave them a few days we can then tell you what we think of them—come in three or four days later, and we will then know. This was done, and the remark then was, I don't know any more what I think of these pictures than I did at first, but if you would like it we will give you an exhibition, and you can have it in two weeks from now. I have no money and no frames, I said. We will supply the frames, was the reply, and the exhibition was far more speedily realized than I could have hoped for, and was my initiation into over twenty years of most remarkable experience, I certainly having the right to call it unique, for here was one man who believed in another man over a space of more than twenty years, and the matter of sincerity was never questioned on either side.

The ensuing weeks were employed sensing this new place, a place which has maintained its physical and spiritual existence for more than forty years, and has been a remarkable, surely a remarkable factor in American art experience.

A sort of hallway between the small room and a large room at the rear was also used for exhibition, and in the rear room all the private talking seemed to be done, and it took me a time to find my place in this room, for it was strewn with fragments of fabrics and wall papers which I learned were the working paraphernalia of the decorating establishment of Stephen B. Lawrence, who had always to rummage around for his materials among a lot of artists, who sat around the drum stove which warmed all of them from the winter's chill.

There was likewise a Parisian tone pervading this place.

We began to hear names like Matisse, Picasso, Cézanne, Rousseau, and Manolo, this last name never heard before, and still none too well known outside immediate circles, and it was from all this fresh influx that I personally was to receive new ideas and new education.

There was life in all these new things, there was excitement, there were healthy revolt, investigation, discovery, and an utterly new world opened out of it all. A new enchantment and satisfaction was to come.

There was, therefore, intense excitement of a visual character in this little room from day to day, and the world flocked in to see what it was all about, to hear a possible explanation of it from someone, or to be intellectually and emotionally dumfounded. Certainly some were to be harassed and annoyed.

The critics came and had begun to laugh and deride.

The brass bowl was being filled with other reverberations, far less whispery than the previous ones, and it was not so long after that the brass bowl disappeared entirely and with it the early softnesses of Marin's water colors, for he too had been overcome—indeed, Marin was among the first in this country to be affected by the new harmonic and the new dissonances.

Drawings and small paintings by Matisse made their first appearance in New York in this room. Matisse's sculpture appeared likewise, also the smaller and, as I recall, only water color pictures of Cézanne, then also the abstractions of Picasso, and the small but very forceful sculptures of Manolo.

It must have been more or less at this juncture that Stieglitz recalled to me, only the other day, my pointing to a Picasso abstraction and saying, this is the way it will go from now on, only an instinctive reaction certainly.

Max Weber had returned with a full understanding of the principles of Cézanne and of cubism. I was ushered into this group as a kind of new hope, with an application of impressionism imbibed through Segantini. Somewhere about this time or later, Mrs. Mary Knoblauch appeared as an old friend of Gertrude Stein, with a heap of manuscript saying, I don't understand anything of all this, I wish someone would look at it and see if he or she can—and some of the now well known portraits of Gertrude's such as "One, One, One" of Picasso were printed in *Camera Work*.

One other day a young lady walked in with a roll of charcoal drawings of a friend of hers who was, she said, teaching drawing in the schools of Texas, this friend having been a pupil of Arthur Dow at Columbia. There was no name on these drawings, and there has never been a name on any of the paintings that have followed, for this artist believes also, as I do, that if there is any personal quality, that in itself will be signature enough, and we have seen a sequence of unsigned pictures over a given space of years permeated with an almost violent purity of spirit. The name of Georgia O'Keeffe was spoken eventually, and soon learned by all of us. It was some time after that this woman herself appeared in our midst, who, according to some persistent voices, has become the leading woman painter perhaps of the world, full of utterly embedded femininity.

There was much talk pro and con about my pictures in this little room, mostly con, I seem to remember, with the dissensions coming largely from the Parisian element. I had no voice in the matter, for I was not a talking person. I only knew I had had some kind of definite experience with nature, the nature of my own native land. I could only tell at what I had been looking and from whom my release had come. Steichen's remark to Stieglitz then was, I don't see, Stieglitz, what you see in those pictures, why you bother about them or him, there is nothing there.

Stieglitz replied, I don't think so, though you may be right—I don't think so—something makes me think something is happening.

New values, as I have said before, have been established, and with the old ones the brass bowl and all that went with it disappeared with a morning wind.

291 had to become a thing of the past, physically speaking, for the building was to be torn down. It was without doubt Mitchell Kennerley who later made it possible for Stieglitz to take room 303 in the Anderson Galleries building. The little room downtown had brought the best there was to light in the world of photography. The whole impetus and interest then seemed to go over to painting and the development of what appeared to be some new American personalities.

Mr. Thomas Craven, in his latest book, would have the world now believe that Mr. Stieglitz has done more evil than good, and that some of us esthetic "snobs" have "gone to the dogs" because of our interest in eclectic notions. We are now placed among the snobs, those awful people, and we are expected to take an interest in the true meaning of art which is "social," as if art was ever meant to be anything else when properly understood, there being no such thing as unsocial art, art being distinctly for anybody who cares to be interested in it, and how really happy must those people be who do not care for it at all, after all the quibbling. Quibbling must, however, be left to the quibblers Stieglitz will tell you, and he has said it a thousand times, that the 291 idea was never meant to be anything but an experiment, "laboratory" is his favorite word; a laboratory where several individuals have been allowed to display their virtues and their defects.

Despite whatever derogatory criticism, and it is the pet mania of certain cynics to destroy annually American values to the American people, this little harmless room of 291 will never be shaken out of its significances. It meant well then, and it means well today. It did a work that was never done before, and one that is not likely to be done again, for the same degree of integrity and faith in one person will not be so readily found. All that one group was able to do was done by the spirit of 291, for that group was never but a single spirit and a single voice. It was never allowed to be broken in upon by a touch of hypocrisy, and the thing that happened was found to be a high and strictly pure American value, and an American contribution to American cultivation. The purpose of Alfred Stieglitz and the famous little room 291 through which I was permitted to enter and pass onward to a given realization which I am still engaged in completing, is as genuine today as it was twenty-five years ago, when we all entered into its trust and were given credence.

If this room ceases to mean anything any longer to an outer and different world, it is because this world is essentially indifferent to the kind of thing it meant and still means.

Something has been done that will never be denied its rightful heritage, which can be no more or less than the admiration of the few who understand and who have admiration and respect to offer.

This little room has become to some of us, then, and it is not too much to say, an enormous room—enormous, I say again, if only because it let a few personalities develop in the way they were believed in, and find the way to develop of themselves.

Arthur G. Dove
A Different One

Once upon a time the same ones could always take the same things to the same places and get the same welcome because the things were the same.

There never was any difference. Any one with any eye could see that.

Even some of those same ones could see that, but they kept on in the same way.

Then there was Stieglitz who at the right time and the right spot threw the wrench.

So by now we have more up-to-now machinery. At least it is not always the same.

There was a great necessity for a live one because there were so many undertakers, and they all made their livings from the dead ones.

The Gentlemen of the Juries would go to Stieglitz's exhibitions and get themselves talked to by an honest man which they never liked any more than they did the paintings.

But it put some of them onto themselves and it put others onto them, so they had to paint modern faces on the backs of their heads, but the knowing ones knew that the undertakers' faces were on the other side so they couldn't go in places where there were mirrors.

And they had to wear snap ties, and all together it was pretty difficult.

And everyone laughed at the wrong moment.

And they forgot to bring their check-book.

So the same ones bought new colors and tried to paint up their spirits but they couldn't reach them—they were too far down.

There was an esthetic revolution going on and they didn't know it, and Stieglitz knew it all the time.

And crowds of people came to hear him talking about the whole condition and they couldn't go back and listen to the same ones talking of their condition.

So the same ones banded together and tried to make the whole condition their condition.

But they couldn't agree because all of them were thinking of their condition, and conditions had changed.

I always hear someone talking of the whole condition.

Someone I always like to hear talking.

Who is always saying something, something that has life rather than value.

It is like the voice of a fine old firm that made fine instruments for the love of their quality.

It is a great voice.

This voice will always be known.

Everyone who has known this voice knows that it will be, I mean the knowing ones.

[This voice is the thing that has changed this America of ours.]

Made something of hope in it.

It has quality.

I have the privilege of knowing the owner of this voice, and—I wouldn't trade it for anything.

I mean that I know Stieglitz, impersonal as any human being so charged with spirit can be.

[And I know that he loves an idea well enough to give his life to that idea all day long every day.]

He loves race horses and does not bet, he is that way about everything.

I like his being a thorn in the crown of the commonplace. And I have always been glad to know him more than any other man.

This man is the greatest photographer, and he has made photography an art.

I have heard O'Keeffe say, "Dove, he's got us beaten."

There was never any compromise in the introduction of ideas, which had been introduced one after the other for the first time in America.

A fine old head with a spirit that can make circles around the younger ones through sheer spiritual energy.

His ears appear as though the roots of his feelings have grown out into the air in the form of hair for more room to breathe.

I have seen some of his feelings, black and white as his photographs, with the same subtle meaning that perhaps even beautiful color could never answer.

Stieglitz was trying to let people see that photography was an art, and at the same time showing Picasso who was trying to make his art "more photographic."

When asked what Stieglitz means to me as an artist, I answer: everything.

Because I value his opinion as one who has always known.

I do not think I could have existed as a painter without that super-encouragement and the battle he has fought day by day for twenty-five years.

He is without a doubt the one who has done the most for art in America.

Charles Demuth
Lighthouses and Fog

For no reason, perhaps a very good reason, after all;—as I start to write this,—I have been thinking, when really not thinking, of lighthouses and fog.

Lighthouses and fog—a lighthouse and many fogs. There really are not many lighthouses, and fogs seem to be always rolling in from most distinguished shores and seas.

Lighthouses are fixed. Sometimes they seem to have moved but—they really haven't. Lights in lighthouses sometimes move but they do not move as lights in a political street parade move. Lights in lighthouses sometimes wink, and I've seen them myself twinkle.

"But you said you were writing about Stieglitz——"

"Well, I am writing about Stieglitz—here, this is what I have been doing—writing about Stieglitz!"

Jennings Tofel
A Portrait

THE PERSONALITY of Alfred Stieglitz has been captivating and perplexing me a long time. I observed the man, his life, his work. I knew that such extraordinary Force should be set down in writing, recorded, but never dared to; feeling it was altogether too big a thing, too complex and varied a nature, made up of so many polarities that would be hard to reconcile in one portrait. But as Stieglitz is growing older and ever more subtle and abstract, soon to extend altogether beyond my capacity as a writer, I will make my first attempt now. To paint his portrait full length properly against the background of these times it would require a master. I can hope to put together only a few simple paragraphs here, a pen portrait of this complex man in a single outline.

What is so remarkable about Stieglitz? In a word, it is the fact that what are two extremes abide in one individual: the active and the contemplative man. The range thus is vast. You cannot at a bound pass from one to the other. You traverse thereby space and time, and along the way lies all life. So authentic an artist as Stieglitz the photographer and so complete a man of the world flourishing side by side in one man command very large quarters indeed for the soul to dwell in in peace.

But if there is any jostling going on within, who knows of it? In one room, on exquisite walls, Stieglitz's exquisite presentation of the ecstatic water colors of Marin, or O'Keeffe's austere passion; in another—in a little cubbyhole, the photographer's dark room—Stieglitz's own lyrics of the sky coming into his exacting view. And think of this artist to whom the thought of money is repellent as an equivalent for his work, talking money freely, almost insensitively matter of fact, to the buyer of the painter's pictures as well as to those who don't buy.

Stieglitz skillfully dissociates the art from the man. Art is invaluable but does not feed the man, who must live. In the next turn of the sentence the man and his work are interchangeable: the picture is a Marin. Then finally the picture is nothing, that is, not an emotional reflex but a symbol, nor even a symbol, merely an index to a man, who, standing somewhere in the midst of facts, paints, suffers, dreams.

Just why does Stieglitz talk so much? Is it in order to teach or to learn or to right some wrong? All of these, but incidentally he is practising an art, the art of the spoken word. Passing through the stages of soliloquy—meditating aloud—and dialogue—conversation

—his talk has entered the phase of dramatic narrative. Where once he needed the interlocutor's "cue," he now is content with his mere presence. And there unfolds itself a story of great power. And the story is this same man Stieglitz unfolding into a drama. A man born in America with the demon within that is art. Therein lies much conflict. And that demon has two heads and one body. One head looks to the past, the other to the future, and the body, I hardly need say, is the present. The creative demon and in the American scene—what a spectacle, what drama!

And Stieglitz, a master of talk, with the unsought and bare word, without gesture, without pauses or poses, but voluminously, portrays, judges, synthesizes these times we live in, this American scene of our struggles. One is overawed by the weight of his pronouncements; one hangs on his periods until he has completed them. There is no stray thought but will be threaded into the scheme of the whole woof. Your one regret is you cannot hold so much. But that does not worry Stieglitz. With Cézanne, he leaves his pictures out in the field where he painted them. However, it is not ever lost, this talk like living seed. It insinuates itself into the soil of America in the most impalpable way.

This rich, copious talk, so sure, so bold, so human—what is its source? What feeds it? What impels it? Above all I would say: Faith. He lashes out at American sentimentality and hardness, out of faith in America. He leaves so much collected art and data—out of faith in the coming men of America. He stands guard over the artists of his choice from their veriest beginnings through all their deviations and gropings. What is it but faith in creative men?

And Stieglitz does not misplace his faith. He knows men. He goes to art by way of the living man, where it is possible. The art may be in a fallow period, in a stage of transition or at its beginning. Not so the man. The man is the soul of the man—a fixed star. He searches him out to the core, to the white glow, where the soul sits rocking on the rhythms of its own music.

Only a prophet would venture to tell from the first tentative efforts an artist's later work, the new garb of acquired rules covering over the natural laws of body and soul. But the character of the man, of every man, stands out from the very first—and perhaps more clearly so at first—naked as daylight, in the full view of those who can see. Only a cataclysm may make a man over. But a man will surely make over his first pictures. All of his life the artist is re-forming his medium, just so it would capture and hold—what?—no more than that true vision of self or that sure awareness of this or that man, woman, or thing.

To the degree that Stieglitz knew men, did he also know himself. He recognized himself very early as just such a man as he later sought round about him. He knew himself, as Adam knew himself, alone and sad, in this Paradise of America. The country had to be sifted and sifted again for what it might yield of the finer spirits among whom to dwell and work. The old men and those grown lazy stayed away. Anyway, they could not have gone through the holes in the sieve that Stieglitz held, any more than the camel long ago could pass through the eye of the needle. Only spirited and visionary young men came. Their coming to Stieglitz was in itself a test of their probity. There was no splendid gallery to draw them, no patrons, no sinecures. They came through an urge within them. It was an art movement in America that has hardly yet begun to be evaluated. And Stieglitz was its First and Chief Mover.

The forces that urge a man on do not exist apart from the man. They shine through in a transfigured way, it is true, but they show through that man only. The forces of vitality, love, and faith, spring from that man. They run over into a manifest physiognomy. They run over into manifest activities. With the artist they run over into the symbols at his command. These are the various ways of knowing a man: from his mask, from his deeds, from the visions he projects. In a simple man, his various ways of manifesting himself are not at variance. Not quite so, Stieglitz. All of Stieglitz does not hover on the surface. And there is so much art and imagination in his activities outside of his art that they body forth still another Stieglitz.

The physiognomy of Stieglitz shows purest, however, in his photographs, the medium in which he is a master. His ideal of clear statement he could bring about best here. But these photographs are not statements only, by which are meant primarily states of the mind; they are states of a soul. No prose enters here. No harshness of voice, but regrettably also they lack that arching of the upper lip, their concept is Apollonian. Stieglitz escapes here to breathe his rarest atmosphere.

As a diver for pearls comes up to breathe the common air again, so Stieglitz comes back into the tumultuous life he obviously loves too. Many an artist knows as well as Stieglitz the void about him which he would so want to encompass about with walls which should retain his music and not let it disperse and mix with the volatile air and so be lost. I mean, they are aware that they must know and love men and women, commune and suffer with them —but somehow they go on living apart, in their shell, and hope to be gods, when they do not dare to be human.

But, though Stieglitz does not carry the Dionysian clatter into the picture, yet he distills life into his art. And a lot of life, and a lot of love too! And it is a fallacy to say that he holds the subject matter as an inferior element. He does not love those heads he portrays? Those skies with sun and clouds? The skyscrapers of New York? Does he employ them only for the "pull and push" of their lines?—that which is the physics of a picture? Away beyond

that reaches out the symbolic—or spiritual—value of the subject matter, which Stieglitz, rooting as he does in life, certainly cannot despise. There is an affinity between the matter and the master.

But as his abundant matter cannot be absorbed into his meticulous and exquisite prints—the Apollonian concept discriminating against much of it—he turns the residue into the stuff of his talk, of which I have already given a glimpse. And so this is another phase of his creative physiognomy.

But for all the fascination of Stieglitz's speech, what would it be but for the body of his talk? Stieglitz's idiom is not brilliant, his phrases in themselves not arresting. His style of speech is casual. One does not know by what art he entrains his listeners. And although one does not at once see the purport of Stieglitz's talk as it begins, one feels, nevertheless, that something of great moment is steadily unfolding. The purport finally becomes clear. It is, to evolve some principle of art, of man, of justice, from his own high plane. The mass of knowledge he has drawn from everywhere, and his own factual experiences inform his talk, though they never weigh it down. He thereby does not formulate any principles, though you feel them forever there. High principles—a sense of art that is religious. Death being as sleep. A sense of responsibility that is heroic. What has been begun is Fate. The perfect thing that is even a blade of grass.

Now those principles are not the rare playthings of the mind of a recluse that lives in some high inaccessible fastness. They are alive at every point, and Stieglitz brings them home to us again and again by his own acts. He is of the company of the great teachers who teach by their own example, by the side of whom good and true things take on an added luster, and ugly and selfish things an added reproach. These men raise the standard of values by their very life. Act upon act they build their life, like a house, in the full view of men. From the ground plan to the finished thing, it is of one irresistible purpose, as if a master mind made it— although as many contrarieties have gone into its composition as disrupts many an ideal scheme: the heart and the curious mind, outer influences and the tides and times.

Stieglitz has made up his life of his acts, acts as tangible as days, as many and as easy to record. Acts mostly of his own initiative, propelled by a flash of intuition—acts of faith. And acts reasoned out and engineered—acts of will. Acts of apparently small account and acts of great moment—all launched with the same care and love, and directed knowingly or unknowingly toward that far-reaching end—The Perfect Life.

As in his photographs and in his talk, so also in his activities, there are no loose ends. It will all be taken care of in due time. The provident eye will not weaken until he sees it through, and the hand will not falter until everything is in its place.

Alfred Stieglitz must know, as well as most of us do, that there is no one else as venturesome and right, as unselfish and just, and as complex a personality as himself, in all the art life of this land at this time, or hitherto.

Edna Bryner
An American Experience

STIEGLITZ BEGAN for one person with Marin.

Marin was what was being taken in by a body inclined dervishly-whirling because of eyes impelled to lightning-rapid adjustments along the eight walls of short-hand performances constituting the great water-colorist's first encompassing show.

What was being taken in was American landscape in all its leaping drama from universal storm menace out of heavy sea floor to that lightest cloud-capering which only American landscape seems foolish enough to indulge in. (And which, "stooping so high," without a doubt tickles the taproot of the country's peculiar *humor* into flinging out beyond its capacious bole of belly-shaking gustiness the very last tenderest laughing-leaf.)

One's head was not so much in clouds as one's body, stanch enough on American earth, went fox-and-goose chasing in American air with its prankish jumps from heavy to light, wet to dry, hot to cold; in American Atlantic pushing ship to air's yea and nay (and to an astute artist's advantage); in American vegetation achieved to its precise size shape texture tone out of just this earth air water.

Sporty landscape, that, poking people too unexpectedly, too hard in the ribs, perhaps; requiring too hasty, too great adjustments of breath intake, blood flow: put down by a man who could take in to the last vibration and deliver to the last quippish delight quick small large slow contrasts.

One stabilized to fondest element-intimacy through long heaping up from earliest impressions of warm sun on soft hair, white snow softness against hard windowpane opaqueness, lustful grit of earth scooped out of wettish spring furrows: That one was boisterously caught up, tossed about, wanted to step hard, push, weep, laugh, so rapidly changeful the impact from performance to performance of LIGHT as living in its mysterious play on paper as actual play of mysterious north light on northern gold-barred sea heaving towards bright midnight.

NEVER BEFORE! an inner voice exulted. But NOW!

YES. From without, answering, a voice curiously alone, impersonal, as if a button pressed had set going mechanism, gave confirmation. Speech, this, evoked from water-color world? No. Came from a man, light on feet approaching, nimble though not dancer, treading to a theme as sporting as that animating wall-shown landscape. YES, assured the upward-going register, throwing out equivocal springboard inviting ensuing leaps and nosedives, WHEN ANYONE gives himself or herself to me, he gives not fifty per cent, not seventy-five per cent, nor even ninety-eight per cent: he or she gives a HUNDRED PER CENT.

Voice, after all, from world of water color!

It came to a person that behind the water color landscape there, ranged a man as sporting in his sponsoring as the artist in that creativeness which let landscape natively sport. That man, rushed into realization for one hitherto thoughtless from too deep absorption in interesting other affairs, that man was Stieglitz.

Stieglitz had existed, had been known to this one, to many, before; had long record of esthetic daring. This particular performance marked for one person a unique coming together of an extraordinary man with an original artist in an esthetic triumph. Stieglitz, American landscape, Marin: three one-hundred-per-centers in closest hand-holding. Emerged out of the intensifications in the high conjunction before one's heightened vision, as a pure water source out of wellings from intricately veined depths into thirst-quenching flow, an indisputable AMERICAN THING.

What, asked the beholder prompt to this amazing rendezvous publicly arrived at on the spur of the moment, what underlay the feeling Stieglitz had for letting Marin's every device of water color in brilliantly syncopated gamut from sea-gashed hardest browns and blues to mist-drenched pink-and-yellow froth tune up full throat? The answer, immediate, was out of what was already known: The sternest history of black and white.

This sounds Puritan. Stieglitz was one when he made black-and-white history.

YES is the great symbol of delivery. No belongs to the by-product of process, to the slipping away of everything not to be wrought into the precious package. The man who said YES to artist's YES in landscape positiveness and to beholder's YES of looking assisted in the delivery of artist, landscape, beholder.

But man Stieglitz had first delivered himself.

A simple thing like this needs to be said.

Art, popularly, is sometimes said to deliver a man of his creativeness consonantly to a woman's bringing forth of children. Art, solemnly, may be a way of man's freeing himself of his feminine rôle in life.

Stieglitz was prolific mother before becoming expert midwife.

His delivery was in black and white.

A piece of black velvet and a white plaster cast. What really black is: what really is white. What does white do to black and black to white under what conditions? When young man Stieglitz gave himself over in an exasperation of a few hundred attempts at putting down black velvet-white plaster values with a machine, he had worried out his main theme. Modern, animating the contemporary scene from Einsteinian physics to new-code morals for all those ill at ease in a tottering subject-predicate world, that theme started into vibration a relevant tone texture resulting in the reaching out to, the drawing in of Marin, O'Keeffe, Dove, as associated major themes in a harmoniously evolving symphony.

Nothing more native has ever come out of America than Marin, O'Keeffe, Dove. Nothing more native has ever been achieved than Stieglitz. For an achievement Stieglitz is, difficult, tortuous, American.

This achievement began, as countless American things began to be, in Europe, where men sent their sons to be educated in a way not thought possible at the time in America. A James, later an Eliot, went thus to Europe; and stayed. Stieglitz, sent thus, returned duly to America. He was, truly, ordered back. A James, an Eliot, in Europe to develop literary talent in the grand old English tradition, did precisely that; and stayed on, caught willing prisoners. Stieglitz, not accomplishing courses calculated to make him into a first-rate engineer, ate up precious time by feeding a newly invented little machine on black velvet and white plaster to see what it could contrive out of such material.

But is not America the land of the MACHINE? Quite in order, then, though ordering be peremptory, that one so machine-involved should be hustled back to the country of machine-involvement!

There was something as quippish in Stieglitz, going out nineteenth-century Puritan returning twentieth-century Pilgrim, as in the landscape he came back to, to document wonderfully in black-and-white notations leading in his own work to the later incredibly intricate Equivalents, laying at the same time subtle basis for his stout sponsoring of Marin.

Just here emerged for the person exhilarated in the unusual rendezvous an obvious center of gravity in this particular American experience. In Stieglitz was a European bias, perhaps born, perhaps deposed by European-born parents anxious for a son's welfare in a still strange land. In Stieglitz was, perhaps is still, a nostalgic longing for the traditional liberal European life of the full-sensed man. (If the actuality today is a mockery, the notion survives.) But there must have been in the youth, there is supremely now in the long-matured man, urge for an Americanization beyond all ordinary conceit. Have we not, here, the Jew set towards utmost deliverance?

The touch of Europe, not the same on a Stieglitz as on a James or an Eliot, had the rare value of pointing off utmost possibility in America. Stieglitz hatched his eaglet in Europe; but it was an American one, going back to the totem bird of ancient American tribes: he must have had its good egg along with him in some precious pocket. (His serpent egg he had along, too; hatched, too, in Europe, yet developing characteristically American!)

The American possibility was not for him great business activity in which numbers of his race have found their deliverance in America, nor in a profession, that which his parents wished for him, nor law, nor medicine to which Jews have made confident contribution in this country. For him it was the possibility of defining with the rigid logic of law the field of activity of a little box machine; of engineering activities in that field; of delivering, finally, he more than any other, the painting world of a lovely incubus—no mean surgical operation!—on which his black box munching in many mouthfuls he let come forth again with consummate skill, the bothering creature, in sharp shining transformation.

The European in Stieglitz, the pent-up American, the Jew yearning for deepest rootedness, was a late thing, already largely at liberty, gargantuan in its push towards absolute fetterlessness: it reached out beyond most things termed American to the furthest reaches to which himself, those chosen to him, could go; thrusting at times paradoxically beyond.

His delivery, then, did not fix him on the thing delivered. Steadying his hands to ever surer development towards full-grown handling of machine medium, it liberated him to the seeing of what was being done in painting that was not merely duplication in color of camera's doing; and with a kind of stone-law logic to the searching out and sponsoring of those artists who had the peculiar fertilizing power to raise up new forms from an incubus-relieved field: in short, to Marin, O'Keeffe, Dove.

The sporting element in him sustained by uncanny knowing could let an artist, a Marin, an O'Keeffe, a Dove, be himself, herself, and himself again and again times over in the open eyes of everyone: furnishing opportunity for experience which many a one may live to regret not having availed himself fully of. Year by year he could let American landscape deliver itself, in all its moods without shadow from the European scene, through Marin and through water color increasing in importance as medium far beyond any level dreamed of as possible. He could let a woman, O'Keeffe, deliver the body of woman's architectural mysteries through flower and fruit sonatas, New York skyscrapers, Canadian barns, white bones of the desert. He could let man Dove deliver himself, in American rawness of machine and elemental scene, of that particular *witness of the body* which emerges ever more significantly as a living element of modern esthetic presentation. Giving, he, all the while, in black-and-white counterpoint, ever newly, more penetratingly, his own passionate yearning for spontaneous union with the quick of livingness.

126

These artists, he, working out of the direct experience of life itself, American; not out of other people, or works of art, schools, books, music. Nothing reminiscent: but at high moments *remembrance back to very ancient life when participation was common and completely satisfying* in accordance with the strictest esthetic integrity, conditioned as in any life process by the exigencies pressing most nearly on the incident occasion.

Stieglitz thus stood forth, for one stirred beholder, out of a prime happy coming together of esthetic significances to remain through many consequent comings together, not a man, not even a human being; but an experience of complicated closely woven texture as American as any experience ever come through by an extremely native person.

Self-creation by liberation, this experience: of enormous moment, extraordinary immediate satisfaction, unending reward; because it is PROCESS. PROCESS is THING. The American PROCESS is the AMERICAN THING. No one has demonstrated that process better than Stieglitz; no educational experiment, no elaborated thesis has so thoroughly set forth the historical self-created fact.

An historical fact presents questions, poses towards a future. So this one:

> Will water color reach, in America, its highest development, unhindered by the dominance of oil-importance?
>
> Will woman attain, in America, her own esthetic destiny untrammeled by the shibboleth of male art dominance?
>
> Will the Jew find, in America, new Palestine, unbruised by the bugaboo of Aryan dominance?
>
> Will the quick of livingness again be captured, in America, by the many, participated in fully, completely enjoyed, beyond the bindings of down-pushing isms?

He sits in his ROOM, this man Stieglitz, as Zarathustra in his Hole, with eagle and serpent. "I sit here, I do not need to go out, the world comes to me." True. He goes not out to his *Jünger;* they come to him, older ones, also. He is troubled by *Weiber,* clever, knowing, sly *Weiber,* as was Zarathustra troubled: he tells them his wisdom, asks of them questions, takes in their answers, gives forth their wisdom. He is not an *Einsiedler,* like Zarathustra, but a *"Zwei-siedler":* hence much sorrow. There is something old, old in him, making more strict the struggle to meet new conditions, make new conditions. He stammers to form new speech for those who come to him in need of it; and moans that always the same thing comes up to strike him in the face in a new way. Thus again, like Zarathustra, he "cooks over and over in his own juice," turning himself more thoroughly into his own historical fact.

And are not men, in final meaning, the true historical facts?

Dorothy Brett
The Room

MY FIRST MEETING WITH STIEGLITZ was, like all meetings with those people who have meant most to me, a moment of anguish. The preparation for this meeting, the long correspondence between Lake George, where Stieglitz was lying seriously ill, and Mabel Luhan about my paintings, my Indian paintings that Mabel thought he ought to see. . . . The tales I had been told filled me with apprehension and dismay. . . . Nevertheless my paintings left Taos for New York, and Mabel and I followed them later. . . . We arrived at the Shelton Hotel the day before Stieglitz and Georgia O'Keeffe. When they arrived the following day, Georgia came down to see us and arranged that she and Stieglitz would come down the following evening to see the paintings if I would have them unpacked and ready. . . .

The following evening with my paintings all round the room, leaning against the walls, perched on tables, and on the backs of chairs, Mabel and I waited, I pacing up and down the room, nervous, horrified, miserable. At last Mabel turned on me exasperated. "For goodness sake," she said, "sit down. He won't eat you." I pulled a heavy armchair round, turning its high back to the room, and sat hidden in it, my cold feet on the boiling radiator. There hidden, I sat, knowing I could neither hear nor see the door open and the entry of these strange upsetting people. . . . I sat silent and remote behind the shield of the armchair until a beautiful resonant voice said to me, "I am Stieglitz." I looked up, and standing looking down at me was a gray-haired dark-eyed man. In the eyes was kindness, in the line of the shapely lips lurked a smile, and over the face lay serenity. . . . I stared back for a moment too astonished by the unexpectedness of the man to move; then I got up and shook the extended hand. "Why," I thought, "did no one tell me he was like this?" . . . and the fear went out of me, leaving only the shyness. Yet is it shyness? Is it not rather the strange desire to keep withdrawn, not to blur with words, until knowledge of the other stands clearer? I don't know, but I did know even then, and nothing has altered one whit what I knew to be the truth in this man. My allegiance and my belief went out to him, and he has never failed to help me all through the ensuing years. Permitting me to test my paintings by placing them round the walls of the Room, gently showing me my direction, as a painter, as a human being: there is no harsh criticism, no attempt to pull down, always the clear-sighted understanding, the endeavor to uphold what has been achieved and to encourage greater endeavor.

For one whole week I was too upset and nervously excited to venture to the Intimate Gallery. At last Mabel took me there in a taxi and left me there. This was the first time I had ever seen a Marin.

Hardly had I recovered from the wonder and beauty of the Marins than Georgia O'Keeffe's paintings were shown. By this time I had become a silent habitué of the Room. I went often, nearly every day, casting an anxious glance at the small man in the large armchair. He would smile encouragingly at me, still leaving me to myself. Georgia would be sitting quietly, a half smile on her lips, a quizzical friendly look in her eyes, her beautiful long white hands folded in her lap, calm and quiet in her black-and-whiteness. My silence deepened. Only in writing could I tell Georgia what I thought of her painting; and that is another tale.

Slowly, somewhat painfully I suppose, owing to my silent approach, a friendship began to grow between us three, but it was when I came back later in the winter to live at the Shelton again that our contact became closer. Four of us would foregather in the cafeteria for breakfast. Stieglitz, Georgia, Claude Bragdon, and I. The ensuing conversations would amuse not only the adjoining tables, but the whole room, as Stieglitz's already resonant voice was raised considerably for my deaf ears. All the voices were pitched in a louder key for my benefit, and the talk never flagged.

Stieglitz with his two profiles. Often have I wondered what his face would have been if the accident of the broken nose had not given him these entirely different profiles, one so flowing, the other so sharp. With his silver hair like an aureole around his head; his serene face, lovely shapely lips, strange dark eyes, eyes with an inner dark light in them; his figure, slight and small, though well proportioned, composed and dignified. Georgia, her pure profile against the dark wood of the paneling, calm, clear; her sleek black hair drawn swiftly back into a tight knot at the nape of her neck; the strong white hands, touching and lifting everything, even the boiled eggs, as if they were living things—sensitive, slow-moving hands, coming out of the black and white, always this black and white. . . . Claude Bragdon, tall, strong, with his full-lidded eyes, close-cropped white hair, full small mouth, a Chinese Buddha, uncanny in his likeness to the Chinese Buddhas in the Metropolitan Museum. Witty, gay, a profound thinker, with a joyous love of life and laughter and the mysteries of life. Thus we four foregathered, foregather to this day when we happen to be all living in the Shelton.

From those early days I have pursued the Room. The Intimate Gallery becoming An American Place. It is An American Place that I have known most closely. It is there that I have lived and learned, have come to discover and rediscover the spirit that presides there, of which so much has been written, so much felt and not felt. For me, as I do not wish to diagnose, to analyze, to presuppose a knowledge that belongs only to the man himself . . . to me, sitting watching, listening, learning, the Room is a pool of serenity, the battleground of peace. Where the spirit of man or woman, expressed in art, meets the presentation worthy of it; where the spirit must be technically well equipped, well presented on the most perfect of walls; where perfection meets perfection, and where the buying and selling are undertaken on lines unique in the world. . . . The Room is an Immaculate Conception. . . .

Stieglitz is a crusader. . . . The Room is the Song of Songs for some of us. The visible half of Stieglitz hangs upon the walls, in his own photography, in the paintings. It is in the tales he tells, in the way of his speech. The other, the invisible . . . lies in the look behind the look in the eyes, in the dark light of them, in the peaceful line of the lips, in the serene face with its halo of silver hair. . . .

Stieglitz standing in the Room, among the many visitors, casting his swift comprehensive glance over them, sending the magnetic power of his voice through them, speaking in parables or else speaking at them . . . witty, brilliant talk, with always that undertone of wisdom, the wisdom of a man who sees all others in himself. . . . To be whole, how rare that is! The wholeness of Stieglitz is rarely broken, his wisdom seldom fails him, except in those moments when he turns away from his own knowledge, when from enthusiasm, from motives outside himself, he recklessly disregards his own wisdom and reluctantly pays the price. . . .

But the wholeness of the man is everywhere. You have but to watch, to see the man who will patiently wait . . . for hours . . . for days . . . for weeks or years . . . the camera ready, for the moment . . . the one moment . . . when sun and cloud meet in the way he seeks, that his inner vision awaits. . . . Thus he awaits other moments . . . the moment for the camera . . . the moment when his door opens . . . and a new expression of his own spirit walks in . . . walks in, and then . . . there must be no compromise, the service given is to life . . . to the beauty of all life, derived and springing out of the love-life . . . and to the untrammeled purity of spirit. . . . There are no half measures, there must be no failure, unless the failure is but one of incomplete power to express; but the other failure when at the final issue the spirit quails and sinks before the exigencies of the world—for those failings there is no help. Recognition of himself and what he upholds is not enough for this man of steel. He demands wholeness in others to match his own wholeness.

In himself he is fearless. He fears no man, no situation. In his bearing he is simple, unaffected, unafraid. He walks among men as a tree stands among trees or as a flower grows upon a desert. . . .

He is always the manifestation of one spirit. It shines from the walls, it shines from the man . . . one's own spirit rushes towards it as it comes, shining, towards one. . . .

Thus the same spirit meets the buying and selling. It is more a passionate exchange rather than the age-old idea of trading. The difference lies in the approach. If the buyer's desire for the painting springs from the heart; and the buyer seeks earnestly a means to meet the demand made for the artist, then, with the welfare of the artist always in mind, Stieglitz advances to meet the buyer; acknowledging the spirit of the buyer and his or her fitness to possess the painting. Thus the passionate exchange is made, and Stieglitz's lifelong endeavor to procure a decent livelihood for the artist momentarily accomplished.

To go to the Room in the early morning is to disturb a peace as the throwing of a stone into a pool disturbs the water. . . . It may be Marin's joyous spirit singing from the walls, or it may be Georgia's trumpet calls to the hidden life of women calling out mysteriously . . . mystically their hidden message. . . . Either way a perfume flows out from the paintings, the colors throw out sound as of music; and sitting quietly at his table, or standing leaning against a bookcase writing . . . is Stieglitz. . . . There is peace around him, the perfume and the music of the paintings is his also. The face is calm, the dark eyes filled with their dark light, and the lips untroubled. . . . The outside world hums far below. The integrity of the man and the Room are impregnable. I lean against the wall wrapped in the stillness, in the immeasurable peace that flows from the paintings, from the undaunted ardent spirit of the man. . . . Spread over it like wings is the mantle of tenderness. It comes hovering from the paintings, hovers round the man, in the clear understanding, the compassionate gesture . . . the gesture that breaks through the stillness to say in that marvelous voice, the timbre ringing through the empty Room . . . "Well, how are you today?" . . . and at that moment, among those paintings . . . in the presence of that man, I have a great longing to reply, "I am feeling beautiful." . . .

Victoria Ocampo
A Witness

. . . Life itself, trying to find out what Life is.
WALDO FRANK.

PERRAULT TELLS THE TALE of Riquet de la Houppe, a prince so ugly that a fairy happening to pass that way when he was born took pity

on such ugliness and gave him, for compensation, the gift of wit: so much wit that he would be able to bestow, on the person he loved most, as much as he had himself. You will remember that Riquet fell in love with a fair princess, a princess fair but stupid! The fairy who attended Riquet's birth was also present at the first appearance of the princess; and she took pity on such dullness and, for compensation, gave her the power to make whomever she loved most as beautiful as she was.

This fairy, who was so sensitive to human ills, had ways of remedying them . . . indirect and mysterious ways . . . no ordinary fairy could have contrived. I vow she was no ordinary fairy. Thus, while she realized that nothing could be done to make so dull a princess bright, or so ugly a prince handsome, she managed the matter in a very simple fashion, by giving to the beauty of the one and to the brightness of the other the power to project itself; thus overcoming the danger that such illumination and such beauty remain each incommunicable and forever bound within itself.

When, three years ago, I went to 509 Madison Avenue; when I stepped from the elevator to a door on which was written An American Place; when I entered a room of white walls filled with light, bare of furniture; when I found myself suddenly at home in this room which resembled what I love the most, and realized that I was feeling, for the first time since I had come to the United States, at home; and when Stieglitz came forward with open hand I was far from being ignorant of the artist he was, but I had no idea of *who* he was.

I was far from suspecting that, after my traffic through immoderate New York whose skyscrapers and noises overwhelmed me, I was to fall (in a Madison Avenue office building) straight into a fairy tale. Or rather, that in these Madison Avenue rooms an old fairy tale was to be told me; a new version of Riquet de la Houppe. And that this tale, which had enchanted my childhood, was to be told to me in terms, this time, of a reality miraculous, like everything real, without intercession of fairies or princesses, by a white-haired man: a man ravaged by love of America, ravaged unto hate, who had no means of expression (if you forget his ardent head and words) except a photographic machine, a machine like any other.

Waldo Frank had said to me: He is perhaps the one great artist that we have today. As Stieglitz drew forth his photographs, one by one, with caressful hands, as from a hiding place, I remembered these words. Skies, trees, faces, bodies, factories, wharves . . . surprised and fixed at a certain angle by a machine, with all the machine's inplacable precision . . . were, after all, not what the machine had seized from the reality; were what Stieglitz had seized of his own dream within reality, through and by the aid of a machine. The continuous exchange between the genial human emotion of Stieglitz before lives and things, and the record, indifferent and incorruptible, of the machine catching details, has made these admirable photographs; so admirable that one is moved to name them otherwise, and yet their fairest title is that they are photographs.

At this moment I have before me two of these photographs. Waldo Frank brought me them as a gift, saying they were the best he could find of his America to carry to South America. They are two tiny squares of sky pasted on much white cardboard. Two "moods" of the sky. The quantity and density of cloud makes the material difference between them. There is just enough sky to fill a lookout. But I have never seen so much sky take up so small a space. Stieglitz has snapped only the sun and a bit of cloud. No trouble in that! But the result is a portrait and a portent of Nature, so nature-sized and of a grandeur so articulate of its model that I want to repeat with Pascal: "The silence of this infinite space affrights me. . . ."

The day I visited his rooms, when Stieglitz had done showing me his photographs and many paintings by Georgia O'Keeffe, Hartley, Marin, Dove, we moved over to the window. New York rose in huge jets of skyscrapers against our eyes. Stieglitz pointed to the city. "I have seen it growing. Is that beauty? I don't know, I don't care. I don't use the word beauty. It is life." . . . I listened, smiling; taken suddenly by that strange need to cry (of which we are ashamed), which comes to us with the happiness of finding what we are no longer expecting. I say "no longer" expecting; instead of "not" expecting. For the need to weep comes precisely from that "no longer"; from the long series of deceptions and defeats that lead us at last to be "no longer expecting" and that, released by this moment of unhoped-for joy, defile dizzily in our mind and make of our joy so sharp a contrast with this self-pity they awake in us that we can hardly bear it. Those who drown know this emotion, at the instant of death, although it is invoked by inverse causes.

An American Place . . . these modest rooms (where the first Cézannes, Matisses, Picassos, found a home on our side of the Atlantic) have been a refuge, I am told, for those who have lost their gods and who suffer in their search for new ones. Was this, perhaps, what I felt as I came into these light-walled rooms? I also was one of those who come for a refuge. We are men and women who suffer from the American desert because we still bear in us something of Europe; and who stifle in Europe because we already bear in us America. Exiles from Europe in America; exiles from America in Europe: we are a little group, scattered from north to south of a vast land, who are afflicted with the malady that no displacement can definitely cure. We are always haunted by the fear of finding the earth, where we need to take root, cease to be earth . . . cease to be nurture (they are the same), and become instead a springboard urging us to leap to a far shore.

An American Place. . . . It would never have occurred to me that I should find an oasis by that name! That is a happiness one no more expects.

"Is that beauty? I don't know. I don't care. I don't use the word beauty. It is life." Stieglitz is telling me the fairy story of Riquet de la Houppe, while from the open window rise the streets of New York, a vague, thick smoke of sound. There he is, leaning over his America, a machine in his hand, telling himself that "there is nothing to do" as regards beauty; but there's "everything to hope" as regards life. He is solving his problem . . . our problem . . . in the way of that extraordinary fairy, the way that is mysterious and indirect. He watches for life; he tracks it; he grapples with it. And when he has caught it, lo! in its place is beauty!

Harold Clurman
Alfred Stieglitz and the Group Idea

IN VIEW OF HIS GREATNESS as an artist, and his importance as a cultural force, comparatively little has been written about Alfred Stieglitz. For Stieglitz is amazingly difficult to write about. Even if the critic has sufficient temerity, he will shy from assertions about "the first photographer of our time" and "the man who brought modern art to America"—they are too bald. But equally unsatisfactory are those aspiring generalizations that appear inevitably to flow from the pen when Stieglitz is the subject.

Is the critical vocabulary so limited or so blunt that no word can define him? No, the difficulty in writing about Stieglitz derives from the inclusiveness of his work. Some artists may be dubbed subjective or objective, painters of nature or portrayers of men, classicists or modernists, realists or abstractionists, but almost any of these devices fit Stieglitz's work equally well and thus lose all value as terms of differentiation. It is fairly simple to discuss a part of something, but language becomes a clumsy medium when it is called upon to delineate a world. The critic used to the half-pint dimensions of most contemporary endeavor is literally lost in the cosmos which is the art of Alfred Stieglitz.

Nevertheless, no one man can be "all" things or represent "all" life. It is still possible to situate this artist, to mark him out from his fellows. But, let us insist, all understanding is violated that does not begin with an appreciation of Stieglitz as an "all-around man" in regard to subject matter, forms of emotion, relation to the past, projection of the future. Later we shall see that this universality of Stieglitz's art is also the touchstone of his symbolic and directive value. . . .

If any quality is absent in Stieglitz's photographs, it is the quality of hate. It is necessary to begin with this negative statement, since its positive would be the proposition that the creative principle of all Stieglitz's art is love, a statement that might give rise to a serious misconception. When we speak of love, we generally refer either to the erotic or to a generalized "humanitarian" sentiment. But though many of Stieglitz's photographs may be variously interpreted from the erotic or social point of view, his art, if we are to accept the conventional use of these terms, is in essence neither.

The love of which Stieglitz's prints are an expression is an infinitely tender, patient concentration on all that life brings before his tireless gaze: an impulse to touch and to understand through touch everything which gives life to an object without ever evincing the desire to make it forcibly other than it is. When this love confronts an evil thing it does not turn to hate but to sorrow. In the case of "small" objects—people or things he does not admire—Stieglitz's love is transformed to a faint caricature. But never in Stieglitz's work are we wounded by that denying bitterness that would destroy any living thing, never are we troubled by a sense that he has made himself superior to any part of life, or that being an artist he assumes he knows more.

This capacity for love has made Stieglitz a *seer*. Because nothing is too unimportant for him to see, and because everything he sees finally becomes the object of an all-embracing and therefore single love, his very simple, always accessible photographs take on a "mystic" quality, and Stieglitz is regarded as a "visionary"! We are unused to such attention in modern times. Stieglitz is incessantly attentive. He is attentive to everything that immediately confronts him. Because he cares for everything, because he loves. . . .

If one recognizes this love as the root feeling of Stieglitz's work, the other aspects of his art and of his activity in general become clarified to an unusual degree. One has only to consider him in the actual environment in which he has lived. Stieglitz is part of a moderately well-to-do American merchant family with cultural traditions that go back to the mellow well-being of bourgeois European civilization in the middle and late nineteenth century. His early photographs, taken in Europe, already show his gentle, sensitive temperament flowering naïvely and yet with mature assurance

in the face of the rich, delicate, strong, very old cultures of the Continental world. Being an American unacquainted with Art, his vision of Europe is unaffected and direct; being of German-Jewish extraction, his nature responds easily to the foreign scenes he photographs. Hence there is nothing in these early prints of the tourist with a camera, and later, in his photographs of New York and Lake George, there will be a kind of emotional subtlety, a spontaneous linking of infinite human associations with every individual object which might be termed "European."

What was the New York that Stieglitz returned to at the end of the century? It was a world in which fragments of Old World grace were lost amid the rising emblems of New World power. But the skyscrapers that were being built and the whole life of which they were the most conspicuous symbols were also fragmentary, lacking the human and social integration that could be read clearly in every detail of European existence. The world that Stieglitz returned to was a lonely world: active, ambitious, pushing its way frantically and fantastically to a goal it did not know. Man was somehow shut out of this world, even while he was helping to make it. The gloomy "city of ambition" that was rising in the early years of Stieglitz's career becomes in the nineteen-thirties an intricate, gigantic tomb. In between, Stieglitz dreams the great dream of his life. It is to build in America a place where men and women too strong to be crushed by the boom development of our civilization may gather to give tribute to the life that is within them and around them, and thus, in the last analysis, to create further life. Here, by an exchange of experiences around a pivot of interest, the work of their hands and hearts—a painting, a piece of sculpture, a photograph—these men and women might grow sure and clear and strong together, might inspire those who saw to other work wrought in the same spirit. Of this place Stieglitz was to be the guardian. Here—it was called "291" at first and later had other names—the artists and their "public" were to find and create the energy and the sense of order that would enable them to live in the barbarous, anarchic world outside—and by so doing to make it livable.

It is not unusual among Stieglitz enthusiasts to speak of his art in almost religious terms. This tendency on the whole has had the unfortunate result of making both his new and old admirers overlook the specific content of his photographs. Because the Equivalents—the sky photographs—have about them something of the prophet's apothegm, a certain habit has been formed of speaking of all his photographs as if their subjects were no closer to us than the sun and the clouds! But if we follow the progress of Stieglitz's photography we see that without being a "social artist" in the sense the term is given nowadays, his photographs, the product of a *photography parallel with o struggle*

profound sensibility amidst the evolving conditions of our American world, really compose a report of our period.

The early European photographs are mostly pictures of humble people who, whatever their position in life, are in harmony with their world, are indeed the "flowers" of their civilization. The fisherwomen, old workers, shopgirls, even the beggars and the girls of indeterminate occupation in the early prints, reveal themselves as complete human beings. In them, whatever the marks of their travail, their simplicity, their apartness from the "big world" of the upper classes, all that was most graceful, honest, homely and gentle in their society finds limpid expression. These pictures date from 1887 to 1889. Beginning with his return to the States in 1890 we see the same tender observation of lowly people at their work—it has rarely been remarked how many of Stieglitz's photographs have workers as their subjects—but already there are signs of a diminution, a feeling that though the artist himself regards these workers with love, everyone else has forgotten them, everything in their background tends to make us forget them, and later, that they are beginning to forget themselves. The outer world—the world of railroads, skyscrapers, aëroplanes, the world of industry and commerce—grows big, grows grim, grows black with determination and sullen will. We do not see precisely what forces are motivating this growth, but that it looms progressively more terrible and hideous, that it exists as a menace and that it leads to tragedy, the order of the prints makes ominously clear. The tone of the pictures—that were peaceful and transparent at first—becomes unemphatically desolate. The workers who come from Europe have somewhat harsher faces; they look out at the new horizon like mute victims or like people resigned to struggle. They are transformed later into the common creatures without substance or character who are herded in ferryboats moving pathetically toward a day of machine-made rest; they are seen taking their pleasure at industrialized seaside resorts, toiling solitary and blind on wet or snowy streets, or in excavations where the only dignity comes from the reality of the heavy work itself.

But Stieglitz is a man who loves; and the lover is a man who hopes. Together with these images of foreboding, Stieglitz photographs faces of people—Americans—in whom there is light and life. These men and women are mostly artists in whom he discovers creative potentialities: the capacity to see, to experience, and to speak. These are the bearers of his hope. These are the people who will bear witness with him to the still remaining (or nascent) human spirit of our country, who will prove in America the reality of the life of man! The artist's approach toward these men and women seems deeply affectionate, humble, thoughtful, and slightly apprehensive. These, for the most part, are the faces of 291.

Moreover, Stieglitz, now arrived at a maturity of years—the maturity of experience seems always to have been his—photographs his knowledge of woman. Stieglitz's prints of the body, face, hands of women are among the truly great achievements of art, because he has made of them the symbol of man's physical closeness to the world itself. Intimacy with woman's body is translated into the equivalent of man's most acute and crucial contact with everything in life. Henceforth, it would seem, all experience for Stieglitz (and for us) must possess the same intensity and depth or it cannot be regarded as experience at all. Unless our relations to objects, ideas, people are as desperately close and completely *involved* as this experience of woman they will forever remain accidental, superficial, mental. Stieglitz's photographs of woman are the image of a total immersion in life.

Profoundly erotic (and dangerously romantic) though this may seem to be, to stamp it as such is to render the effect of these photographs altogether static. One of the distinctions of Stieglitz's work lies in his ability to make each photograph a complete thing in itself and at the same time part of a process toward something beyond. Indeed, is not Stieglitz's extraordinary sense of line the plastic manifestation of his sense of continuity—of association and of correspondence in life? So that we can hardly think of Stieglitz's nudes and other portraits of women without desiring to see the sky pictures beside them. These pictures of the clouds and the sun are the graphs of Stieglitz's spirit creating in "remote" figures the generalizations—ideas of attraction and repulsion, struggle and unity, peace and conflict, tragedy and deliverance—that emerge from every individual experience to become part of our knowledge and preparation for other experiences. For each man draws from the "moments" of his life a "metaphysical" sum of understanding that seems to be greater and more important in relation to his progress into the future than the "moment" itself. Thus we give evidence of the perpetual "becoming" of life, and in the sense of that "becoming" lies the token of our present aliveness.

The war came, and Stieglitz stood apart from its hysteria and nonsense. There was an interruption in his work, and a rude awakening from the dream of 291. Stieglitz did not lose faith in the men he had revealed to America. But some of the early collaborators fell away: they were sucked into the whirlpool of the art business which with the after-the-war gold rush and its atmosphere of international exchange became a part of all other business. Stieglitz's places, of which his own photography was but a function, was another kind of business: that of American life itself. There were fewer people now, but their work was the ripe expression of experience uncontaminated by fashions or by the desire to wink flatteringly at the snobbism of the new "art public." At the Anderson Galleries, where I first saw Stieglitz in 1924, the whole of the first period of his effort (which means of course the work of his fellow artists as well as his own photographs) took on the aspect of a classic reminder of the past, and a challenge to the future. Here I first heard Stieglitz proclaim his comrades like a man battling on the barricades. But—I remember it very clearly —he was battling alone. The work at the Anderson Galleries was interrupted too, and Stieglitz repaired to An American Place.

His own art at this time (1929) becomes veritably majestic not only by virtue of an unsurpassable perfection of statement, but through a vision of an absolute grandeur, a vision of a life-and-death combat. At first this was mirrored in more cloud prints, but later (1930–1931) in new pictures of the city: built up now to a pyramidal splendor, crowded, immutable, and terribly, terribly deathlike. The New York of Stieglitz's recent photographs is far more magnificent than the old; more glittery, erect, indomitable. It is a city in which man has almost completely disappeared; despite all its metallic precision, it is like an enormous graven image of some very ancient civilization in which all signs of humanity have withered and everything is wrapped in silence. There is no denying it: the New York which we saw in the early photographs shadowed by a strange doom has reached its apogée of pride, and it is stricken beyond recall.

This picture of New York is simply the landscape that Stieglitz photographs by focusing his camera outside the window at Madison Avenue and Fifty-third Street. And since Stieglitz is the kind of artist who finds all his subjective intuitions embodied objectively in his immediate surroundings, so that we are never quite sure whether his photographs are "merely" factual records or entirely personal interpretations, we may justifiably conclude that these photographs represent what Stieglitz feels as he looks out from An American Place as well as what actually exists. The former "city of ambition" is now the city without hope.

Yet *he* is there, Stieglitz himself, and the room with its paintings by Marin, O'Keeffe, or Dove, in whose creative value he has never ceased to believe. They are there to prove the presence of passion, of purity, of gusto, and of imagination. If Stieglitz has been able to do his great work in America and has provided for others to do theirs, why has he come to see the world outside his window in terms of death and to think of his Place as a kind of forgotten chapel? Why does Stieglitz constantly repeat—and his photographs voice the sentiment more eloquently than anything he may say— "We are out of it, we are out of it, we are out of it?"

Has art lost its capacity to speak to men? Has beauty no persuasion? We are sometimes asked to believe that the domain of creativeness has passed entirely into the hands of "practical" men.

But this is an adolescent distortion. Art is an action, and no action that has its roots in man's fundamental need can ever be accounted futile. Is painting *passé?!* Though the situation of the painter today is an anomalous one, the fact remains that there are people who cannot speak at all unless they paint, and that painting acts upon many as surely as literature or music. We cannot dismiss anything as "outmoded" which really exists. The answer to Stieglitz's dilemma must be sought elsewhere.

The artists of Stieglitz's generation and even of the generation that succeeded him (the men who today are forty or fifty) did not heed the lesson that was inherent in his work. They "adored" Stieglitz's effort, but hardly any used it. Many became almost professionally "sensitive" to his artistry but did not transform it into their own equivalent of action.

Stieglitz said, "You can work with any medium and make it creative." Stieglitz worked with a machine and made it speak of the life around him. Stieglitz said, "Look out of your window, cross your threshold, tell me what you see there." And like the simplest cameraman he photographed the streets of New York and the hills of Lake George where he spent his summers. Stieglitz said 291 is not an "art gallery," it is a place of contact. Contact of people. The art work must talk like a person. People must "agree" with it or "disagree." They must react to it as to a living object. Stieglitz's photographs were "things": he wanted them to be as available as postage stamps and to go further. He wanted people on looking at them to know something, to think something, to do something, as they would on the receipt of a letter.

291 and the other "places" were to be a center, a meeting place— not for artists particularly, but for everybody, and he spent as much time talking to a stenographer, a teacher, a business man as he did to his colleagues. What did he talk about? The "line" of the picture? Their composition? Their relation to Cézanne? He wanted to find out if the pictures he was showing were really alive—what they said to people, and what people would become from having seen them. Stieglitz was interested in the *life* of the picture, which included the life of those who made them and those who saw them. For Stieglitz, the picture's final significance was just as much in the artist's "bread-and-butter" problems, the use that the buyer was going to make of it, the house it was going into, the people who were going to see it there, as in the painted canvas itself or in his own personal reaction to it.

Stieglitz, we have said, is a "universal" artist. And the "universe" that he would have us think about in relation to a work of art is precisely the world in which it is produced, and the world into which it is to go. The artist's work is simply the focus of the world around him; therein lies its importance. The art work is not something static and finished, something to be passively admired: it must be an activizer, something which sets things in motion. Art is the completion of one experience—the artist's—but if it is to be alive it must become the beginning of another—the beholder's—an experience that leads back into life again. If it does not it will die, and the artist with it.

In a word, Stieglitz's whole work, from his photographs to his conversations, clearly reveals that classic conception of art that today we call *collective*. The men who were close to Stieglitz did not understand this. To them 291 was a haven in a storm. It should have been an outpost. There they sought shelter from the unbearable world from 1905 to the present. There they healed their wounds by looking at the lovely and exciting images Stieglitz showed them and by listening to the ecstatic words that Stieglitz spoke which soothed and lulled them. Without knowing it or wishing it, they turned Stieglitz into a decorative artist, a creator of "beauty" like so many contemporary European artists, and they thought they flattered him by saying that he was their equal or their superior. They should have looked closer, and then turned their eyes again on the subjects which Stieglitz photographed. How could these sad streets be made joyous? How could these dreary objects that the "hand of men" had wrought be converted into magnificence? How could the world they lived in become the reflection of Stieglitz's spirit and vision? How could they change the world?

For something of the sort was in question. If they were really aware, these artists, critics, connoisseurs, fine-feelers, and fine-thinkers, and they had spoken aloud, they would have said, "We are the best in America. Our values are sound, our way is the most vital. We want a rich life and a healthy humanity. The builders of railroads, the men of affairs in America have only half the truth, and with that half they are killing all the rest. We are right though we have no power. They are wrong though they own the world."

Such a thought must be unbearable to any sane man. That the sensitive, the intelligent, the natural man should be the victim of the brutal, the blundering, and the blind is a monstrosity, and nothing can be right in a world in which such a situation is tolerated. Who shall make it right if not those who suffer the hurt of this imposition?

Stieglitz had said that that which was going on in his "places" must be as real as that which was going on outside. Otherwise everything that had been done would become worthless. And if there was realness here would it not necessarily reflect on the world outside? ... But people argued about "photography as an art," extolled Stieglitz's ability to make his prints as delicate as a paint-

ing, discussed dead distinctions, indulged in all the heavenly small-talk that has made art galleries the world over a cozy corner for idle dilettantes. They did not see that Stieglitz was not concerned with the refinements of their exegesis; that he was as much interested in the dirigible he photographed as in the "art" that resulted from it. The railroads and skyscrapers that Stieglitz photographed were not mere "subjects": they were part of his life, they controlled the conditions under which he had to work, and they shaped his work. To be an artist in such a world one had to be as strong, as persistent, as shrewd as those active tireless men who built the railroads and skyscrapers. ... To Stieglitz art was a serious job; to most of his friends it was a divine game which they played because they were too weak, too incompetent, or too frightened to play any other.

Perhaps there was some flaw in Stieglitz's presentation of his ideas. Though the meaning of his words was unmistakable, perhaps that residue of nineteenth-century romantic individualism which dwells within him brought too great a personal emphasis to his teaching. A tendency to dramatize his thought in terms of his own destiny, the prestige and magnetism of his own personality, deflected certain energies from the common goal to become simply a solicitude for the master. Despite Stieglitz's insistence on the anonymity of their task, the disciples could not see beyond their leader. To "understand" Stieglitz, that is, to suffer sympathetic pains while he struggled with chaos, became willy-nilly the lifework of his lieutenants. That tension and dialectic which must exist between the leader and the members of a group for it to fulfill its progressive function was not preserved in the collective of 291. The faithful served Stieglitz but did not know how to collaborate with him. It seemed impossible for the stronger workers to retain their independence without breaking altogether. Moreover, there can be no discipline where all debate of will and idea among the members of a group fails to be resolved because of a mutual worship of the leader; and no doubt the thought of a formal organization would have shocked the mystic sense of the free souls that all intellectuals at the beginning of the century considered themselves to be. Yet without such organization no group can exist. The philosophy, the material, the form of a group were all present, yet the group ideal as such was never clearly established in the minds of the individual artists. Practically speaking, 291 was therefore never quite a group, it was more a protective association.

Then too a certain virtue of Stieglitz's sentiment began to exert a crippling influence on the soul of his friends. Nothing that was less complete, less forced, or less necessary than a natural phenomenon could sincerely be approved. Nothing less than the "ultimate" could be fought for wholeheartedly. In our America, where the approximate, the imitation, the comfortable short-cut, and the expedient "just as good" is always threatening to rob everything of its essential reality, Stieglitz's ceaseless pursuit of perfection both in art and in personal relations, became a symbol of utmost constructive value. But a perfectionism that is not combined and balanced with an even greater need for going forward according to the demands of immediate situations assumes a negative aspect. However sound its roots, whenever the quest for perfection becomes an end in itself, it will finally resolve itself into preciosity. Though it was composed of natively passionate beings, there was something precious in the Stieglitz environment. It was incumbent upon Stieglitz's followers to do, but doing in existing circumstances always implies the ability to swallow and to digest all manner of discrepancies, contradictions, vulgarities—dross. Such a diet was too coarse for men who had systematically cultivated a stomach for only the finest nurture. Their hunger for the absolute—their fear of being wrong—was imperceptibly converted to a kind of hyperesthetic, ultracritical refusal. They forgot that, despite his high standards, their master had been able to work with people who were often something less than first rate: but *his* "perfection" absorbed the greater part of their fervor and devotion. A number of potentially vital men were thus rendered impotent beyond the confines of their own "perfect" world.

But aside from these considerations, it is certain that the consequences that followed from the premises of Stieglitz's example were not drawn by the people around him. With his innate understanding of the interdependence of all things and of all beings, Stieglitz, in organizing 291, had meant to indicate that no artist can exist in isolation: he must be part of a group, which implies the collaboration of other artists of his own kind and of an audience related to him. But this is not enough. The man who in his art could show the interrelation between a woman's face and the automobile she drives, that is, the man who saw at all times the action of the so-called external world on the life of the spirit, knew also that in the last analysis, *no group can exist by itself*. To live, one group must link itself with another, doing in another medium what the first has begun to do. Each group thus complements and clarifies the other.

If Stieglitz's work had been truly understood it would not have inspired reverence and vows of purity so much as acts. An influential magazine might have grown out of 291. (Of course there was *Camera Work,* in which Stieglitz gave his literary colleagues a hint of what might be done.) A publishing house might have developed through the needs of the magazine. And there might have been more than this: a musical group, a theater—and all of these assisting one another, forming and sharing a public together.

But this is not yet the end. If Stieglitz's thought were applied it must lead further than he himself might imagine. Our arts cannot live separate from the world, and if we feel that art such as Stieglitz's and those he sponsored has a right to be, we must have some conception of the kind of world that would give it nurture. We cannot do this without considering the whole structure of society. We must finally find a political equivalent for the ideal we discover in our artists. And to the political group whose aims are consonant with ours we must give our support and lend our talents. An art that cannot be integrated with every human activity is a sick art.

The men of Stieglitz's generation were "individualists" who saw the artist in the guise of the lone "genius" emerging miraculously out of nowhere, working obscurely and rather contemptuously till one day the world took notice. They cultivated their differences. We have seen that in the presence of Stieglitz they humbled themselves (too much) only to continue on their "individualistic" way, which essentially is not Stieglitz's way. Thus they ended by frustrating the master they love: But they have also frustrated themselves, for the logic of life takes little account of "individualities." Today most of them write for those "others" whom they do not respect, and who are indeed very often their inferiors, lecture for "others," play for "others," or are altogether silent because they have no place of their own. They should have learned to cultivate their agreements, and on such a foundation built organs of expression and of work to which they could have felt morally attached.

We must create collectives which will include artists of our own kind, and be associated with groups of related workers. Unless we do, our world shall always be "theirs." Unless we do, serious effort in the arts will dwell in catacombs and die there. The paintings that hang on the wall of An American Place are surely not commodities, but in a sense they no longer function as works of art; since they do not form a part of any social unit, they do not belong to any complete world. They have become passwords by which one lonely brave soul signals to others to let them know that people free enough to be moved by life still exist in America. Unless we learn to work together we shall all be crying that "we are out of it."

The collective way is the only road forward. When this is completely realized—and the younger generations are at the beginning of such a realization—when artists and craftsmen will submit to a collective discipline and establish collective organisms seeking their own audiences, identifying themselves with a cause or a movement on the broadest basis of collective activity, Stieglitz will become known to all such workers as the great pioneer of American group work in the arts. And then perhaps will the Stieglitz photographs —for me at least the greatest individual achievements in American art—find a home and a *place.*

Gertrude Stein
Stieglitz

IF ANYTHING IS DONE and something is done then somebody has to do it.
Or somebody has to have done it.
That is Stieglitz's way.
He has done it.
He remembers very well our first meeting.
But not better than I do.
Oh no not better than I do.
He was the first one that ever printed anything that I had done.
And you can imagine what that meant to me or to any one.
I remember him dark and I felt him having white hair.
He can do both of these things or anything.
Now that sounds as if it were the same thing or not a difficult thing but it is it just is, it is a difficult thing to do two things as one, but he just can that is what Stieglitz is and he is important to every one oh yes he is whether they know it or not oh yes he is. There are some who are important to every one whether any one knows anything of that one or not and Stieglitz is such a one, he is that one, he is indeed, there is no question but that he is such a one no question indeed, but that he is one, who is an important one for every one, no matter whether they do or whether they do not know anything about any such thing about any such one about him.
That is what Stieglitz is.
Any one can recognize him.
Any one does know that there are such ones, all of us do know that Stieglitz is such a one.
That he is one.
291
I am sorry that I can not go on longer and tell all about and more and more what Stieglitz is, but they never told me what they were all doing because Stieglitz had said do not bother her she is in France, but now just in time and I am so glad I find out I could just say what I know, I like to say what I know, and how could I know, how could I not know what Stieglitz is.

[handwritten marginalia:] he is a question (about truth?)

Photography

Paul Strand
Alfred Stieglitz and a Machine

THE LIFE WORK OF ALFRED STIEGLITZ, covering a period of almost fifty years of creative experiment, projects a complete analysis and synthesis of a machine, the camera. Using the methods and materials which belong exclusively to photography, Stieglitz has demonstrated beyond doubt that when the camera machine is guided by a very sensitive and deeply perceptive artist, it can produce perfectly embodied equivalents of unified thought and feeling. This unity may be called a vision of life—of forces taking form in life.

His is a monumental work. There are but two other such artists in the photographic past, whose works, though of lesser scope and less conscious, are also great landmarks in the development of photography: the Scotsman, D. O. Hill (1843), and Atget, who died in relative obscurity in Paris but a few years ago. For the history of photography, despite its numerous and varied phases, is almost entirely a record of misconception and misunderstanding, of unconscious groping, and a fight. The record of its use as a medium of expression reveals for the most part an attempt to turn the machine into a brush, pencil, whatnot; anything but what it is, a machine. Men and women, some who were painters, others who were not, were fascinated by a mechanism and material which they unconsciously tried to turn into painting, into a short cut to an accepted medium. They did not realize that a new and unique instrument had been born of science and placed in their hands; an instrument as sensitive and as difficult to master as any plastic material, but requiring a complete perception of its inherent means and of its own unique approach, before any profound registration was possible. There is no evidence in the work of the celebrated photographers (with the exceptions just noted), whether American, English, German, or French, of such a fundamental perception. The

freshness and originality of their seeing, the fineness of their feeling for life, was always, to some degree, muddied and obscured. They did not understand their own material, therefore they never respected it, never accepted it fully; they suffered from an inferiority complex which either limited or destroyed them. Possibly this complex might have been resolved in some cases, if the assertion had not been made that photography is not "art." This dictum was in reality the defense mechanism of an Erewhon of art, no less fantastic than the land of Samuel Butler's imagination: Erewhon feared the machine. Instead of impelling the photographers to find out what photography is, this assault only intensified their original feeling of inferiority. In the fight which ensued, they compensated by suddenly discovering themselves to be second Holbeins, Rembrandts, and Whistlers, always anything but photographers. Their work became inevitably a still greater mixture, deservedly unrespected, because it was neither painting nor photography. They never questioned the criteria of painting and could not perceive that basically photography could negate ninety-nine per cent of what was, and still is, called painting.

When that assault was made over twenty-five years ago, Alfred Stieglitz led the photographic cohorts, arranged exhibitions in the art museums of Europe's capital cities as well as in America. But he soon sensed the implications of the fight, soon realized that he and his co-workers were not working for the same thing. He tells a significant anecdote from a time when, in 1884, as a' student of engineering in Germany, he discovered photography for himself. The fervor and passionate intensity with which he experimented with the then undeveloped process soon attracted attention. His fellow pupils began to ask questions, and finally his instructor. Then many painters, some of them well known, became interested and said: "Of course, this is not art, but we would like to paint the way you photograph." To which Stieglitz replied: "I don't know anything about art, but for some reason or other I have never wanted to photograph the way you paint." This is the keynote, the essential leitmotif of his work. From the beginning, Stieglitz accepted the machine, instinctively found in it something that was almost a part of himself, and loved it.

So that later on, as a leader of the workers in photography, he was fighting not for the admission of photography into Erewhon, because he questioned Erewhon; not for the social climb into the Four Hundred of art, because, not knowing what art was, he questioned. He fought for the machine and for its opportunity to channel the impulses of human beings, for the respect which was due it because it could so claim their interest. He fought for its unique potentiality of registering the world directly, through the science of optics and the chemistry of silver and platinum, translated into tonalities subtle beyond the reach of any human hand. Stieglitz was interested in establishing photography and not photographers, not even himself. And then quite naturally and consciously he went further. Photography became for him the symbol of a great impersonal struggle. This machine toward which he so freely moved, through which he was impelled to register himself, was a despised, a rejected thing. It became a symbol of all young and new desire, whatever form it might take, facing a world and social system which tries to thwart and destroy what it does not understand and fears. Photography became then a weapon for him, a means of fighting for fair play, for tolerance of all those who want to do anything honestly and well. Stieglitz was affirming laws of change and growth, by defending the right to exist and to grow, of those who, as the years have proven, were bringing a new vision into human life.

The fight for all free expression led him, in 1906, to a battle-ground of two simple little rooms, on Fifth Avenue, in the heart of New York, which people called "291." There he fought for and gained recognition for modern painting, anti-photography: the attempt to use paint and canvas, and an abstract method of color, form and linear arrangements, to divest painting of literary and other extraneous elements; to come closer to a knowledge of what this medium's intrinsic qualities and special instruments of expressiveness really are; and with this knowledge to explore the thoughts, ideas, and feelings at work in the world of our time. The paintings, at that time seemingly without commercial value, and for that reason unable to find a hearing—work which Americans therefore had no opportunity to see—Stieglitz hung with respect, with sensitiveness, and with intelligence. Photography and this expression of painting were both rejected and despised; in that way they were deeply related. 291 became a laboratory for examining and clarifying this relativity, of ascertaining what they meant, in terms of each other. Here the experiments of photographers and painters were presented with scientific detachment, with interest directed completely towards discovering the meaning and significance contained in the works themselves. There was no commercialism, no ballyhoo, no list of patrons, no publicity campaigns. For the first time perhaps in the history of art, a conscious effort was made here to measure

esthetic values impersonally, that is, in terms of the spontaneous reactions (whether hostile or friendly), of the many different kinds of people who came from every walk of life—every social stratum —to the little laboratory.

It is from this background of passionate struggle and search that Stieglitz's photographs come, a record of his intellectual and spiritual growth. The work itself is complete—esthetically satisfying. The machine and its own special technique are here mastered without any tricks in the use of materials, no diffusions, no evasion in any way of the objective world in front of the camera. And there is no slightest trace of brush or pencil either in handling or, what is more subtle, in feeling; in his own words: "no mechanicalization but always photography."

The evolution of this life work is thus a picture of the direction and quality of his life. Its direction reveals an uninhibited approach to people and things; its initial quality is that of an intense desire to affirm them as beautiful. As these two primary impulses evolve, they meet the impacts of reality without resentment or bitterness, without disillusionment, and penetrate the reality. The direction of this life continues unequivocally the same, but the affirmation becomes deepened and fibered by a critical, especially a self-critical, intelligence, which recognizes neither beautiful nor ugly, because it has seen the causal forces of which such concepts are the effects. So Stieglitz turned the "mechanical eye" of the camera from the things which people do or build, directly to the things which people are. He has given portraiture, in any medium, the new significance of a deliberate attempt to register the forces whose sum constitutes an individual, whose sum therefore documents the world of that individual. These amazing portraits, whether they objectify faces or hands, the torso of a woman, or the torso of a tree, suggest the beginning of a penetration of the scientific spirit into the plastic arts. Through photographic line, form, and tonal values, Stieglitz has gone beyond mere picture making, beyond any empty gesture of his own personality made at the expense of the thing or the person in front of him. He has examined our world of impulse and inhibition, of reaching out and of withdrawal, in a spirit of disinterested inquiry oriented by a wistful love. Photographs of things and people—of sun and cloud shapes—become equivalents of a deeply critical yet affirmative inquiry into contemporary life. They are the objective and beautiful conclusions of that inquiry.

Stieglitz does not label his work "art," he does maintain that it is photography. The question is an academic one and can be left to those who are greatly worried about whether this or that is or is not art. One needs but to go to the Boston and Metropolitan museums, see their few but fine examples of Stieglitz's work, to feel grateful that life has been again enriched by a new beauty, another heritage being preserved for future generations. And beyond what these photographs give in themselves they may also be seen as symbols of the machine used not to exploit and degrade human beings, but as an instrument for giving back to life something that ripens the mind and refreshes the spirit. They give hope of, and perhaps prophesy, a new world, humanly speaking, which is not an absurd Erewhon; but one in which people have learned to use machines with a different attitude towards them and towards each other. In such a world the machine would take its place, not alone as an invaluable tool of economic liberation, but also as a new means of intellectual and spiritual enrichment.

Evelyn Scott
A Note on the Esthetic Significance of Photography

DURING THE LAST HUNDRED YEARS, the methodology of natural science has increasingly influenced procedure in all departments of learning. As we, *qua* social units, become more and more aware of our interdependence, a working agreement on what we will assume "true" becomes a paramount necessity. And the testimony of the senses affords a common denominator for assessing the validity of reports on experience. Thus science and democracy go hand in hand.

Social relationships are primarily those of convenience, and, for their success, a currency of understanding is requisite. Practical accomplishment would, we presume, be heightened were we able to come to decisions for action on the basis of results to be infallibly forecast.

The old moral laws, which were rationales from ideals of conduct in a social surrounding, seldom rested on any demonstrable inference from observed behavior; but the speculations of science attempt to establish "principles" after the recognition of constantly apparent aspects in the conduct of the phenomena examined. In particular, when man is able, himself, to duplicate the conditions of some original observation in a way that compels the reëmergence of a factual sequence previously noted, and now foreseen, he is prepared to assert a "law of nature."

A conquest of environment would inevitably depend on forecasts, and it is the hope extended to the masses that demonstration may establish all action as predictable which gives science its forceful emotional appeal to the general today. Science is to make man master not merely of his present but of his future.

Important to this program, by means of which humanity will cease to be victimized by chance, has been the progressive elaboration of machine invention, evolved from the application of logic to demonstrable premises, to the end of predictable effects. The quantitative advantages of machine output over those of human labor could carry no seeming message of emancipation were it not that certain results of mechanization, related to intentions assumed in advance, being demonstrable, can be foretold. This has encouraged a widespread belief that all function in nature can, and soon will be, similarly exploited.

A corollary to current reverences for techniques of science is a growing theoretic contempt for pursuing speculation on any theme beyond demonstrable limits. And there is with this a tendency to discard any data of fact, however well attested, which cannot at present contribute to a demonstrable forecast. While a pure science awaits with humility the assembling of *all* facts which *may* prove relevant to the solution of the problem discussed, bigotry has no such willing patience. Exaggerated optimism inclines men to accept as evidence what will seem to confirm their hopes, and to ignore utterly equally pertinent data if these threaten the finality of their theories.

Philosophy, under what amounts to the pressure of public opinion, has largely abandoned its metaphysic of pure reason, since the function of reason, as apart from demonstrable results after its specific application, is nondemonstrable. At this stage, science lags far behind what would conceivably be data adequate for a demonstrable "system," which would be universal and complete; and the abnegating gesture of the philosophers may presage at least a partial atrophy of a function involved, also, in scientific procedure, though not present in its "proof." We seem about to suffer a loss for which full compensation cannot now be offered. And the arts, as well, and like philosophy, under the same influence, are falling into disrepute.

True, there is, for art, a criticism which lays claim to a scientific methodology in finding support for its judgments. But this Marxian stammering after a functional diagnosis of art expression is an extension only of an antecedent social-economic theory to interpret history, and its exponents approach art expression not to search out principles for demonstrable effects which will constitute art, but for evidence which will seem to corroborate an intention on the part of the artist which is presumed in their own theory of history.

And surely a science of esthetics must take for its material, first, those art objects which have survived the centuries, and note the most constant and obviously recurrent aspects of art expression before intention can be imputed and defined, or the degrees of relevance in those facts which may bear on intention allotted.

We look to the demonstration of a principle after we have noted what is least and not most variable in the behavior of the phenomena we take as data. The examination of art objects, when it is made without prepared reference to a theory based on other data, will show what we term "content" (which may be referable, as we proceed, to history), as, apparently, variable and unpredictable, whereas the fusion of what is so named in the sensational element of a medium is constant in all descriptions of any art whatsoever. And this without consideration of whether the hypothecated artist was a Chinaman of a thousand years ago or is a contemporary in Europe or America.

The association of art expression with a medium, which shall be its projection and vital "embodiment," beyond the subjectivity of its inception, is equally characteristic of the written word and of painting and the sound waves of music; even though in writing sensation must be invoked by allusion, since the impact on our sensory equipment of a literal medium is absent.

Yet because expression, before it is art, must be conditioned in a medium, the art object, either directly or by inference, must meet sensational requirements paralleling those which establish fact elsewhere. And even the art we call "phantasy," in which antecedent sequences of fact are reflected as in a distorting mirror, must carry that requisite "illusion of reality" before we identify it as a work of art.

The pseudo-scientific esthetician of the present does not search out the uninvestigated constitution of what establishes, in that conviction of reality we experience with the fusion of content references in a medium, the *fact* of a work of art, which is its constant character, and not seemingly affected by the secular altering of social environments; rather does he deny to art objects any character of fact, since he relates art expression to the subjectivity of logic only, confining his description of art to consistence with a premise, and thus exempting himself from the conditions of objective demonstration. He goes even further to contradict scientific methodology, and demands an expression which he will assume to be art solely because it will typify and extend the logic of his presumption—a presumption as to content that shall carry implications as to intention relating it to his theory of history.

The spontaneity of natural laws is not assailed by an understanding of a conditioning of phenomena to produce evidence of function, and even that forecast of intention which guides the inventor when constructing a machine is an exploitation of spontaneous principles in nature previously demonstrated. Yet Marxian critical dictation, since its standards for art do not take into account principles underlying that sensational conviction of reality accompanying all experience of expression in a medium, anticipates laws of esthetics not, so far, demonstrated at all. Nor can these be demonstrated in Marxian terms, which remove the problems of art

from those spheres in which scientific method can be applied, and are, indeed, rational conclusions from ideal fixities which are without demonstrable inferences as to function, and parallel the dogmas of an abstract moral law.

And the blind alley into which we are led recalls that into which many have followed academicians of the past, who, not concerned with demonstrations in fact, left consideration of art's "illusion of reality" out of their reckoning altogether, and made their approach to understanding art expression dependent on consistent dogmas which would be a theory of form.

For form, indicative of selection, is referable to reason and is its interpretive reflection in art. Scientific procedure is itself contingent on acceptance of the function of reason as nondemonstrable, though it is through reasoning that the scientist arrives at the demonstrable inference. An attempt to remove reason out of its subjectivity will be a contradiction of the spontaneity which recognition of a function presumes. Conclusions adduced after such a denial, to reason, of functional significance, will therefore be dogmatic, and contingent on the substitution of fixity for function. The standards of a dead "classicism" were evolved on the basis of such a denial.

Yet, though the formalists have both ignored the demonstrable inference and disallowed form to be evidence of function, and though the so-called functionalists, deflected from scientific methodology, have developed a logic from their own presumptions, and no more, the possibility of a scientific diagnosis of the esthetic problem is not thereby negated.

Though scientific methodology may not yield a knowledge we shall in future accept as the ultimate to be attained, it is plausible to suppose that we have still far to go before we are confronted with the necessity for a final judgment on its worth to ourselves. The critic who today pleads for an esoteric evaluation of art, while abiding only by the demonstrable inference when assessing "truth" in other experience, is making of criticism a theology, and is robbing science of data that will be essential when its philosophic report on life is, if ever, made.

To attribute art expression to a functioning not yet fully understood, or to the results of a conditioning not now demonstrable, would seem at this stage like arrogating to the artist privileges of personality not at present to be brought under that mass direction which intends to control humanity's environmental resources. And it is to satisfy democratic aspiration without loss of time that the Marxian critic has essayed, prematurely, to bring the production of art objects into line with the production, by mechanical contrivance, of goods in general.

It is not, strangely, the introduction of machinery as a tool of the artist that Marxian theorizing brings under discussion, but, rather, the Marxian's own tendency to regard human nature as itself already so well understood that we may now assume it to be in the machine stage of direction and control. In brief, the Marxian has swept aside such questions as have previously occurred to both psychologists and philosophers, and has substituted, for inevitable intricacies of speculation, a simplification by abstraction. In the light of such ideal simplicity we are to take for granted a demonstration of esthetic function, which has not occurred, and apply its undemonstrated "principles" even as we apply physical principles, that have been tested, when we construct machinery for specific use.

However, even should we approach, with unscientific haste, and in advance of a study of more obvious, and also undemonstrated, aspects of art experience, that consideration of the historic reference in art which is the Marxian obsession, we would first have to establish both the manner and measure in which the antecedent literal experience of the artist, of whatever description, reëmerges as art content.

That first apparent variableness of content reference, as opposed to the *in*variable persistence of art's expressive association with a medium, may itself be the basis for inferring something constant, such as environmental influence in the life of the artist. It may well be that the tracing of content references to their source, at the appropriate time to do so, will substantiate some part of the Marxist interpretation. But even though, at some stage in future demonstration, certain elements of Marxian theory are shown to have a bearing on esthetics, present premature acceptance of any part of the theory is contrary to scientific methodology.

If, then, the function of the literal in art is to be scientifically resolved, the readiest examples of art to be tested for an illumination of the enigma will be those in which mechanisms previously demonstrated as recording the literal are exploited for the art effect. For in precisely such degree as the attainment of the effect is subject to demonstration will the attempt to diagnose the conditioning requisite for art functioning be made easier. And though there is demonstration of but a single aspect of what may be involved in the hoped-for solution of the whole problem, the dissipation of one relevant ambiguity advances explanation in general.

In at least two arts, those of music and photography, mechanisms have been introduced for the realization of mediumized expression. Musical composition is adapted to a preconsidered instrumentation of sound, yet, while this demands of the composer an adaption of end to means (which is part of a conditioning to any medium whatever), it cannot be said that there is a functional participation of a mechanism in the art effect. For the art work evolved is complete before its rendition on any instrument.

In photography, however, content itself is supplied by the literal recording of the camera, and that distortion of the literal which is unavoidable when there is a time intervention between experience of the fact which is the content reference and the projection of impressions from this experience in the medium (in the guise of a fresh reality) is not a condition of the art. This, indeed, has been the basis of most efforts to discredit photography as art, since such literalness would seem to contradict certain ancient assumptions as to the primary distinction between art expression and all other.

Yet, if we are able to demonstrate that in music, painting, poetry, and so on, all reference which is in content is an effect of a happening *to* the artist, and is the translation of his unelected recording of impacts sensuously registered, then the assertion of a fundamental difference between photography, in which such passively received imprints are mechanically preserved, and other arts will be less tenable. Then the coincidence of impression with expressive function will not seem to place photography beyond the category of fine arts.

Perhaps the disparagement of photography's literal content may be traced to esoteric attitudes previously deplored, and to the false conceit which would disallow all attempts to discuss esthetics by scientific method. For the single indisputably mystic ingredient in art effects may well turn out to be interpretive and reflected from a functioning reason, the operation of which is implied in photography, as in painting, music, poetry, and all other arts. Conceivably, the photographer's preference for certain materials may be shown to proceed, in all specified instances, from what is, demonstrably, an unelected bias, determined by previous impacts of fact on the artist; when this bias may, again, be related to those processes which, via the senses, impress artists subjectively and determine content whether it is conveyable as a literal record or not. Yet the significant aspect of comparison between, say, photography and painting cannot be described as merely the photographer's preference (which still smacks too much of a "free will" of which science makes no admission), but is indicated in the pure passivity with which the photographer, with the camera his proxy, accepts unperjured evidence of the external, as mechanically witnessed—a passivity largely paralleling that of the painter who receives, every day, and whether it is his decision to do so or not, impressions informing him of an outer world.

And to the very degree in which it can be demonstrated that art is functional, and so determinable, will the validity of standards based on dictated conformity to a theory of arbitrarily preferred content be undermined. For surely, in such measure as content references may be revealed as the inevitable product of conditioning, will judgments by preference become inappropriate, and Marxian dogmatizing exposed as like that of the Victorian moralists, who ineffectually attempted to impose theory on the spontaneity of the natural, and regarded that "good art" which extolled "Christian" sentiment.

Without exposition not appropriate to an essay devoted to comment on a general theme, my individual estimate of Alfred Stieglitz as one of the greatest artists of our times must stand as opinion and no more; yet, since it is rational to suppose that a diagnosis of the function of the literal in art expression might be advanced through attention to, and demonstration with, the camera, and since Alfred Stieglitz is a notable example of dedication to a pure employment of the medium he has chosen, I suggest his work as data for the commencement of such a study. Early experimenters with the camera, and, indeed, some more recent, having held literal recording to be disadvantageous to art, have adopted an attitude of apology and attempted to disguise it by putting forth what were, actually, faulty prints, hoping these might suggest effects attained without resort to mechanization.

But it will be plain that, since art relies, for its "illusion of reality," on the association of content references with a medium, our conviction as to this reality diminishes when there is a failure to utilize fully exclusive attributes of the medium adopted in the particular instance. Thus there is a degree of ineffectualness in efforts to render sound, which should reach the ear, symbolically, in pigment, or visual impressions in so-called descriptive music.

In America, Alfred Stieglitz has been the great outstanding pioneer among photographers who have a true devotion to a specifically camera expression. He has not essayed imitation of the techniques of drawing, painting, or lithography, but, far from deprecating the literal accuracy of the machine, has exploited its peculiar possibilities without reservation. Thus, though we infer from his work a reason functioning to discriminate, he has deferred to the machine's testimony on content material with a passivity that parallels inevitable human passivity in experiencing fact.

It is not by reducing machine efficiency that he has achieved his memorable portraiture and the exquisiteness of his skies; and his photographs of commonplaces of nature not before represented with this precise literalness in art work, are, I believe, admitted to gain in their moving attributes through our very recognition of an exploration in forms reprojected without psychic intervention.

And, since scientific procedure is a method of determining, and its appeal to emotion the vision of an understanding of the existent which will bring us into harmony with our surrounding in a way equivalent to control of the circumstances inescapably affecting us, there is more than a hint, in the experience of such photography, of points of intention at which artist and scientist meet. If speculation, in our own age, is still vague, what is adumbrated, even in a brief survey of camera expression, should, I think, merit the attention of future estheticians.

City Plowman

Jean Toomer
The Hill

THEY TELL ME that what is now called The Hill was once a farmer's place. On this place were pigs. Pig stench drifted down to the big house of the Stieglitz family on the shore of Lake George. To get rid of this stench the family bought the farm. Thus they acquired the house and grounds which later, when financial reverses set in, they themselves occupied. Thus the place was linked with the life of Alfred Stieglitz. Once this happened, the linkings became so many and various that the old farm must have felt that the world had come to settle within its borders.

I wonder what the old house felt when rooms and baths were added, when furnishings which it had never seen the like of were moved in, when the complexities of the Stieglitz family began weaving in and out the rooms and into the simple old wood and farmer's plaster. Surely it knew that an unexpected fate had overtaken it. Surely it gazed with amazement at Alfred Stieglitz and his camera, at Georgia O'Keeffe and her paints and canvases. And it affirmed the transformation and felt satisfied because the photographer and the painter, like the farmers before them, were producers, producers of things for America.

One may guess, too, at the surprise of the flowers when they saw O'Keeffe first paint them. At the surprise of the trees and weeds when they became important before Stieglitz's camera. Something new had come to pass in this Lake George place. The farm had become The Hill.

At The Hill the windows are uncurtained. Each window is all window. The outside can look in, the Lake George landscape, near-by trees, an old red barn, floating clouds. The house rests upon its earth, inviting this part of the American countryside to enter. And the countryside does enter, and something of the great earth, and something, I feel, of the great world.

What is of equal importance, the inside can look out—and this, particularly, is Stieglitz. The inside looking out unhindered, the human spirit being, with a permanent intensity to perceive, feel, and know the world which it inhabits, to give a sheer record of experiences.

I always see his eyes, those ever alert instruments of a consciousness whose genius is to register both the details and the vastnesses of life, of this part of the universe where now we happen to be dwelling—all with an extraordinary sense of significance, a feeling of relatedness.

Nothing for him is unrelated; even twigs and pebbles fit in as constituents of the universe. Even human stupidity, for he can see its function in relation to intelligence. An accepter, an affirmer, a rich nature with a generous interest in all that exists.

One of my pictures of him is Stieglitz in a deep chair, people around him, his body relaxed, hands unoccupied, gray hair in whatever way it happens to be, but his head poised as if it were the prototype of all cameras, recording with uncanny sensitiveness all that is visible and much that is not.

There are deep chairs at The Hill, deep chairs in his rooms at the Shelton, one deep chair in his room at An American Place, and I see him in them. This actual or apparent physical immobility is an instructive feature of the man who has *done* more for modern art in America than any other single person, who has established a standard of truth.

Obviously his way of doing is not that which we ordinarily advertise and idealize. No one would mistake him for one of our publicized men of action. No, he has the dynamics of *being*—hence he can do. In this he is in striking contrast to those who believe they can do without being, and who are, therefore, under the awful delusion that is wrecking Western civilization.

Wherever he is, *he is*. I cannot picture him elsewhere. I cannot envisage him going anywhere. In the midst of people, many of whom bustle and scamper about nothing, he is with something. So surely does the center of him proclaim, "I am," that it is difficult for me to think of him in terms of growth, change, becoming—though I know he has grown.

Quite early he must have found the places on this earth which belonged to him; and he must have recognized that he belonged to them. Or, for all I know, he may have felt he was an essential stranger on this planet; hence, that all regions were, on the one hand, equally alien, and, on the other, equally meaningful as locales where one could see the cosmos in epitome. In any case, within what some might call a circumscribed habitat (mainly Lake George and New York City) he has remained, relaxed from the urge to go elsewhere, yet never resting.

Never resting. Always doing. Carrying on his own individual life and work, helping carry on the individual life and work of others, always initiating, always pressing against whatever tends to hinder his aim of sensitizing the world, deeply powered by a sense of what is beyond, the great potentiality.

He will sometimes tell you that he feels uprooted. From one point of view this is true. He has not had a fixed establishment. What is more to the point, he is not a tree. The human nostalgia to revert to vegetable may occasionally move him, but with him as with so many of us, it has come to nothing. Yet I do not feel he is suspended or unplaced. Always I feel he is rooted *in himself* and to the *spirit* of the place. Not rooted to things; rooted to spirit. Not rooted to earth; rooted to air.

If he is at The Hill at Lake George, I do not have the feeling that he has come from New York or that he may be going there. No, here he is, capable of sustaining and fulfilling himself with what is present. Now and again he may walk to the village, but even this short going seems foreign to him, and he usually does it with an air which makes one feel he is walking with an illusion of Stieglitz in a black cloak.

He lives in his house, the house with uncurtained windows, bare gray-white walls, deep chairs, tables, uncovered blue-white lights, and in this house he creates an atmosphere. A delicacy, a sensuousness, an austerity.

No ornaments anywhere, nothing that isn't used. No "oughts" or "ought nots" governing the running of the house except those which relate to the work of O'Keeffe, of himself, of whoever may be his guests at the time, his fellow experiencers. No ought even in relation to work. No ought in relation to life—providing you do not hinder someone else. Just life.

My first visit to The Hill I was soon struck by a feeling that came from him constantly and filled the house. I particularly remember one morning.

We were having fruit, Zwieback, and coffee in the kitchen. O'Keeffe and Paul Rosenfeld were there. Stieglitz was at the table, silent, his head lowered, eyes pensive on something not in sight, absently dipping Zwieback in coffee before eating it.

Outside, snow was on the hills, a cold hidden landscape; and to my eyes it seemed that we were four people far away from every-thing, practically lost in a remote frosty region of the earth, uncon-nected with wide living. But I *felt* warmth and a most amazing sense that life was coming into us, that the wide world was imme-diate out there, that we were in the midst of happenings in America, that Stieglitz had an interior connectedness with life, that through him I also felt connected.

Feeling, I believe, is the center of his life. Whatever he does, he does through feeling—and he won't do anything unless feeling is in it. Whatever he thinks, he thinks with feeling—and he won't think anything unless feeling is in it. His words convey it, his miraculously clear photographs, his silences, his sitting relaxed in a deep chair.

Feeling is being. Stieglitz can evoke the one and therefore the other; and this is why he can help people find and be what they are, why he can move people both into and out of themselves, why we value him, we who are younger than he but old enough to realize that thought and action are nothing unless they issue from and return to being.

I wondered when he would begin photographing. O'Keeffe was painting. Paul and myself were writing. Stieglitz was simply in the house. I wondered how he would be when working. In due time he began.

A natural happening. His working tempo was but a quickening (though what a quickening!) of his usual tempo. All he did was but an intensification of what had been in The Hill all the while. Work and life were the same thing, and life and art. No casual observer would have thought that anything "great" was going on. His camera was in evidence. Out he would go with it. In he would come. And soon the large table in the front room was filled with his materials and prints. It was that simple—and that real.

Only it wasn't simple at all. The search for truth and reality is a complex search, the attempt to extend consciousness is a difficult attempt, the effort to determine and demonstrate by experiments the possibilities of a comparatively new instrument and medium is intricate and it must be sustained—and all of these he was doing with and through the camera while I looked on at the apparent simplicity of it.

Though at various times to various people he has told, so to speak, the partial history of this or that photograph, the full genesis of his pictures is unknown, and perhaps it is just as well. Like himself, his photographs are explicit in themselves, direct communicants with one's feelings.

A genius of what is—this is Stieglitz, and this is why he uses a camera, and this is why he will never use a *moving*-picture camera.

The *treeness* of a tree . . . what bark is . . . what a leaf is . . . the *woodness* of wood . . . a telephone pole . . . the *stoneness* of stone . . . a city building . . . a New York skyscraper . . . a horse . . . a wagon . . . an old man . . . a cloud, the sun, unending space beyond . . . the *fleshness* of human flesh . . . what a face is . . . what a hand, an arm, a limb is . . . the amazing beauty of a human being . . . the equally amazing revelation of the gargoyle that hides in all of us but which he and his camera devastatingly see. . . .

Here in these prints our earth is as it *is,* our dwellings as they *are,* ourselves, we humans, as we *are.*

If I were commissioned to travel through space and inform the beings of some other planet on the nature of this earth-part of the universe, I would take Stieglitz's camera works along, and I would feel confident that those beings would get, not subjective picturings and interpretations, but objective records, and I'd feel confident too that if, later on, they paid a visit to this planet, they would recognize it.

From Lake George to New York City is not far. But from the house that rests upon its earth to the 17th and 29th floors of the skyscrapers in which Stieglitz lives in New York, there is a great distance, a difference of a century. By means of the continuity and singleness of his life he connects them. The Hill, his rooms at the Shelton, An American Place on Madison Avenue, are but variations of the same thing—the world he has built and is building.

The beginning-structures of this world: 291 and *Camera Work,* those manifest crystallizations of his deep resources which had such vital functions in the life of their time, which have carried forward like good blood into the living body and spirit of today. I did not experience them; I do sense them now as they exist in the present in him, as they and their effects exist in present-day America which owes to them an important part of its cultural being.

The past is a solid life behind him. The future is a solid life before him. He is solid in today.

If he is in his rooms at the Shelton, there he is. From these uncurtained windows of a skyscraper he can see the weather before it reaches the city pavements—and when I think of him looking out I remember the artists he has seen and recognized before they became known to most of us, before they were solid figures on the horizontal earth. He saw them, he recognized them, he did something so that they were aided in becoming such figures.

Here in these personal rooms of his one can sense the richness of his private life, his friendships and devotions, affirmations of this one, lashings against that one, his warmth, his clean kindliness, his humor—in fine, his dimensions in human experience.

If he is at the gallery, there he is. Behind him are other galleries. Before him, maybe more. But here, now, in this one, he is; carrying it on from day to day, from year to year through personal, economic, and spiritual vicissitudes.

Here the world comes to meet and experience his world. Here life comes to meet life. Here he meets what comes in.

There is, let us say, a show of Marins. One day I go up and many people are about. Stieglitz is himself. He talks and makes things happen or says nothing and lets things happen, according to how he feels. Another day I go up and the place is vacant. Stieglitz is himself, relaxed in his deep chair, neither more nor less himself because of what others do or don't do.

Yet no one has such a profound (and, sometimes, such an anguished) sense of what is involved—the entire life work of an extraordinary human being. Here on these walls is *Marin.* We can understand what Stieglitz feels—and feel with him—when he sees the place vacant, or, what is worse, when he sees some candidate for humanity come in, glance around for ten minutes, and go out, feeling that he has seen everything and knows it all.

And no one cares so deeply. Ever since he discovered himself, Stieglitz has been working for truth and people, to demonstrate certain things about life, to make for art a substantial place in America, to aid certain people bring forth the best from themselves, and of course he is concerned if what happens is less than what is possible.

And he tries to do something about it, and if he can't—he accepts, with the knowledge that there is an inevitability in life and events, that what must be must be, that because it happens (or fails to happen) there is a certain rightness in it. Then he tries again. It is rare to find anyone in whom the two attitudes—"I will," "Thy will be done"—are so balanced.

As a creator, the "I will" is stronger. "I will" and the opposite, "I won't." By affirming he has done what he had to do. By denying he has kept himself unimpeded.

This man who is living in the spirit of today will have nothing to do with the things of today that distract from this spirit. Sometimes it is a fiery rejection. Sometimes it is a natural unconcern, as if in past lives he had experienced and become disillusioned with the vanities of the world, as if now in this life they simply do not exist for him.

In these days of "great personalities," of small souls and swollen egos, he is a simple man, a sincere man, uncompromising, a quiet man who comes into the house and you hardly know he has come in, who has come into this ambitious world of ours, who exists and has his being in it, unmindful of its scurryings, its advertisements and publicities.

He has no place for what is unrelated. Others may be interested, the thing may be valuable, the person may be promising, but he seems to know by intuition what is his and what is not, how far he can go, how far he can't, and he keeps to what is related to him, and he remains faithful to the high task of building his world with the materials and the people who belong to this world—all the while knowing, of course, that what he does carries beyond the boundary of his immediate aims and reaches people near and far.

A man in his world. A world which he has made, not found already made. No one, no group, no race, no nation could have built it for him. His function in life was not to fit into something that already existed but to create a new form by the force of his growth. Now he calls this form, "An American Place"—which it is, authentically. Whoever goes to room 1710 of 509 Madison Avenue or to The Hill at Lake George will find certain American essences in the paintings, in the photographs, in the very life and atmosphere too. Yet deeper than the national reality is the human reality. He himself and his form are of the great body and spirit of mankind.

An *individual* who is himself, who is for those of the wide world that claim him by similarity of spirit and of values.

Sherwood Anderson
City Plowman

THEY HAVE ALL BEEN TRYING to stand up on their feet. I have been trying. I have seen others trying. It has been going on since I was a child.

The cities try to stand on their feet. The buildings in the cities try.

There is a great uncertainty, roots trying to go down into American soil.

I remember when I was a young man and first went to Europe. I saw much there. There were the cities, the cathedrals, old kings' palaces, all of the things we wide-eyed Americans go eagerly to see, to come home and talk about. Water from the river Jordan, a swim in the Seine. Here the Disciples walked. There marched Napoleon. There, at a desk in a room in that great building, sat Bismarck.

These things to be seen and wondered over, but there was a greater wonder. I saw it in the body, in the eyes . . . it was in the hair, in the clothes, of a French peasant, driving a dust cart along a French country road, under trees.

It was in a man in a field near an English village. He was binding grain into sheaves. He arose from the ground and stretched. I remember standing in a path near by and watching . . . feeling something I find it hard, even yet, to put down.

It was English skies in the Englishman, French skies in the Frenchman, sense of fields, horizons, of place in man. Man in a place he knows, feels related to. "Life has gone on a long time here. Our sins on our own heads.

"We are men standing here. We will not pretend to be something greater, more splendid than we are.

"I will accept myself in my own place and time, in this moment, under these skies. My feet walk on the soil of this field. I will not leave this field. I will stay here.

"There will come bad years and good years. I am a man who belongs in this country town, on this farm. I am a man of this city.

"The city streets are mine. I am walking in the streets of this city. Watch my feet go down.

"In the city my feet strike upon stone, cement, asphalt. What does it matter? Something within me, tiny sap roots in me, go down through stone, cement, asphalt, to the dark ground.

"I admire my place. I want it.

"What does it matter to me that life constantly changes? The old relationships, man to man, man to woman, woman to woman, go on. I need the tiny veins in me, reaching down, to bring sap of earth up . . . that I may live, love . . . be brother, be sister . . . be friend, be foe.

"I need my own land, my place, my city.

"Let them change it, remodel it. 'Go on, men. Build your great buildings, bring your machines.' We men and women remain. We ourselves will get it or lose it."

There is something that constantly gets lost, that is occasionally, in a man, in a woman, regained. I have seen proud men in America, a few of them, a few proud women.

What gives me pride, life pride, is ability to love, vitality to love.

If I am a painter, this canvas can be my home, my place, my field, my hill, my river . . . if a sculptor this piece of stone, if a writer these white sheets, here before me. I have dirtied too many white sheets myself, seen others dirty city streets, American streams, dirty farms, dirty towns.

Something spoiled things too much for us here in America.

I declare it isn't our own fault. That, I know, doesn't let us out, but still I declare it.

They asked too much of us . . . Goddam 'em . . . giving us this.

They didn't give it. It happened. No one is to blame. As you live along you find that out. No one is to blame for anything.

Still. Still. Still.

It was too much. It was too splendid.

You have to think of men coming here, to this America . . . not supermen.

Just men . . . and women . . . their old European sins thick on them. Your grandfather and mine . . . to say nothing of grandmothers . . . Jews, Germans, Irish, Swedes.

Roumanians, Poles, Italians.

New blood mixtures, new streams forming.

Here the deep rivers, the forests, the rich valleys.

Wealth coming. It had to come. All the things men wanted and needed . . . or thought they wanted and needed . . . were here in abundance. Is it any wonder we got out of touch? The wealth was outside man, in forests, mines, rich earth, slowly built up by nature through thousands of years. One of the great crimes against the Holy Ghost . . . is the crime of soil destruction that has gone on here. Thirty million acres of it in one state I know of, land once rich thrown aside.

Cities built blindly, factories stuck in anywhere, railroads stealing river fronts, blind building, building, building . . . never for the inner man.

It takes so long, so long here to get a bit of ground under your feet. "What is my relationship with all this?"

They tell themselves so many little lies. Where is the man who will not lie to himself or others?

I used to feel man's ultimate lie so much, in myself and others when I was a younger man, out in Chicago. I had come there from the backwoods, was what Henry Mencken loves to call "a Yahoo." I didn't care. I didn't feel much like apologizing to the city Yahoos.

I remember that just before I came to the city for the first time I went out along the Sandusky Pike to Uncle Jim Ballard's farm near my home town in Ohio, for a last visit. Uncle Jim was not my real uncle, and Aunt Mary was not my real aunt. I had adopted them. I walked out, the seven miles, and stayed overnight.

It was in the spring. I remember that the dogwood was blooming. I had been out there a week before to leave my clothes. Aunt Mary was mending them for me, getting me ready for my city adventure. Uncle Jim had laughed at me. "I guess you think you have to do it. You have to go. All the young fellows think they have to go."

He chuckled, making me uncomfortable. "You want to turn out to be something big, eh?" he said. Why, whenever I think of my friend Alfred Stieglitz do I think also of Uncle Jim, of Uncle Jim in relation to his farm, his barn and house, his friends?

There was a field that went away from the barn to a distant wood and, on the next morning, during my visit there, Uncle Jim was plowing in the field. He was a little wiry old man, just such a figure as Stieglitz is now. He was hatless in the field. The spring wind was blowing through his thin gray hair as he followed his team along a plowed furrow.

Uncle Jim always had a good team. He came down along a furrow toward the barn, and I am quite sure that, even then, I felt something of the splendor in the breasts of the great work horses, in the clean furrow rolling up as the plow marched.

He turned the team at the furrow's end and stopped. He went into the barn. It may have been a call of nature. Anyway, I put my hand to the plow in his field. "I'll make a few rounds for him," I thought. I wasn't really a plowman. What I did to his field might have passed unnoticed by any other farmer along that road.

A slight twist to my furrows. I spoiled the clean lines across the face of his field and it hurt Uncle Jim as though I had made an ugly mark on the face of his wife.

I remember the hurt look in his eyes as he stood looking at the field. It was something to remember. He cared. It wasn't in Uncle Jim to throw the hurt back to me by cursing, but I had spoiled his day's work. A little perhaps I had spoiled all the work of the year for him there in that field.

And what has all of this to do with this other man, this Alfred Stieglitz? There was Uncle Jim's relationship to the fields he had already plowed for some fifty years when I first knew him, and Stieglitz's to the city where I found him. He also made a clean furrow. There was the man and his environment, something fitting, going together. They were both men unashamed. They belonged.

It must be something very hard to get, and that most of us, here in America, never do get. I myself have been a passionate traveler, a lover, but where has it brought me in the end? I am here, facing these white sheets, as Uncle Jim his field and Stieglitz his white sheets. It must be nonacceptance that has brought this mouth-weariness, eye-weariness to so many of us. There are voices crying, "Accept, accept."

Other voices—a few . . . "Put it down. Put it down."

Stieglitz is a voice. He is a putter-it-down.

Fear of not making good. Who ever heard of Uncle Jim? Who ever bothered about him? What did he care? The young full of the disease: "I must make a noise, get big."

"But I don't want to."

"But you must. You must."

I think there must have been too much big talk in America, long ago. "America, the new sweet land," etc., etc. All the earlier ones flocking here from old Europe, the old human shame on them.

"Land of opportunity."

"Land of opportunity."

"Make good now, make good."

"If you can't do it really, make a bluff. Turn out showy work. Get attention."

Uncle Jim, back there, on his Ohio farm, never got off any of that stuff they were so full of in town. "Boy, I know you are going to make good now." He would have asked, "What's the matter with you as you are now?" He wasn't ashamed of his own position, on his little farm, warm with it, alive with it . . . his little strip of woodland, little fields, barns and sheds. "It's in me, and I am in it."

Later Stieglitz, in a city street walking. The man in his workshop. He catching, with his photographer's plates, city lights, significance of tall skyscrapers, light on the face of stone, on skies. There is an old gelding, standing weary after the day's work—something to make your throat hurt looking. How are you going to tell the story back of such work?

A dead tree by a road near the little house in the country to which he has gone in the hot months for thirty, forty, fifty years. He in his environment as Uncle Jim in his. "Make it yours, then give.

"Give them a farm, wide Ohio horizons. Give them the city. Make it your city and then give it."

Uncle Jim, by the clearness and honesty of his relationship to a field, giving me, standing and watching, sense of all fields, stretching away in a flat country, skies above fields, towns in the distance, so that later, fields and towns could live also in me, my own fancy released, my own imagination playing over farms, going into farm houses, going into streets in towns. . . .

And so Stieglitz to me. He in the city releasing the men about him, turning the imaginations of other men loose in his city. I get him so, as I get Uncle Jim . . . his workroom and the city, the fields he plows, he giving me thus also the city, as Uncle Jim the fields.

Making the city live as reality.

His relations with others, men and women, artists, his photographs. . . .

Himself asserting, sometimes preaching. His preachings and his assertions haven't mattered half as much to me as his devotion. . . .

Just brother, I think, to the devotion of my uncle Jim. . . .

That bringing in something healthy . . . love of work, well and beautifully done . . . the work of others as well as his own work.

Nonsense, eh?

It is the thing for which America cried out. It is the thing the city needs. A few more New Yorkers like Alfred Stieglitz and the city would change.

Take him away and the city will again change. I never did dare go back to Uncle Jim's farm after he and Aunt Mary turned up their toes to the daisies.

APPENDIX

Chronology

1864 Born January 1, Hoboken, New Jersey.

1871 Family moved to New York.

1871–79 Attended Charlier Institute, then New York Grammar School No. 55.

1879–81 Attended College of the City of New York.

1881–82 Studied at Realgymnasium, Karlsruhe, Germany.

1882–90 Studied at Berlin Polytechnic and University of Berlin. Took mechanical engineering courses; studied photochemistry under Professor H. W. Vogel. Dropped engineering for photography, 1883. Spring and autumn trips to Munich, Vienna, Italy, Tyrol, Switzerland. Constantly photographed, experimented, becoming own teacher.

1885 Began writing for German photographic magazines.

1887 Won first prize (silver medal and two guineas) in "Holiday Work Competition" of *The Amateur Photographer* (London), awarded by Dr. P. H. Emerson. First official recognition.

1888 Brief visit to family at new summer home, Oaklawn, Lake George.

1890 Returned to New York. Entered photoengraving business with Joseph Obermeyer and Louis Schubart, his roommates in Berlin.

1890s Began to arrange numerous photographic exhibitions. Continued to write articles for photographic and other magazines. In rapid succession won over 150 medals for photographs entered in competitions throughout the world. Among most important awards in '90s: three Royal Photographic Society (London) medals; three Joint Exhibition medals in Boston, Philadelphia and New York.

1891 Joined Society of Amateur Photographers (New York).

1893 Married Emmeline Obermeyer.

1893–96 Co-editor: *American Amateur Photographer*.

1894, 1904, 1907, 1909 Trips to Europe. Last trip 1911.

1895 Withdrew from business.

1896 Society of Amateur Photographers amalgamated with Camera Club of New York.

1897–1902 Founded and edited *Camera Notes* (organ of the Camera Club of New York).

1897 *Picturesque Bits of New York,* portfolio of photogravures, published by R. H. Russell, New York.

1902 Resigned editorship of *Camera Notes.* Founded the Photo-Secession; founded, published and edited the quarterly *Camera Work* (first issue dated January, 1903). Became recognized as international leader in photography. One of first American members (1894) of Linked Ring (avant-garde British photographic society).

1905 Founded, with cooperation of Edward J. Steichen, the Photo-Secession Gallery, 291 Fifth Avenue, New York. Honorary Member, Royal Photographic Society.

1908 Held first public exhibition of modern art in United States at Photo-Secession Gallery, which became known as 291.

1915 Published the periodical, *291,* March, 1915–January, 1916, with cooperation of Marius De Zayas, Agnes E. Meyer and Paul Haviland.

1917 Gallery 291 closed. Last number of *Camera Work* published.

1922–23 Publication *MSS* issued under Stieglitz's auspices.

1924 Married Georgia O'Keeffe. Received "Progress Medal" from Royal Photographic Society.

1925 Founded The Intimate Gallery (1925–29), Room 303, Anderson Galleries Building, 489 Park Avenue, New York.

1929 Founded An American Place, Room 1710, 509 Madison Avenue, New York.

List of Exhibitions

Photographic, Photo-Secession, 291, 1917–25, The Intimate Gallery, An American Place

1897-1902: Under Stieglitz's jurisdiction, the Camera Club of New York and *Camera Notes* presented the then radical departures of such Americans as Gertrude Käsebier, Edward J. Steichen, Frank Eugene, Clarence White, Joseph T. Keiley and himself.

1902: At the request of the recently organized National Arts Club of New York City, Stieglitz arranged the first Photo-Secession exhibition. Beginning in the same year, museums and other organizations in various countries called upon him to select and send work by Photo-Secessionists to important international photographic exhibitions.

Prints chosen in this way were shown in Paris, Brussels, Glasgow, Turin, Dresden, St. Petersburg, The Hague, Vienna, Pittsburgh, Washington, Buffalo, Toronto and San Francisco.

1905–17: Among the outstanding photographers shown at the Photo-Secession Gallery (291 Fifth Avenue): Stieglitz, Steichen, Robert Demachy, C. Puyo, René Le Bègue, Annie W. Brigman, Käsebier, White, Eugene, D. O. Hill, J. Craig Annan, Frederick H. Evans, Heinrich Kühn, Hugo Henneberg, Hans Watzek, Alvin Langdon Coburn, Baron A. De Meyer, Paul Strand.

Pamela Colman Smith's 1907 exhibition constituted the first show of paintings held at the Photo-Secession Gallery, soon to be known simply as 291. Among the outstanding non-photographic exhibitions that followed:

AUGUSTE RODIN DRAWINGS. First American exhibition, 1908. Second exhibition, 1910.

WILLI GEIGER AND D. S. MCLAUGHLAN. 1908.

HENRI MATISSE. First American exhibition, 1908. Second exhibition, 1910. Third exhibition, first Matisse sculpture shown in the United States, 1912.

MARIUS DE ZAYAS CARICATURES. First American exhibition, 1909. Further exhibitions in 1910 ("Up and Down Fifth Avenue") and in 1913.

ALFRED MAURER. First exhibition anywhere, 1909.

JOHN MARIN. First American exhibition, 1909. Except for 1912 and 1914, annual one-man exhibitions.

MARSDEN HARTLEY. First exhibition anywhere, 1909. Further exhibitions in 1912, 1914, 1916, 1917.

JAPANESE PRINTS FROM F. W. HUNTER COLLECTION (Sharaku and Utamaro, etc.), 1909.

HENRI DE TOULOUSE-LAUTREC LITHOGRAPHS. Their introduction to America, 1909.

YOUNGER AMERICAN PAINTERS (G. Putnam Brinley, Arthur B. Carles, Arthur G. Dove, Lawrence Fellows, Hartley, Marin, Maurer, Steichen, Max Weber), 1910.

LITHOGRAPHS BY PAUL CÉZANNE, AUGUSTE RENOIR, EDOUARD MANET AND TOULOUSE-LAUTREC; RODIN DRAWINGS; SMALL PAINTINGS AND DRAWINGS BY HENRI ROUSSEAU (introduction to America), 1910.

GORDON CRAIG ETCHINGS AND DRAWINGS. First American exhibition, 1910.

WEBER. First comprehensive exhibition, 1911.

CÉZANNE WATER COLORS. First exhibition of his water colors in America, 1911.

PABLO PICASSO DRAWINGS AND WATER COLORS (complete evolution through Cubism). First one-man show in America, 1911.

CARLES. First one-man exhibition, 1912.

DOVE. First one-man exhibition, 1912.

DRAWINGS, WATER COLORS AND PASTELS BY UNTAUGHT CHILDREN AGED 2 TO 11. First exhibition of its kind in New York, 1912.

CARICATURES BY ALFRED J. FRUEH. First one-man show, 1912.

ABRAHAM WALKOWITZ DRAWINGS AND PAINTINGS. First comprehensive exhibition, 1912. Further exhibitions in 1913, 1916, 1917.

FRANCIS PICABIA. First American one-man show, 1913. Second exhibition in 1915.

CONSTANTIN BRANCUSI. First one-man show in America, 1914.

FRANK BURTY. First one-man show anywhere, 1914.

AFRICAN SCULPTURE. First exhibition in America to present African sculpture as art, 1914.

DRAWINGS AND PAINTINGS BY PICASSO AND BY GEORGES BRAQUE, 1914.

KATHARINE N. RHOADES AND MARION BECKETT, 1915.

OSCAR BLUEMNER. First one-man show in America, 1915.

ELIE NADELMAN. First one-man show in America, 1915.

GEORGIA O'KEEFFE, CHARLES DUNCAN, RENÉ LAFFERTY. First O'Keeffes shown anywhere, 1916.

GINO SEVERINI (Futurist). First American exhibition, 1917.

S. MACDONALD WRIGHT PAINTINGS. First American one-man show, 1917.

FIRST ONE-MAN O'KEEFFE EXHIBITION, 1917.

In the interval between the closing of 291 and the opening of The Intimate Gallery in 1925, Stieglitz arranged to have Marin exhibited at the Daniel Gallery (1920, 1921) and at the Montross Gallery (1921, 1922, 1923). In 1923 and 1924, he organized O'Keeffe exhibitions at the Anderson Galleries. In 1921, 1923, 1924 Stieglitz held one-man shows of his own work at the Anderson Galleries. An exhibition of Seven Americans was arranged by Stieglitz in 1925 at the same Galleries: Marin, O'Keeffe, Charles Demuth, Dove, Hartley, Stieglitz, Strand.

Stieglitz founded The Intimate Gallery, 489 Park Avenue, in 1925.

Exhibition I	MARIN. December, 1925.
Exhibition II	DOVE. January, 1926.
Exhibition III	O'KEEFFE. February, 1926.
Exhibition IV	DEMUTH. April, 1926.
Exhibition V	MARIN. November, 1926.
Exhibition VI	O'KEEFFE. January, 1927.
Exhibition VII	GASTON LACHAISE. March, 1927.
Exhibition VIII	MARIN. November, 1927.
Exhibition IX	DOVE. December, 1927.
Exhibition X	O'KEEFFE. January, 1928.
Exhibition XI	BLUEMNER. February, 1928.
Exhibition XII	PEGGY BACON. March, 1928.
Exhibition XIII	PICABIA. April, 1928.
Exhibition XIV	MARIN. November, 1928.
Exhibition XV	HARTLEY. January, 1929.
Exhibition XVI	O'KEEFFE. February, 1929.
Exhibition XVII	STRAND. March, 1929.
Exhibition XVIII	DOVE. April, 1929.
Exhibition XIX	DEMUTH. April, 1929.

Stieglitz established An American Place in 1929. Between that date and the autumn of 1934 the following exhibitions were held there:

MARIN. December, 1929.

O'Keeffe. February, 1930.

Dove. March, 1930.

O'Keeffe, Demuth, Marin, Hartley, Dove (retrospective). April, 1930.

Marin. November, 1930.

Hartley. December, 1930.

O'Keeffe, January, 1931.

Dove. March, 1931.

Demuth. April, 1931.

Group Show (impromptu exhibition of selected paintings), Marin, Hartley, O'Keeffe, Dove, Demuth. May, 1931.

Marin. October, 1931.

O'Keeffe. December, 1931.

Stieglitz (photographs—retrospective). February, 1932.

Dove. March, 1932.

Strand (photographs). Rebecca Strand (paintings on glass). April, 1932.

Impromptu Exhibition of Selected Paintings (Dove, Demuth, Marin, O'Keeffe, Hartley). May, 1932.

S. Macdonald Wright. October, 1932.

Marin. November, 1932.

O'Keeffe. January, 1933.

Dove and Helen Torr. March, 1933.

Selected Early Works of O'Keeffe, Dove and Marin. May, 1933.

Marin Retrospective Exhibition. October, 1933.

Marin New Work. December, 1933.

O'Keeffe Retrospective Exhibition. January, 1934.

Dove. April, 1934.

Selected Bibliography

PUBLICATIONS

Edited by Alfred Stieglitz:

American Amateur Photographer. A Monthly. New York, 1891–96.

Camera Notes. Published quarterly by the Camera Club of New York under Stieglitz's direction. New York, 1897–1902.

Camera Work. A Quarterly. Edited and published by Alfred Stieglitz. 50 numbers. New York, 1903–1917.

Published under the sponsorship of Stieglitz:

291. Published at 291. 12 numbers. New York, March, 1915–February, 1916.

Manuscripts. 6 numbers. New York, 1922–23.

BOOKS

Sherwood Anderson. *A Story Teller's Story.* Dedication, pp. 375, 395. New York, 1924.

R. Child Bayley. *The Complete Photographer.* London, 1906. (1932 Latest Revised Edition.)

Claude Bragdon. *An Introduction to Yoga.* Pp. 18–19. New York, 1933.

C. J. Bulliet. *Apples and Madonnas.* Pp. 54–55, 201–204. Chicago, 1927.

Charles H. Caffin. *Photography as a Fine Art.* New York, 1901.

Sheldon Cheney. *A Primer of Modern Art.* Foreword, pp. 232–33. New York, 1924.

Thomas Craven. *Modern Art.* Pp. 166, 311–14, 316, 325–26, 331. New York, 1934.

Arthur Jerome Eddy. *Cubism and Post-Impressionism.* Pp. 1, 116, list of *291* exhibitions 217–19. Chicago, 1913–1919.

P. H. Emerson. *Naturalistic Photography.* London, 1888.

Waldo Frank. *Rediscovery of America.* Pp. 140, 177–78. New York, 1929.
Salvos, P. 232. New York, 1924.
Time Exposures. Pp. 175–79: "Alfred Stieglitz the Prophet." New York, 1926.
Our America. Pp. 180–87. New York, 1919.
Primer Mensaje á la América Hispana. Madrid, 1930.

A. E. Gallatin. *American Water-Colourists.* Pp. x-xi. New York, 1922.

Marsden Hartley. *Adventures in the Arts.* Pp. 102–111. New York, 1924.

Sadakichi Hartmann. *History of American Art.* Pp. 151–59. Vol. II. Boston, 1902.

C. Lewis Hind. *Art and I.* Pp. 45–56, 153. New York, 1921.

Samuel Kootz. *Modern American Painters.* Foreword. New York, 1930.

Alfred Kreymborg. *Troubadour.* Pp. 162, 168. New York, 1925.

John Marin. *Letters of . . .* New York, 1931.

Lewis Mumford. *Brown Decades.* Pp. 232–35. New York, 1931.
Technics and Civilization. Pp. 339–340. New York, 1934.

Dorothy Norman. *Dualities.* Pp. 76–78. New York, 1933.

Ralph Pearson. *Experiencing Pictures.* P. 117. New York, 1932.

Duncan Phillips. *A Collection in the Making.* P. 59. Washington, 1926.

Paul Rosenfeld. *Port of New York.* Pp. 237–279. New York, 1924.

Harold Rugg. *Culture and Education in America.* Pp. 198–200, 206, 273. New York, 1931.
The Great Technology. P. 221. New York, 1933.

Gertrude Stein. *Autobiography of Alice B. Toklas.* P. 119. New York, 1933.

Willard Huntington Wright. *Modern Painting.* P. 341. New York, 1915.

ARTICLES

SHERWOOD ANDERSON. "Alfred Stieglitz." *New Republic*. New York, October 25, 1922.

EGMONT ARENS. "Alfred Stieglitz. His Cloud Pictures." P. 15, *Playboy*, No. 9. New York, 1924.

ALEXANDER BLACK. "The New Photography." *Century Magazine*. New York, October, 1902.

GUIDO BRUNO. "The Passing of 291." *Pearson's Magazine*. Vol. 38, No. 9. New York, March, 1918.

CHARLES H. CAFFIN. "Photography as a Fine Art." Ten Essays beginning March, 1901. *Everybody's Magazine*. New York.

JAMES B. CARRINGTON. "Night Photography." *Scribner's*. New York, November, 1897.

THEODORE DREISER. "A Master of Photography." *Success*. New York, June 10, 1899.

 "The Camera Club of New York." *Ainslee's*. New York, September, 1899.

 "A Remarkable Art: The New Pictorial Photography." *The Great Round World*. New York, May 3, 1902.

GUY EGLINGTON. "Art and Other Things." *International Studio*. New York, May, 1924.

WALDO FRANK. "Alfred Stieglitz." Pp. 24, 107–108. *McCall's Magazine*. New York, May, 1927.

GEORGE GARFIELD AND FRANCES O'BRIEN. "Stieglitz, Apostle of American Culture." *Reflex Magazine*. New York, September, 1928.

SADAKICHI HARTMANN. "The Photo-Secession. A New Pictorial Movement." *The Craftsman*. New York, April, 1904.

 "Aesthetic Activity in Photography." *Brush and Pencil*. Chicago, 1904.

A. HORSLEY HINTON. "The Work and Attitude of the Photo-Secession of America." English *Amateur Photographer*. London, June 2, 1904.

MARMADUKE HUMPHREY (RUPERT HUGHES). "Triumphs in Amateur Photography. 1. Alfred Stieglitz." *Godey's*. New York, December, 1897.

J. NILSEN LAURVIK. "New Color Photography." *Century*. New York, January, 1908.

 "Alfred Stieglitz, Pictorial Photographer." *International Studio*. New York, August, 1911.

WARD MUIR. "Alfred Stieglitz. An Impression." *Amateur Photographer and Photographic News*. New York, March 24, 1913.

HENRY McBRIDE. "Modern Art." *Dial*. New York, April, 1921.

LEWIS MUMFORD. "Alfred Stieglitz, '84." Pp. 149–151. *City College Alumnus Bulletin. Fine Arts and Architecture*. No. 5. Vol. 25. New York, May, 1929.

 "El Arte en los Estados Unidos." Pp. 49–82. *Sur*, No. 3. Buenos Aires, 1931.

H. R. POORE. "The Photo-Secession." *The Camera*. Philadelphia, 1903.

ROLAND ROOD. "The Three Factors in American Pictorial Photography." *American Amateur Photographer*. New York, 1905.

PAUL ROSENFELD. "Stieglitz." *The Dial*. Pp. 397–409. New York, April, 1921.

 (PETER MINUIT) "291." *The Seven Arts*. New York, November, 1916.

 "Photography of Alfred Stieglitz." *The Nation*. New York, March 23, 1932.

HERBERT J. SELIGMANN. "A Photographer Challenges." *The Nation*, New York, February 16, 1921.

 "Alfred Stieglitz and His Work at 291." Pp. 83–84. *American Mercury*. New York, May, 1924.

PAUL STRAND. "Photography and the New God." *Broom*. New York, November, 1922.

 "Photography." *The Seven Arts*. New York, August, 1917.

 "The Art Motive in Photography." *British Journal of Photography*. London, October 5, 1923.

HORACE TRAUBEL. "Stieglitz." *Conservator*. New York, December, 1916.

WHAT IS 291? Number 47. *Camera Work*. New York, January, 1915.

PAMPHLETS AND CATALOGUES

BOSTON MUSEUM CATALOGUE. Ananda Coomaraswamy. "A Gift from Alfred Stieglitz." Pp. 14–15. Vol. XXII, No. 130. Boston, April, 1924.

HUTCHINS HAPGOOD. "Fire and Revolution." (Reprinted from the New York *Globe*: July 11, 1912.) Free Speech League. New York, 1912.

"IT MUST BE SAID" and "IT HAS BEEN SAID" pamphlet series. An American Place. New York, 1932—.

MARIUS DE ZAYAS, PAUL B. HAVILAND. "A Study of the Modern Evolution of Plastic Expression." 291. New York, 1913.

METROPOLITAN MUSEUM CATALOGUE. William Ivins, Jr. "Photographs by Alfred Stieglitz." Pp. 44–45. Vol. XXIV, No. 2. New York, February, 1929.

PHOTO-SECESSIONISM AND ITS OPPONENTS. 5 Letters by Alfred Stieglitz. New York, August, 1910.

 A 6th Letter by Alfred Stieglitz. New York, October, 1910.

The Publications which Stieglitz edited and which are here listed, contain many of his early photographic articles. Other articles that he wrote are scattered in photographic journals in different parts of the world, and to give a few selected articles as references would be to give a false, rather than a true, picture of the nature of these variegated writings, about experiments and technique, as well as about exhibitions and policy. Late nineteenth- and early twentieth-century photographic journals should be consulted, in addition to the *American Amateur Photographer, Camera Notes,* and *Camera Work,* herewith listed.

No newspaper articles, and few foreign publications or writings on the work of artists mentioned are included, since they are too numerous to list in a partial bibliography.

Notes on Contributors

SHERWOOD ANDERSON is a novelist, poet, and writer of short stories and essays. Among his numerous works are *Winesburg, Ohio; Poor White, Story Teller's Story, Dark Laughter, Beyond Desire, Mid-American Chants.* He was born in Camden, O., September 13, 1876.

R. CHILD BAYLEY was assistant secretary of the Royal Photographic Society from 1892–98. Ever since this period he has been editor of what is now known as *The Amateur Photographer.* He has done extensive newspaper work. He is Honorary Life Fellow of the Royal Photographic Society. He has written a number of books on photography, the best known of which is *The Complete Photographer.* He was born in Hertfordshire, England, 1869.

THE HONORABLE DOROTHY BRETT is a painter and the author of *Lawrence and Brett.* She was born in England, November 10, 1891, and lives in New Mexico.

EDNA BRYNER is a novelist and writer of short stories. Among her published novels are *While the Bridegroom Tarried* and *Andy Brandt's Ark.* She has contributed short novels and stories to the first and second *American Caravan, The Dial, The Bookman,* and other magazines. She was born in Tylersburg, Pa., September 1, 1886, and lives in New York.

HAROLD CLURMAN is one of the organizers and directors of *The Group Theatre* and has written many critical essays and reviews. He was born in New York, September 18, 1901.

CHARLES DEMUTH is a painter in oil, tempera, and water color. He has exhibited in New York chiefly at the Daniel Gallery, Kraushaar Gallery, at the Intimate Gallery and An American Place. Among the museums in which his work is represented are the Metropolitan Museum, Brooklyn Museum, Cleveland Museum, Chicago Fine Arts Institute, Barnes Foundation, Phillips Memorial Gallery. He was born in Lancaster, Pa., 1883.

ARTHUR G. DOVE is a painter in several media and an illustrator: he has also farmed. He has exhibited his work at *291,* The Forum Show—1916, The Intimate Gallery and An American Place. He is represented in the Phillips Memorial Gallery. He was born in Canandaigua, New York, August 2, 1880, and lives in Geneva, N. Y.

RALPH FLINT has been art critic for the *Christian Science Monitor, Creative Art,* and Editor of the *Art News.* He is also a painter and has exhibited at the Harriman Galleries and the Jacques Seligmann Gal-

leries. He was born in Boston, Mass., August 22, 1885, and lives in New York.

WALDO FRANK is a novelist, cultural critic, writer of short stories and a lecturer on cultural subjects. Among his numerous works are *City Block, Rahab, The Death and Birth of David Markand, Our America, Virgin Spain, The Rediscovery of America.* He is an associate editor of the *New Republic.* He was born in Long Branch, N. J., August 25, 1889, and lives in New York.

MARSDEN HARTLEY is a painter in several media. He is the author of *Adventures in the Arts, Twenty-Five Poems,* and numerous poems and essays published in various anthologies and periodicals. He was born in Lewiston, Me., January 4, 1877.

DR. EVELYN HOWARD is an instructor in physiology at Johns Hopkins Medical School, Baltimore, and has published papers on the general physiology of the organization of living matter and on endocrinology. She was born in Bangor, Me., May 14, 1904.

JOHN MARIN is a painter in oils and water color, and an etcher. His evolution has been demonstrated in almost regular yearly exhibitions since 1909 at 291 Fifth Avenue, the Intimate Gallery, and An American Place. In the interval between 1917 and 1925 Alfred Stieglitz arranged exhibitions of his work at the Daniel and Montross galleries. A Collection of his letters was published in 1932 under the title of *The Letters of John Marin.* Among the museums in which his work is represented are the Metropolitan Museum, Brooklyn Museum, San Francisco Museum, Chicago Art Institute, Fogg Art Museum, Gallery of Living Art. He was born in Rutherford, N. J., December 23, 1871.

ELIZABETH McCAUSLAND is art editor of the *Springfield Republican* and has contributed articles to magazines. She was born in Wichita, Kan., April 16, 1899.

LEWIS MUMFORD is the author of works of cultural, esthetic, and architectural criticism. Among his books are *The Story of Utopias, Sticks and Stones, The Golden Day, Herman Melville, The Brown Decades,* and *Technics and Civilization,* and he is the author of innumerable essays in periodicals and symposiums. He is an associate editor of the *New Republic.* He was an editor of *The American Caravan.* He was born in Flushing, L. I., October 29, 1895.

DOROTHY NORMAN is the author of *Dualities* and of other poems. She was born in Philadelphia, Pa., March 28, 1905, and lives in New York.

VICTORIA OCAMPO is the author of a volume on *Dante* and other critical works, is an architect, and the editor of *Sur,* published quarterly in Buenos Aires. She was born in Buenos Aires, Argentina, April 7, 1890, and lives in Buenos Aires and Paris.

PAUL ROSENFELD is a novelist and is a critic of and lecturer on music, literature, and art. Among his books are *The Boy in the Sun, Port of*

New York, Musical Chronicle, By Way of Art, Musical Portraits, Men Seen. He was an editor of *The American Caravan,* and his critical essays have appeared in numerous periodicals. He was born in New York, May 4, 1890.

HAROLD RUGG was a civil engineer and is at present a Professor of Education at Teachers College of Columbia University. He is the author of many books on educational and cultural subjects, among them *Culture in America, Changing Governments and Changing Cultures, The Child Centered School, The Great Technology.* He was born in Fitchburg, Mass., January 17, 1886.

EVELYN SCOTT is the author of novels, short stories, essays, poems, and a drama. Among her books are *Escapade, The Narrow House, The Wave, Eva Gay, Breathe Upon These Slain, Precipitations.* She has published critical essays in various periodicals. She was born in Clarksville, Tenn., January 17, 1893.

HERBERT J. SELIGMANN is a poet, critic, and publicist. He is the author of *D. H. Lawrence, An American Interpretation;* two volumes of poetry: *Firebird* and *Suns and Tides,* and many critical essays. He edited, with introduction, *The Letters of John Marin.* He was born in New York, November 13, 1891.

GERTRUDE STEIN is the author of numerous works, among them *Three Lives, Matisse and Picasso (Camera Work,* Special Number, 1912), *Tender Buttons, Autobiography of Alice B. Toklas, Four Saints in Three Acts, Portraits and Prayers.* She was born in Allegheny, Pa., February 3, 1874.

PAUL STRAND is a photographer; he has also made motion pictures. He has written critical essays on photography and art. Exhibitions of his photographs have been held at 291, The Intimate Gallery, An American Place, and recently in Mexico. He was born in New York, October 16, 1890.

JENNINGS TOFEL is a painter, essayist, and writer on esthetic subjects. He has contributed to *The American Caravan* and is the author of a study of *Benjamin Kopman.* He was born in Poland in 1891 and came to America in 1905.

JEAN TOOMER is a novelist, short-story writer, poet, and critic. Among his published works are *Cane, Essentials,* and contributions to the second and third *American Caravans,* and other periodicals.

WILLIAM CARLOS WILLIAMS is a poet, novelist, essayist, author of short stories; and a practising physician. Among his numerous works are *Al Que Quiere, A Novelette and Other Prose* (1921–31), *Poems,* 1921–31, *In the American Grain, A Voyage to Pagany, Kora in Hell.* His work has appeared in many anthologies and periodicals. He was born in Rutherford, N. J., September 17, 1883.

Acknowledgments

The publisher wishes to express deep appreciation to the following individuals without whose help and support this revised edition of *America and Alfred Stieglitz* would not have been possible:
Mrs. Dorothy Norman, the original editor of this volume, was generous in making available many of the images which appeared in the first edition; Mrs. Ethel Bobb conscientiously provided assistance in organizing material for reproduction; Lynn Kaufman researched sources for additional images. Aperture acknowledges with gratitude the contributions of the Andrew Crispo Gallery, New York City; Anita Duquette, Rights and Reproduction, and Peter Freeman, Curatorial Department, Whitney Museum of American Art; Georgia O'Keeffe and Juan Hamilton, Abiquiu, New Mexico; Gail Levin, Whitney Museum of American Art; Elizabeth Pollock, Philadelphia Museum of Art; Malcolm Varon Associates, New York City; Cheryl Wacher, Photographic Services, The Metropolitan Museum of Art; Joan Washburn, Washburn Gallery, New York City; Zabriskie Gallery, New York City.

Credits

The Bibliography and Notes on Contributors are reprinted from the first edition of this work. Later material can be found in *Alfred Stieglitz: An American Seer* by Dorothy Norman, Aperture, 1978.

Index

Adams, John, 18.

Adamson, Robert, 43, 53.

Adventures in the Arts, 64.

"Alfred Stieglitz and a Machine," by Paul Strand, 137–39.

"Alfred Stieglitz and the Group Idea," by Harold Clurman, 130–35.

Amateur Photographer (London), 44, 63, 151, 153.

American Amateur Photographer, 46, 151.

"American Background, The," by William Carlos Williams, 17–26.

"American Experience, An," by Edna Bryner, 125–27.

American Photography, 46, 151. *See also* PHOTOGRAPHY.

American Place, An, 66, 67–77, 89, 98–99, 128, 129–30, 133, 135, 146, 151; list of exhibitions, 151–53.

"American Place, An," by Dorothy Norman, 67–77.

Anderson, Sherwood, 61, 63; "City Plowman," 146–48; Note, 155.

Anderson Galleries, exhibitions of Stieglitz's work, 48, 62–63, 64, 152; of O'Keeffe's paintings, 63, 152; Room 303, the Intimate Gallery, 64–66, 121, 133, 151, 152; exhibition of Seven Americans, 152.

Angelus (Millet), 87.

Annan, J. Craig, 43, 48, 53, 54, 151.

Armory Show (1913), 87.

Art, Modern, *see* MODERN ART; French, 81.

Art Essays, Burnet's, 55.

"Artist and the Great Transition, The," by Harold Rugg, 91–99.

Art Now: An Introduction to the Theory of Modern Painting and Sculpture, 82–83, 85.

Atget, contemporary of Stieglitz, 33, 48, 137.

Bacon, Peggy, 66, 152.

Ballard, James, 147–48.

Bayley, R. Child, 48, 63; "Photography before Stieglitz," 51–57; Note, 155.

Beckett, Marion, 152.

Beethoven, 42.

Bell, Clive, 82.

Bennett, James Gordon, 28.

Bergson, 42.

Berkeley, Sir William, 17.

Berlin Polytechnic, 40, 41, 151.

Bernhardt, Sarah, 45.

Bibliography, 153–54.

Black Monk, The, Chekhov's, 74.

Blake, William, 107, 109.

Bliss Collection, 82, 84.

Bloch, Ernest, 61, 63.

Bluemner, Oscar, 48, 64, 66, 152.

Bonheur, Rosa, 60, 87.

Boone, Daniel, 19, 21.

Bossert and Guttmann, *"Les Premiers Temps de la Photographie,"* 53.

Boston Museum of Fine Arts, 64, 87, 138.

Bouguereau, 87.

"Boy in the Dark Room, The," by Paul Rosenfeld, 38–50.

Bragdon, Claude, 128.

Brancusi, 65, 152.

Braque, 59, 85, 88, 152.

Brett, Dorothy, "The Room," 127–29; Note, 155.

Brooks, Van Wyck, 88, 89.

Brown, John, 116.

Bryant, William Cullen, 31.

Bryner, Edna, "An American Experience," 125–27; Note, 155.

Buffalo Exhibition (1911), 53.

Burnet, *Art Essays,* 55; *Treatise on Painting,* 56.

Butler, Samuel, 20, 137.

Caffin, Charles, 48.

Calotype, 52, 53.

Camera Club, of New York, 46, 58, 151; of London, 56.

Camera Notes, 47–48, 58, 151.

Camera Work, 36; history of publication, 47–48, 151; Gertrude Stein a contributor to, 48, 60, 120, 154; description of Hill Collection quoted from, 53; prints of Mrs. Cameron reproduced in, 54; a record of the evolution of Stieglitz's idea, 58, 135, 145; Stieglitz honored for publication of, 59; Sir Purdon Clarke quoted from, 60; work of Paul Strand represented in, 60; Stieglitz's work included in, 60; No. 47, "What Is 291?" 61; Expulsion from Camera Club, (No. 22), 151.

Cameron, Julia Margaret, 43, 48, 53; contribution to photography, 54, 56.

Carles, Arthur B., 151, 152.

Carlyle, Thomas, 54.

Cary, Elisabeth Luther, 48.

Cassirer, Bruno, 47.

Cézanne, Paul, 48, 60, 116, 123; introduction to America, 59, 88, 120, 130, 152; the turning point in modern art, 82–85, 86; compared with Stieglitz, 89; list of exhibitions, 152.

Charlier Institute, 39, 151.

Chekhov, Anton, 74.

Chronology (Alfred Stieglitz), 151.

"City Plowman," by Sherwood Anderson, 146–48.

Clarke, Sir Purdon, 59, 60.

Clurman, Harold, "Alfred Stieglitz and the Group Idea," 130–35; Note, 155.

Coburn, Alvin Langdon, 43, 47, 151.

College of the City of New York, 40, 151.

Communism, Stieglitz on, 74.

Confucius, 106.

Cook, Jay, 28.

Cortissoz, Royal, 48.

Craig, Gordon, 152.

Crane, Stephen, 32.

Craven, Thomas, 121.

Crystal Palace Exhibition (1851), 43.

Cubism, 60, 84–85, 120; Picasso exhibition showing evolution through, 152.

Culture, beginning of American, 17ff; American addition to world, 20; defined, 25; the metropolitan milieu, 27ff.; the problems of the new culture, 96, 97.

Dadaism, 60.

Daguerre, 52.

Darwin, Charles, 54.

Day, Holland, 151.

De Casseres, Benjamin, 48.

De Fourment, Hélène, 36.

DeKay, Charles, 151.

Dégas, Edouard, 35.

Demachy, Robert, 48, 151.

De Meyer, Baron, 48, 151.

Demuth, Charles, 63, 90; one of the "Seven Americans," 64, 65; "Lighthouses and Fog," 122; list of exhibitions, 152–53; Note, 155.

D'Ors, Eugenio, 86.

Dérain, 85.

Detaille, 87.

Dewey, John, 93–94, 97, 107.

De Zayas, Marius, 48, 152.

Dickens, Charles, 21, 27.

Dickenson, Emily, 24, 116.

"Different One, A," by Arthur Dove, 121–22.

Dodge, Mabel, 48, 61.

Dove, Arthur G., 60, 61, 62; one of the Seven Americans, 64–65; his work an embodiment of the Stieglitz idea, 89, 90, 126, 133; American quality of, 116, 126; "A Different One," 121–22; list of exhibitions, 152–53; Note, 155.

"Dualities," by Dorothy Norman, 66.

Duchamp, Marcel, 63.

Dufy, 85.

Duncan Charles, 152.

Duse, Eleonora, 45, 119.

Eakins, Thomas, 33, 90.

Edison, Thomas, 81.

Einstein, Albert, 101.

Eliot, T. S., 126.

Emerson, Dr. H. P., medal awarded Stieglitz by, 44, 57, 151; not represented in *Camera Work*, 48; his *Naturalistic Photography*, 56–57.
Emerson, Ralph Waldo, 24, 33, 98, 116.
Equivalents (Stieglitz), 64, 89, 126, 131.
Eugene, Frank, 43, 47, 151.
Evans, Fred H., 48, 151.
Exhibitions, representative list, 151–53.

Fading Away (Robinson), 54, 55.
Fauves, 84–85.
Field, Marshall, 38.
Five Points (Stieglitz), 46.
Flammarion (Paris), 53.
Flatiron, The (Stieglitz), 47.
Flint, Ralph, "Post-Impressionism," 81–90; Note, 155.
Foord, John, 45.
Frank, Waldo, "The New World in Stieglitz," 106–11; quoted, 129; estimate of Stieglitz as artist, 130; Note, 155.
Franklin, Benjamin, 18–19.
French, Herbert G., 151.
French art, 81–82.
Freud, Sigmund, 107.
Frueh, Alfred J., 152.
Fuller, George, 36.
Futurism, 60.

Gauguin, 83, 84.
Geddes, Patrick, 30.
Geiger, Willi, 152.
Glackens, 120.
Goethe, 39, 42.
Goetz, Fritz, 45.
Going to the Post (Stieglitz), 35.
Great Transition, Stieglitz and the, 91–99; traits of the modern industrial and social revolution, 92ff.
Great War, see WORLD WAR.
Greco, El, 85.
Greene, Belle, 61.
Greene, General Nathanael, 39, 72.
Grueze, 60.
Guttmann, Bossert and, *"Les Premiers Temps de la Photographie, 1840–1870,"* 53.

Hals, 87.
Hand of Man, The (Stieglitz), 47.
Hartford Museum, 87.
Hartley, Marsden, 60, 62; essay on O'Keeffe, 64; exhibition of the Seven Americans, 64; Room 303 in the Anderson Galleries, 65; "291—and the Brass Bowl," 119–21; list of exhibitions, 151–53; Note, 155.
Hartmann, Sadakichi, 48.
Haviland, Paul, 48.
Hegel, Georg W. F., 31.
Heliochrome Engraving Company, 45–46.
Helmholtz, Hermann von, 102.
Henderson, L. G., 102, 103, 104, 105.
Henneberg, Hugo, 48, 151.
Herschel, Sir John, 54.
Hill, David Octavius, 43, 48, 52, 53–54, 56, 137, 151.
"Hill, The," by Jean Toomer, 143–46.
Homer, Winslow, 65, 90.
Horse Fair (Bonheur), 87.
Houston, Sam, 19.
Howard, Evelyn, "The Significance of Stieglitz for the Philosophy of Science," 100–05; Note, 155.
Huneker, James, 48, 59.
Hunt, Holman, 54.
Hunter, F. W., 152.
Huxley, Aldous, 34.

Icy Night (Stieglitz), 46, 47.
Impressionism, 82, 84; in work of Stieglitz, 88, 89.
Inness, George, 87.
Intimate Gallery, 65–66, 89, 98, 128, 151; exhibitions, 152.
Ives, American composer, 24.

Jackson, Andrew, 19, 23.
James, Henry, 126.
James, William, 88, 89, 93.
Jefferson, Thomas, 18–19.
Juhl, Ernst, 48.

Karlsruhe Realgymnasium, 40.
Käsebier, Gertrude, 43, 47, 151.

Keiley, Joseph T., 43, 47, 48, 53, 151; quoted on Buffalo exhibition, 58–59.
Kennerley, Mitchell, 62, 63, 64, 121.
Kerfoot, John B., 48.
Kirnon, Hodge, 61.
Knoblauch, Mary, 120.
Kühn, Heinrich, 48, 151.

Lachaise, Gaston, 61, 66, 152.
Lafferty, René, 152.
Lake George, The Hill at, 143–46.
Lawrence, D. H., 101.
Lawrence, Stephen B., 120.
Le Bègue, Renée, 151.
Leighton, Frederick, 43.
"Letters of John Marin," 66, 154.
Liebovitz, David, 61.
"Lighthouses and Fog," by Charles Demuth, 122.
Linked Ring, 47, 58, 151.
Lippmann, Walter, 61.
Liszt, Franz, 40.
Lowell, Amy, 25.
Luhan, Mabel, 127–28.

Maeterlinck, 48, 119.
Male Figure (Cézanne), 84.
"Man and the Place, The," by John Marin, 118–19.
Man in a Blue Cap (Cézanne), 82.
Manet, Edouard, 152.
Manolo, 48, 120, 152.
Marin, John, 48, 60, 61, 123; Stieglitz's sponsorship of, 61–62, 100, 126; exhibitions at the Montross Gallery, 62; portraits by Stieglitz, 63; exhibition of Seven Americans, 64; opening exhibit at the Intimate Gallery, 65; estimate of him as artist, 65, 89–90, 100, 126; "Letters," 66, 154; his work an embodiment of the Stieglitz idea, 89, 133; his American quality, 116, 126; retrospective exhibition (1933), 116; "The Man and the Place," 118–19; Stieglitz experienced through a show by, 125–27; his work first seen by Dorothy Brett, 128; list of exhibitions, 152–53; Note, 155.
Mark Twain, 41.

Martin, Paul, 58.
Marx, Karl, 106, 107, 110.
Matisse, Henri, 48, 60, 116; introduction in America, 59, 88, 120, 130; his place in modern painting, 85; sculpture, 120, 152; list of exhibitions, 152.
Maurer, Alfred, 60, 152.
Mauve, 87.
McCausland, Elizabeth, "Stieglitz and the American Tradition," 115–17; Note, 155.
McLaughlan, D. S., 152.
Meissonier, 60, 87.
Melville, Herman, 23, 28, 31.
Memling, 43.
Mencken, Henry, 147.
"Metropolitan Milieu, The," by Lewis Mumford, 27–37.
Metropolitan Museum of Art, bequest of Frank Munsey to, 26; Stieglitz's prints in 47, 138; reactionary attitude, 60, 87; Marquand Bequest, 87; popular buys of the 'eighties and 'nineties, 87.
Meyer, Eugene, 61.
Millet, 87.
Modern Art, *Camera Work* a record of, 48; the exhibits at "291," 59; Post-Impressionism, 81–90; Cubism, 85; beginning with Picasso, 86; in America, 86–90; Alfred Stieglitz, 87–90.
Modern Painters, Ruskin's, 81.
Monet, Claude, 81–82.
Montross Gallery, 62, 152.
Morgan, J. P., 60.
Morris, Roger, 20.
Moussorgsky, 43.
Mumford, Lewis, "The Metropolitan Milieu," 27–37; Note, 155.
Munsey, Frank, 26.
Museum of Modern Art (New York), 90.
"Music—A Sequence of Ten Cloud Photographs" (Stieglitz), 63.

Nadar, 43.
Nadelman, Elie, 60, 152.
National Arts Club, 151.
National Gallery (London), 81.

Naturalistic Photography, 44, 56–57, 58.

Newton, Sir W. J., 54.

"New World in Stieglitz, The," by Waldo Frank, 106–11.

New York City, in the period of Alfred Stieglitz, 27ff., 131; Stieglitz photographs of, 32ff., 46, 89, 133.

New York Society of Amateur Photographers, 47.

Nietzsche, 107.

Norman, Dorothy, 66; "An American Place," 67–77; Note, 155.

"Note on the Esthetic Significance of Photography, A," by Evelyn Scott, 139–42.

Obermeyer, Emmeline (Mrs. Alfred Stieglitz), 45, 151.

Ocampo, Victoria, "A Witness," 129–30; Note, 155.

Official Report on Virginia, An (1671), 17.

O'Keeffe, Georgia, her work first shown to Stieglitz, 60, 121; relationship with Stieglitz, 61–62, 126, 151; portraits by Stieglitz, 63; exhibition in Anderson Galleries (1923), 63; estimates of, 63–64, 89–90, 100; one of the Seven Americans, 64, 65; her work the embodiment of the Stieglitz idea, 89, 133; American quality of, 115–16, 126; retrospective exhibition (1934), 116; work described, 123, 126; described by Dorothy Brett, 128; at The Hill on Lake George, 143, 144; list of exhibitions, 152–53.

"One, One, One," by Gertrude Stein, 120.

O'Sheel, Seumas, 119.

Painting, American, and the French tradition, 25.

Pan, 47.

Papin, 92.

Paris International Exhibition (1867), 55.

Pascal, 130.

Paul of Tarsus, 106, 107.

Peirce, Charles, 93–94.

Penseur, Le (Rodin), 152.

Perrault, 129.

Philebus, of Plato, 83.

Philipse, Mary, 20.

Photography, Stieglitz's introduction to, 41; early experiments in, 43; Stieglitz the liberator of, 43; artists contributing most to the development of, 43, 137; evolution of Stieglitz's work, 43ff., 88; American Photography, 46; exhibitions of Stieglitz's work, 48–50, 62–63; from the beginning to 20th century, 51–57; its birth as a means of artistic expression, 57; Stieglitz's contribution to, 58, 64 (*see also* STIEGLITZ); *versus* art, 137–42; list of exhibitions, 151.

"Photography Before Stieglitz," by R. Child Bayley, 51–57.

Photo-Secession, 47, 58, 72, 151; Little Galleries of the, 59; 291 Fifth Avenue, 59ff., 151 (*see also* 291 FIFTH AVENUE); list of exhibitions, 152.

Picabia, Francis, 48, 59, 66, 152.

Picabia, Gabrielle, 48.

Picasso, Pablo, 48, 60, 116, 122; introduction in America, 59, 88, 120, 130; leading protagonist of Cubism, 85; embodiment of modern art, 86–87; loan exhibition at Hartford Museum, 87; Gertrude Stein's portrait of, 120; list of exhibitions, 152.

Picturesque Bits of New York (Stieglitz), 151.

Plato, 83.

Poe, Edgar A., 21, 36.

Pointillism, 84.

Police Gazette, 46.

"Portrait, A," by Jennings Tofel, 123–25.

Portraiture, Stieglitz's conception of, 62–63.

Post, William B., 47.

Post-Impressionism, the exhibits at "291," 59; history, 81–90; in America, 86ff.; Stieglitz and, 88.

"Post-Impressionism," by Ralph Flint, 81–90.

Pound, Ezra, 19, 25.

Pragmatism (or pragmaticism), of Peirce, 93.

"Premiers Temps de la Photographie, Les," 53

Prendergast, 120.

Proust, Marcel, 25.

Puyo, 48, 151.

Pythagoras, 107.

Ray, Man, 43.

Read, Herbert, 82–83, 85.

Rejlander, 54.

Rembrandt, 84, 87.

Renoir, Auguste, 152.

Reuleaux, Professor, 40, 151.

Rhoades, Katharine N., 152.

Rimbaud, Jean Arthur, 107.

Robinson, Henry Peach, 54, 55.

Rodin, 48, 59, 88, 119, 152.

Roebling, Washington, 31.

Romanticism, as a philosophy of art in America, 115–17.

Rood, Roland, 48.

"Room, The," by Dorothy Brett, 127–29.

Rosenberg, Paul, 85.

Rosenfeld, Paul, "The Boy in the Dark Room," 38–49; at The Hill, 144; Note, 155.

Rouault, 85.

Rousseau, Henri, 59, 120, 152.

Rousseau, Jean-Jacques, 107, 117.

Royal Photographic Society, 48, 53, 54, 57, 153; medals conferred on Stieglitz, 58–59, 151.

Rubens, Peter Paul, 36, 44, 87.

Rugg, Harold, "The Artist and the Great Transition," 91–99; Note, 156.

Ruskin, 81, 89.

Russell, R. H., 151.

Ryder, Albert Pinkham, 31, 33, 90.

Salomon, Adam, 53, 55.

Sandburg, Carl, 61.

Santayana, 42.

Sargent, John Singer, 43, 65.

Sayn-Wittgenstein, Princess, 40.

Schopenhauer, 42.

Science, the significance of Stieglitz for, 100–05.

Scott, Evelyn, "A Note on the Esthetic Significance of Photography," 139–42; Note, 156.

Seated Woman (Picasso), 86.

Seeley, George, 151.

Segantini, 120.

Seligmann, Herbert, J., "A Vision Through Photography," 58–66; Note, 156.

Seurat, 84.

"Seven Americans," 64–65.

Severini, Gino, 59, 152.

Sex, in American society, 35–36; in the work of Stieglitz, 36–37; in Rubens's paintings, 36.

Sharp, Virginia, 48.

Shaw, Bernard, 43, 51.

"Significance of Stieglitz for the Philosophy of Science," by Evelyn Howard, 100–05.

Sketches in Criticism, by Van Wyck Brooks, 88.

Smith, Pamela Colman, 59, 152.

Socrates, 106.

South Street (Stieglitz), 46.

Spiritual America (Stieglitz), 64.

Steffens, Lincoln, 22, 23.

Steichen, Eduard J., 43, 47, 48, 59, 151; comment on work of Marsden Hartley, 121.

Stein, Gertrude, a contributor to *Camera Work*, 48, 60; portrait of Picasso, 120; "Stieglitz," 136; Note, 156.

Stewart, A. T., 38.

Stieglitz, Alfred, effect of his life and work, 26, 37; the New York background of, 27ff., 131; Berlin, 31, 40–44; returns to New York, 32, 44; discovery of New York with the camera, 32ff., 46, 88, 133; symbolism in his work, 33, 34–37; parentage and early life, 38–40, 126, 131; education, 39ff.; goes with family to Europe, 39, 40; musical and literary tastes, 41; introduction to photography, 41–42; Italy, 44; receives prize in *Amateur Photographer's* competition, 44; earliest known specimens of his work extant, 44; decision to make profession of photography, 45; New York (1895), 45ff.; marriage, 45; the Heliochrome Engraving Company, 45; decision to retire from business, 46; editor of *American Amateur Photographer,* 46; publishes *Camera Notes,* 47; honors, 47, 58, 59; prophetic prints, 47; as moralist, 47; founder of the Photo-Secession, 47; publishes *Camera Work,* 47–48, 61; opens Photo-Secession gallery, 48; artists introduced by him, 48, 59, 60, 88, 130; exhibitions of his work, 48–50, 62–63, 64, 151ff.; quality of his work, 48–50, 62–63, 64, 100, 107–11, 116, 124, 130; his work exhibited in England, 57; contribution to photography, 58, 64; first period of his evolution, 58, 133; the experiment at 291 Fifth Avenue, 59ff., 88, 119–21, 131, 133, 134, 138, 145; relationship with O'Keeffe, 60, 61–62; the center of a group of workers, 61; his sponsorship of American artists, 61–62, 126; the Marin exhibitions, 62; conception of portraiture, 62–63, 138; statement of his ideal, 62, 65, 73; explanation of Cloud Music, 63; presents work of O'Keeffe, 63–64; Boston Museum acquires his photographs, 64; opens center in Anderson Galleries, 64; exhibition of Seven Americans, 64; the Intimate Gallery (q.v.), 65–66; An American Place (q.v.), 67–77; the man, 67–77, 107–11, 115, 122, 123, 128, 145; exponent of art in the New World, 87–90; as teacher, 91, 124; his idea embodied in work of Marin, O'Keeffe, Dove, 89, 133; his importance to the new culture, 91, 97–99, 106; his significance for the philosophy of science, 100–05; symbol of the American tradition, 115–17; meeting with Marsden Hartley, 119; Thomas Craven's judgment on, 121; a master of talk, 123, 124; knowledge of men, 123; experienced through a Marin show, 125–27; illness at Lake George,

127; meeting with Dorothy Brett, 127; appearance, 128, 143, 147; estimates of him as artist, 129, 130, 132, 135, 142; review of his photography, 131ff.; photographs of woman, 132; period of the war, 132; conception of art, 127–35; the presentation of his ideas, 134–35; conception of photography *versus* art, 138; at The Hill on Lake George, 143–46; at work, 144; Chronology, 151; list of exhibitions, 151–53; bibliography of material relating to his life and work, 153–54.

Stieglitz, Edward, career, 38–39, 46; takes family to Europe, 39, 40.

"Stieglitz," by Gertrude Stein, 136.

"Stieglitz and the American tradition," by Elizabeth McCausland, 115–17.

Stirling, Edmund, 47.

Stokowski, Leopold, 61.

Strand, Paul, 43, 48, 60–61; one of the Seven Americans, 64, 65; "Alfred Stieglitz and a Machine," 137–39; exhibitions, 151, 152–53; Note, 156.

Strand, Rebecca, 153.

Strauss, Francis, 47.

Sullivan, Louis, 31, 98.

Surréalism, 60, 86.

Swan, 52.

Talbot, Fox, 52.

Tennyson, Alfred, 33, 54.

Terminal, The (Stieglitz), 46.

Terry, Ellen, 54.

Tofel, Jennings, "A Portrait," 123–25; 154, Note, 156.

Toomer, Jean, "The Hill," 143–46. Note, 156.

Torr, Helen, 153.

Toulouse-Lautrec, 59, 152.

Treatise on Painting, Burnet's, 56.

Turner, J. M. W., 81, 87.

Tweed, Boss, 28, 29.

"291—and the Brass Bowl," by Marsden Hartley, 119–21.

"291: A Vision Through Photography," by Herbert J. Seligmann, 58–66.

291 Fifth Avenue, the Stieglitz "laboratory" at, 59ff., 88, 119–21, 131, 133, 134, 138, 145; list of exhibitions, 151–52.

Two Ways of Life (Rejlander), 54.

Van Dyck, 87.

Van Eyck, brothers, 43.

Van Gogh, 83, 84–85.

Velasquez, 84.

Verlag, Bruckmann, 45.

Vlaminck, 85.

Vogel, Prof. H. W., 41, 151.

Wagner, Richard, 100.

Walkowitz, Abraham, 48, 60, 152.

Washington, George, 18, 19–20, 23.

Watson-Schütze, Eva, 47.

Watt, James, 92.

Watts, G. F., 54.

Watzek, Hans, 48, 151.

Weber, Max, 48, 60, 120; exhibitions, 152.

Webster, Noah, 18.

Werner, Hedwig (Mrs. Edward Stieglitz), 39, 40.

Weston, 43.

Whistler, James McNeill, 43, 44, 60, 83, 119.

White, Clarence H., 43, 47, 151.

Whitman, Walt, 31, 33, 37, 98, 107, 116.

Williams, William Carlos, "The American Background," 17–26; Note, 156.

Wilson, Woodrow, 20, 24.

Winter—Fifth Avenue (Stieglitz), 46, 57.

"Witness, A," by Victoria Ocampo, 129–30.

Women, American dearth in culture among, 24; as symbols in Stieglitz's work, 34; Stieglitz's photographs of, 132.

World War, modern art after the, 85ff.; effect on economic-social system, 94–95; an interruption in Stieglitz's work, 132.

Wright, S. Macdonald, 152.

Zola, 41.